Urbanization and Environmental Quality

STUDIES IN APPLIED

REGIONAL SCIENCE

URBANIZATION AND ENVIRONMENTAL QUALITY

Isao Orishimo
Toyohashi University of Technology

Kluwer • Nijhoff Publishing
BOSTON / THE HAGUE / LONDON

DISTRIBUTORS FOR NORTH AMERICA:
Kluwer Boston, Inc.
190 Old Derby Street
Hingham, Massachusetts 02043, U.S.A.

DISTRIBUTORS OUTSIDE NORTH AMERICA:
Kluwer Academic Publishers Group
Distribution Centre
P.O. Box 322
3300 AH Dordrecht, The Netherlands

Library of Congress Cataloging in Publication Data

Orishimo, Isao, 1923–
Urbanization and environmental quality.

(Studies in applied regional science)
Includes index.
1. Urbanization. 2. Central places. 3. Pollution. 4. Quality of life. 5. Residential mobility. I. Title. II. Series.
HT119.074 307.7′6 81-9635

ISBN-13: 978-94-009-7394-7 e-ISBN-13: 978-94-009-7392-3
DOI: 10.1007/978-94-009-7392-3 AACR2

CONTENTS

LIST OF FIGURES

LIST OF TABLES

ACKNOWLEDGMENTS

This monograph is largely the outgrowth of my studies at MIT and Washington University as a Fulbright exchange researcher from 1978 to 1979. I am indebted to Professors Brian J. L. Berry and Mark J. Roberts of Harvard University and Ralph Gakenheimer, M. O'Hare, and Jerome Rothenburg of MIT for their contributions to the empirical and institutional analyses and to Professor H. Noguchi and his former student K. Sawada (of Waseda University) for their help with the theoretical material. My thanks go also to Professors C. Leven and M. Beckmann for their valuable comments at an earlier stage of this study, to Professor P. O'Donoghue, who read through the manuscript in detail and provided many helpful comments, and to H. Hansen, N. Cousino, T. Ogawa, and Associate Professor T. Kanesawa of Rissho University, who are among the many people to whom I am indebted for assistance in the data collection and processing.

Finally, I want to express my sincere gratitude to Professor Y. Oishi (University of Tokyo) for his constant encouragement.

INTRODUCTION

The purpose of this monograph is to clarify the effect of environmental change on the process of urbanization. The research attempts to uncover the similarities as well as the differences across countries of the characteristics of environmental effects on cities and metropolitan areas during the process of industrial development.

Over the past several decades, a notable behavioral shift has been observed in many developed countries. People appear to be switching from an almost exclusive concern for material (commodity) consumption to a broader set of concerns that includes interest in so-called environmental problems and in improving the quality of life (USEPA 1973). These new areas of concern include, of course, the problems of pollution, congestion, and, in general, environmental degradation in urban areas.

People seem to be becoming increasingly conscious of the physical as well as the social environment. Richard L. Morrill described the situation in the United States as follows:

> Evidently many are still moving [their residences] for amenity values, into regions they like, irrespective of job opportunities. While movement to the traditional amenity areas of Florida and Arizona continues, there has been a dramatic shift away from California, or from metropolitan areas generally, to

> the Pacific Northwest, the Rocky Mountains, upper New England, and even to the Ozarks, Appalachia, and Upper Michigan. [Quoted in Berry and Gillard 1977, p. 9]

In the case of Japan, demographers have noticed a U-turn population movement; people who once looked for higher-paying jobs in the big metropolitan areas are returning to the smaller metropolitan areas as well as to their native communities. The research presented in this monograph investigates the cause and effect relationship of these characteristics of recent population movement in terms of the influence of environmental degradation in metropolitan areas. This relationship is extremely complicated and not easy to determine. The research consists of three types: theoretical (Chapters 1 and 2), empirical (Chapters 3, 4, and 5), and institutional (Chapter 6). The main points are summarized briefly below.

THEORY

Theoretically, we are primarily concerned with the incorporation of environmental quality into the theory of consumer location. In regard to the location of individual consumers, a number of economists have further developed land use theory with respect to rent theory (after Alonso 1964). The framework of the theory derives from the utility function, the variables of which have two contradictory factors. One variable is private goods, and the other is distance from the city center or central business district (CBD), where, according to the so-called Thünen assumption, job sites are concentrated.

Agglomeration phenomena consist of external and diseconomy effects. Distance from the CBD similarly reflects two elements: the inconvenience of the distance and the value of the amenity of the surrounding area. The urbanization process is influenced by the many changing characteristics of environmental quality at each location, in addition to physical distance from the CBD. Environmental quality can be reflected in part by its effect on the location choice of the individual, where environmental quality means air quality, levels of noise pollution, open space, and other neighborhood qualities, physical as well as social.

We cannot assume that a community's environmental quality level is reflected entirely in the local tax mils, nor that it is completely embodied in the rent of the property at the location, even though much theoretical research has assumed that it is. Location choice is closely related to the existence of desirable environmental qualities, such as open space; this is not necessarily embodied in rent or tax. Accordingly, considering the location behavior of an individual, we develop a model with location parameters, the attributes of which are reflected in neither rent nor tax (Chapter 1). The parameters should explain location choice in an urban area on grounds other than rent and commuting cost, given a set of commodities. The model is developed as an application of Debreu mapping. Using this model, we attempt to explain the changing behavior of the location choice of individuals.

Similarly, as in the case of the individual location model, we assume that two contradicting factors, such as the wage rate and degradation of environmental quality, are working in the urbanization process. Both factors are represented in the control space. In the behavioral space, which considers the psychological tendencies of residents, locational behaviors are shown. A model of the urbanization process, based on the probability model and applying elementary catastrophe theory, is developed in Chapter 2.

EMPIRICAL ANALYSIS

From an empirical point of view, when we focus attention on the common features of the urbanization process among countries, we would expect our observations to be in line with the following statement:

> The macro-location of industry and population tends towards an ever-increasing concentration in a limited number of areas; their micro-location, on the other hand, towards an ever-increasing diffusion or "sprawl." In this case it is convenient to describe under the heading of macro-location the analysis of the location of population and industry as between regions and groupings of industrial towns; and the term micro-location to describe in more detail how they are located within such areas. [Clark 1968, p. 280]

In Clark's context of the urbanization process, the so-called macro-location and micro-location phenomena — or, in other words, sprawl-suburbanization and spreading of metropolitan areas — appear to be interrelated. A number of people are entering the city, and at the same time, a number of people are dispersing to suburban areas. The phenomenon of the city population movement can be recognized as a kind of dynamic process. We could reasonably describe the phenomenon as "metabolic" in reference to Thom's research (1975, p. 323). From this dynamic viewpoint, Hoover's notion of a relative rate of adjustment seems to play an important role in the urbanization process (Hoover 1937).

In terms of the intracity or micro-location supposition, it has been well recognized that urban dwellers will tend to reside in suburban areas in response to (1) increases in income, which are generally accompanied by a relative rise in the marginal utility of housing space and amenity, and (2) technological change in transportation and other communication means. For these intra-urban phenomena, we examine the changing behavior of the population density gradient, the rent gradient, and the adequate form of the equation in Chapter 3. We follow the secular changes in the parameters of the equations, which approximate the shifts of the population densities in the New York and Tokyo metropolitan areas. The content of Chapter 3, though it is based on empirical research, is closely related to the location-choice behavior of individuals presented in Chapter 1 as a one-parameter family of utility functions. In Appendix 3.2, we observe that the economic behavior of individuals, including their location choice, changes discontinuously at a certain point in the process. This discontinuity is observed in the transportation modal choice, which relates closely to location choice. In this case, the so-called systems variable — including environmental quality — is changing continuously. We present empirical research that applies probit and logit analyses to modal choice behavior.

In Chapter 4 the theory of the hierarchical distribution of cities, or central place theory, is treated from the viewpoint of intercity commodity flows. We use the model to establish that the distribution of cities depends not only on the transportation network, but also on the differences in per capita income or in the productivity of each city and, accordingly, on the degree of environmental degradation — within the context mentioned in Chapter 2 — and on demand generated by rural areas and foreign trade.

In the appendix to Chapter 4 we make some preliminary observations, based on the Weberian or historical approach, on the differences between countries with respect to the environmental effects of urbanization. This approach is useful because many differences originate from historical and social factors in the urbanization processes. Each region and country is different, and industrial-location behavior cannot be adequately explained solely on the basis of population concentrations. This Weberian approach to industrial location seems to explain the main differences in urban agglomeration in different countries. Differences in the distribution of the resources among the countries explain the different characteristics of industrial location behavior in the various countries.

Another focus of our empirical research is on the relationship between city size and the degrees of the physical environmental qualities of the city with respect to population movements. In Chapter 5 we explore two elements of this relationship. First, we use data from fifty-four U.S. SMSAs to estimate the degree to which certain elements of environmental quality — specifically, air, water, and noise pollution, solid waste management, and park area — are related to city size. Second, since it is not merely the level of environmental quality that influences the location behavior of a potential immigrant or emigrant, we investigate the "price" of environmental quality that residents must pay, usually in the form of taxes and charges for public expenditures on environmental quality control. In Chapter 5 the "price" is first developed in a theoretical model and then examined empirically, using three U.S. cities.

INSTITUTIONAL ANALYSIS

In Chapter 6 we address the question of social responses to environmental degradation. Social responses to environmental change (e.g., voting, moving, and activism) can be studied from various viewpoints. First, they can be identified and understood through the concepts of traditional economics — externality or public goods. From a second point of view, they are recognized as responses to Murphy's "ecosystem," which refers to nature's ability to renew. Third, the way social responses are conveyed is also becoming more and more complex because of the multi-objective nature of our society. The policy-implementation process can also be characterized by a variety of social responses.

Furthermore, specific cultural features of each country are reflected in the characteristics of the social responses and the implementation process with respect to environmental degradation. These phenomena not only reflect the urbanization process, but they also work by themselves. So, as Isard (1969) mentioned, it is important for us to recognize all the processes of urbanization, environmental degradation, social responses, and policy implementation. Each should be grasped as synthetic streams of economic, social, and institutional equilibria.

In this book, we develop a theoretical perspective on the changing character of location choice in terms of a general equilibrium context. On the basis of this recognition, we review the recent changing trend of the urbanization process, intracity as well as intercity, and compare similar data in the United States and Japan. Although we cannot completely demonstrate this dynamic process in our framework, we can simply prove the necessity of our hypothesized relationship between environmental degradation and the urbanization process. In terms of environmental policy formulation, we review the general composite view of the institutional background of the country, especially comparing the special characteristics of the Japanese policy process with that of the United States. In sum, our main theme is to clarify the nature of the urbanization process with respect to environmental degradation and to stress that partial equilibrium analysis is not necessarily appropriate for the judgment of the adequacy of a policy in the total system.

Urbanization and Environmental Quality

1 A LOCATION MODEL WITH RESPECT TO ENVIRONMENTAL QUALITY

Our main interest in this chapter is the individual's problem of location choice with respect to the environmental quality of the location. We set environmental quality as a key concept that is determined by the location.

Many previous models of urban location theory have been developed with respect to rent theory since Alonso's publication (1964). In most cases they have explained individual location on the basis of the utility function, represented by distance from the CBD, a single measure of the location in the usual Thünen-type model. Although location choice is closely related to the existence and quality of such physical environmental attributes as open space as well as to social environmental quality, only a few models, among them research done by Schweizer, Variya, and Hartwick (1976), have explicitly included this relationship.

We emphasize this relationship because we recognize that the urbanization process (particularly with respect to individual location choice) is strongly related to the rapidly changing character of local environmental quality in addition to distance from the CBD. In terms of economics, some aspects of environmental quality may be expressed as public goods, while other aspects may be reduced to externalities (Ellickson 1973). The quality of the environment is relative and depends on the viewpoint of the agent. For example, perception of environmental quality may vary according to community size, as Buchanan (1965) suggested for the case of public goods.

Although some attributes of the environmental quality of a location are reflected in the land or property rent (Smith 1978) and others are reflected in the local tax level through the public expenditures for environmental quality control in a location (Richter 1978), these embodiments are not necessarily complete. Accordingly, we look at aspects of environmental quality that are not embodied in the rent or in the tax level of the location. In this case, therefore, we consider that all such environmental qualities of a location should be reflected in a different type of utility function for the location.

Therefore, we consider one-parameter families of utility functions generated by a parameter, which expresses the location, or the set of environmental qualities. Our model is a pure exchange economy with l commodities and m consumers. The following assumptions are basic for the economy: (1) free location option: each consumer can move and live where he likes; (2) free consumption option: each consumer can consume any commodity wherever he lives. By assumption (1) each consumer's location choice does not depend on the choices of others, and by assumption (2) his location choice does depend on his holding (e.g., his commodity bundle may constrain location choice).

In this paper, under some specific conditions, we derive a location equilibrium for households, given an initial resource endowment. We apply equilibrium theory as developed by Debreu (1970) and Balasko (1975), as illustrated in Figure 1–1.

STATEMENT OF THE THEOREM

Each consumer's utility function is parameterized by the interval $I = (0, 1)$ considered as the set of the locations. In this case the ith consumer's utility function u_i is a C^r-function, $r \geqq 2$, of $I \times R^l_+ \subset R \times R^l$ into R, where R^l_+ is a commodity space such as

$$R^l_+ = \{(x^1, \ldots, x^l) \in R^l \mid x^j > 0 \text{ for all } j\}.$$

Throughout this chapter we assume the following:

1. For any $t \in I$, the correspondence $u_i^t : x \to u_i(t, x)$ is a C^r-function of R^l_+ into R such that:
   i. $Du_i^t(x) \in R^l_+$ (differential monotonicity) (see Figure 1–2);
   ii. $D^2u_i^t(x)$ is negative definite on kernel $Du_i^t(x)$ (differential convexity) (see Figure 1–2);

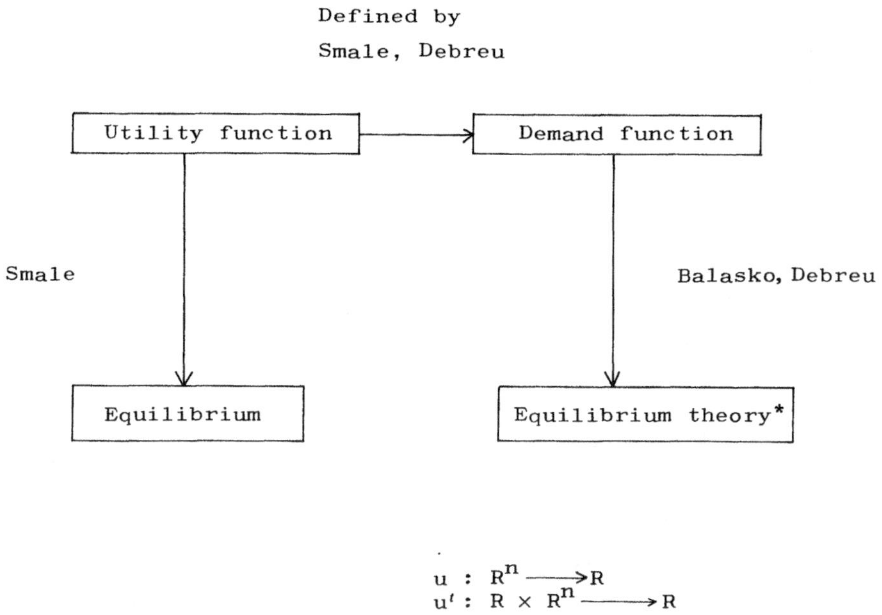

*One-parameter family of utility functions

Figure 1–1. Equilibrium Theory

iii. for any $c \in R$, closure of $(u_i^t)^{-1}(c) \cap \partial R_+^l = \phi$ (boundary condition) (see Figure 1–2).

2. For any $x \in R_+^l$, there is a unique point $t \in I$ such that $(\partial u_i / \partial t)(t, x) = 0$, and then $D^2 u_i(t, x)$ is negative definite on kernel $Du_i(t, x)$.

Remark. Condition (2) implies that for any $x \in R_+^l$, there is a unique location t to maximize u_i (see Figure 1–3).

The first derivative $Du_i(t, x)$ at $(t, x) \in I \times R_+^l$ is a linear map from $R \times R^l$ to R, which, by using coordinates of $R \times R^l$, can be considered as a vector in $R \times R^l$, the gradient of u_i. We shall use $Du(t, x)$ to denote ambiguously a linear map and a gradient.

The space of the states of this economy is expressed by

$$W = \{(t_1, x_1, \ldots, t_m, x_m) \in (I \times R_+^l)^m \mid \sum_{i=1}^{m} x_i = s\},$$

where $s \in R_+^l$ is the fixed vector of total resources.

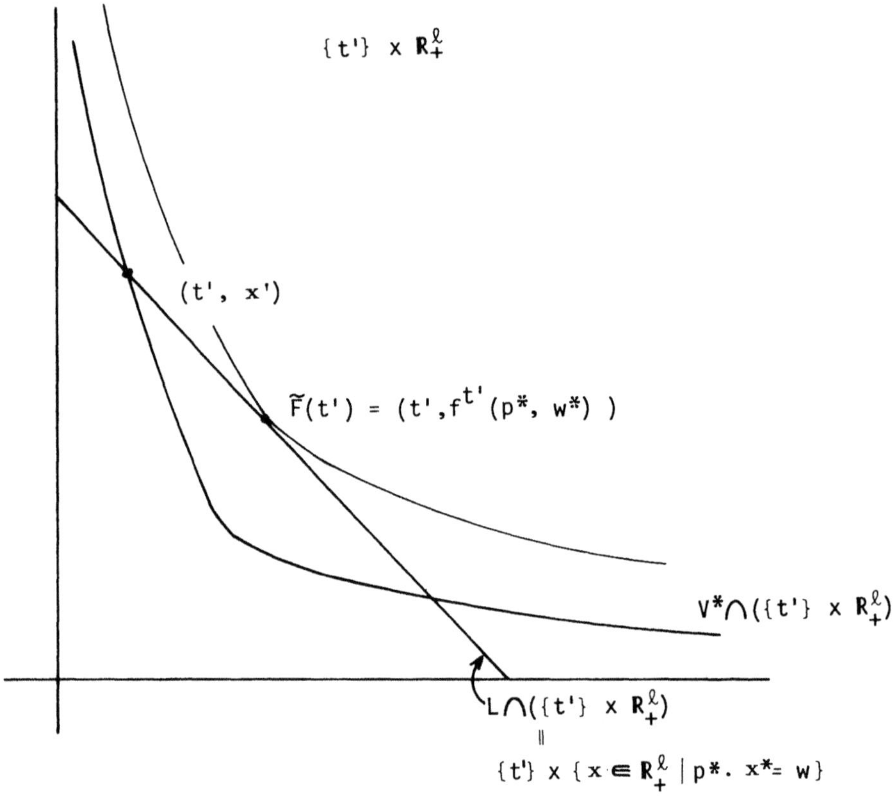

By differential monotonicity,

$$u(t', x') = u^{t'}(x') \leqq u^{t'}\ (f^{t'}(p^*,w^*)) = u \circ \tilde{F}_1(t').$$

Figure 1–2. Differential Monotonicity

Let $S_+ = \{(p^1, \ldots, p^l) \in R^l_+ \mid (p^1)^2 + \cdots + (p^l)^2 = 1\}$ and $\Omega = \{(r_1, \ldots, r_m) \in (R^l_+)^m \mid \Sigma_{i=1}^m r_i = s\}$, say, the set of initial endowments. Then $(t, x, p) = (t_1, x_1, \ldots, t_m, x_m, p) \in I \times W \times S_+$ is said to be a *Walras price equilibrium with locations* for $r = (r_1, \ldots, r_m) \in \Omega$ if u_i has (t_i, x_i) as maximum on the set $\{(t_i, x_i) \in I \times R^l_+ \mid p \cdot x_i \leqq p \cdot r_i\}$ for all i.

THEOREM. *For any $r \in \Omega$, there is a Walras price equilibrium with locations, and its number is finite over open dense set Ω^* in Ω.*

The proof of the theorem is reduced to Balasko (1975) and Debreu (1970) through the lemmas given in the appendix to this chapter.

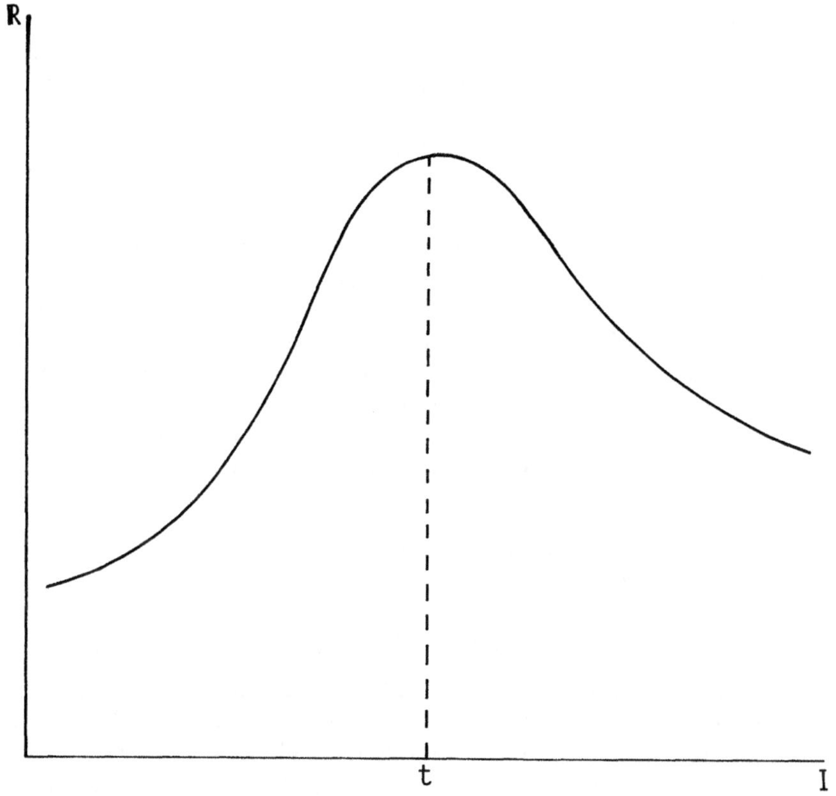

$$u(t, x) \geqq u(t', x) \quad \text{for any } t' \in I$$

Figure 1–3. Graph of the Map $u(\cdot, x)$: $t \rightarrow u(t, x)x \in R^l_+$

IMPLICATIONS OF THE MODEL

In this section we clarify the nature of the environmental quality problem for theoretical development and give some perspective on how this chapter relates to the rest of the book. If we look at the environmental quality of an urban location, we find that various characteristics have been recognized as public goods. But we soon recognize even open space and fresh air as explicitly public goods. Some public goods are embodied in the rent of the location as amenity value. The phenomenon has attracted many researchers' attention (see Smith 1978).

Certainly some elements of the attributes of a location are reflected in the land rent, while other elements are not necessarily so reflected. In other words, a location has many attributes, which we can consider as a continuum between two poles; the elements at one end are completely included in the land rent while those at the other are not. Over time, the number of elements of the attributes of a location that are included in the land rent apparently increases.

On the other hand, there is a relationship between the rent and the tax level of the jurisdiction, which is necessary to cover the expenses of the local public goods. Open space should be considered as a local public good. For example, there are many open spaces in a suburban area in the early stages of the urbanization process. After development advances, in order to preserve the environmental quality of the earlier stages, a great deal of public expenditure is needed to preserve the open spaces as parkland. We can illustrate the situation as follows:

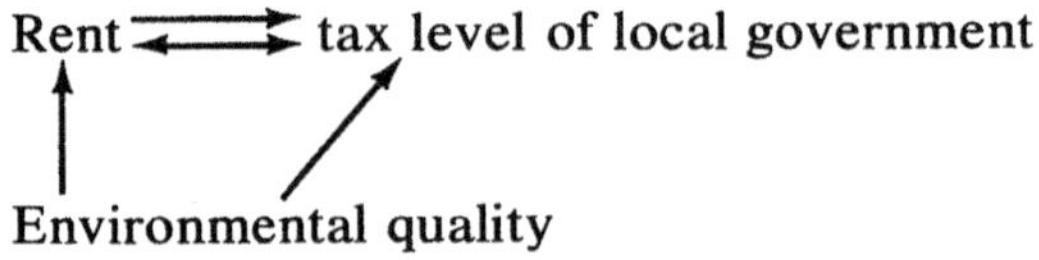

In one of the two extreme cases, all of the environmental quality of the location is embodied in the rent; in the other case, it is all embodied in the Lindahl price of the public goods through local government taxes.

Thus, with respect to the preservation of environmental quality, the urban land rent should represent a location's environmental quality directly as well as indirectly through the local tax level. Usually the degrees of this representation shift over time.

If we assume that all of the environmental quality is embodied in the land rent, previously developed location rent theory should adequately consider the situation. On the other hand, if all of the environmental quality is embodied in the tax level as public expenditure for public goods, Lindahl equilibrium should reasonably explain the resource allocation (Ellickson 1973; Richter 1978; Bergstrom 1976).

However, with respect to the concept of public goods, we must recognize that pure public goods and pure private goods are, as Samuelson suggested, two poles of the concepts that represent the goods of the real world. On this point, when developing his theory of clubs or cooperative membership, Buchanan (1965) mentioned that spectrums of ownership-consumption possibilities range from the purely private or individualized activity to purely public or collective activity.

It should be noted that, in general, whether goods are private or public depends on our coordinate, which determines the extension of ownership-consumption rights over differing numbers of persons. Regarding the land use problem, the environmental quality of the location is closely related to this coordinate.

From the point of view of community size, the concept of public goods is itself relative with respect to our coordinate; that is, for the smallest community family, most of the goods are consumed collectively. In other words, from the viewpoint of the coordinate of the family, many private goods have more or less the meaning of public goods. For instance, a beautiful historical garden may be privately owned. Hence the rent is bid at the market level. This garden is an element of the environmental quality of the vicinity. From the owner's point of view, the garden is a private good, but from the broader viewpoint of the community, it is a public good, and thus externality forces are also at work. Probably some part of it should be reflected in the tax level of the area. If the central government regards the garden as a historical monument and subsidizes it, then the garden becomes a public good at two different levels.

Only when we restrict our attention to a community of fixed size, which is authorized to levy local taxes exactly corresponding to the supply of local public goods, under the assumption of free population movement, can we recognize the reasonable meaning of Tiebout equilibrium (Tiebout 1956; Richter 1978). But in the real world, population movement is not completely free, and land rent also reflects the price of public goods in the local tax level.

To simplify, we can suppose that land rent is a numeraire. The extent to which environmental quality is reflected in this numeraire of the private goods price system depends on community size. For instance, there may be a forest in a suburban area. For the region the forest constitutes an important element of environmental quality. But for the smaller community it might be regarded as an object for development, which relates directly to the numeraire. So, in order to capture different numeraire impacts, we can establish some composite coordinate of a set of viewpoints of communities of different sizes. Also, we expect that the extent to which environmental quality is reflected in the price of local public goods will probably decrease over time and become more embodied in the numeraire.

If we shift our assumed coordinates for community size and time, then there is another reflection of environmental quality in the rent. This is the reason, from our point of view, that "crowding problems" affect the location's environmental quality. It is apparently impossible for the rent of a location to reflect simultaneously all of the viewpoints of communities of various sizes.

Furthermore, with respect to the crowding problem, the concept of externalities should be considered. To cope with externalities, groups tend to form governmental institutions to achieve efficient allocations. For instance, real estate covenants that restrict all land use within a certain area for certain purposes represent an attempt to deal with the externalities involved in the appearance and general environment of whole neighborhoods. Here the tax is levied implicitly, since there is a loss in not being able to put land to its most profitable use. This tax pays for such public goods as quiet and beauty of surroundings (Buchanan 1965).

Thus, location theories that have been formulated in a general equilibrium context have not been fruitful because these models have merely added a subscript to the conventional competitive model (Foley 1967). We must recognize that, in addition to the points mentioned above, it is very difficult to assume convexity and divisibility in the case of location activities.

The tax levels for local public goods and for environmental quality are closely related and form an extremely relative base on the coordinate of the viewpoint of the community. In addition, this relationship is regarded as an adjusting process; in Hoover's (1937) terminology, it is denoted as a relative rate of adjustment.

In order to gain some perspective on all of these points, our model is composed from a set of utility functions, the parameter of which is variable. The parameter is considered to represent an individual's motive for location choice in an urban area, given a set of commodities and the dimensions of a set of community sizes. As far as the parameter is concerned, the attributes of the location are not reflected completely in land rent or in public expenditures. Theoretically, the parameter is sufficient for the indivisibility and nonconvexity of location activities, which until now were the most difficult aspects to deal with.

The parameter is represented as a variable of the control space of individual location choice in the urbanization model developed in Chapter 2 as an application of elementary catastrophe theory. It is illustrated more practically in Appendix 3.2, where it represents a system variable in the modal choice model. Empirically, a hypothesis presented in the study of intra-urban population distribution behavior in Chapter 3, which presupposes some dynamic adjusting process of individual location choice, is developed on the basis of the static considerations presented in this chapter.

CONCLUSION

We have dealt with a one-parameter family of utility functions, although more generally this one-parameter-family approach should be extended to an n-parameter family of utility functions. In the case of an n-parameter family, these parameters should represent location, local public goods (including transportation facilities), various environmental qualities (such as open space, air pollution, noise, and amenities), and the public services of the location. Furthermore, the crowding parameter, which might represent the number of people and the area of the jurisdiction, could be included.

In this model we have considered the situation in which there should exist some parameter, t, which is an objective measure, either optional or not, and which is not capitalized as rent or property values of the location. In such a case, are there some equilibrium conditions or is there disequilibrium? This was our sense of the problem. Finally, under the reasonable condition, $(\partial u/\partial t)(t, x) = 0$, $(\partial^2 u/\partial t^2)(t, x) < 0$, we may not necessarily find equilibrium.

When we set a stricter condition, assumption (2), there are equilibria containing the parameter. So, in considering the parameter, which represents location or environmental quality, there might be a possibility of disequilibrium, and, under more restrictive conditions, whose meaning is unknown, there should always be equilibria in terms of the general equilibrium context.

Discussion of policy issues under the assumption of the existence of general equilibrium is possible, as in the case of cost-benefit analysis. However, we find it not necessarily reasonable to make policy issues relate so directly to the general equilibrium context, as will be elaborated in Chapter 6.

What has been presented in the body of this chapter is a simple application of so-called Debreu mapping to location theory. This application enables us to consider the existence of an optimal spatial arrangement of households, given an initial endowment. Thus, if the initial endowments change, or if the location-environmental qualities change, the spatial arrangements change (see Figure 1–4). Furthermore, we can consider the changes in urban population distribution caused by environmental quality.

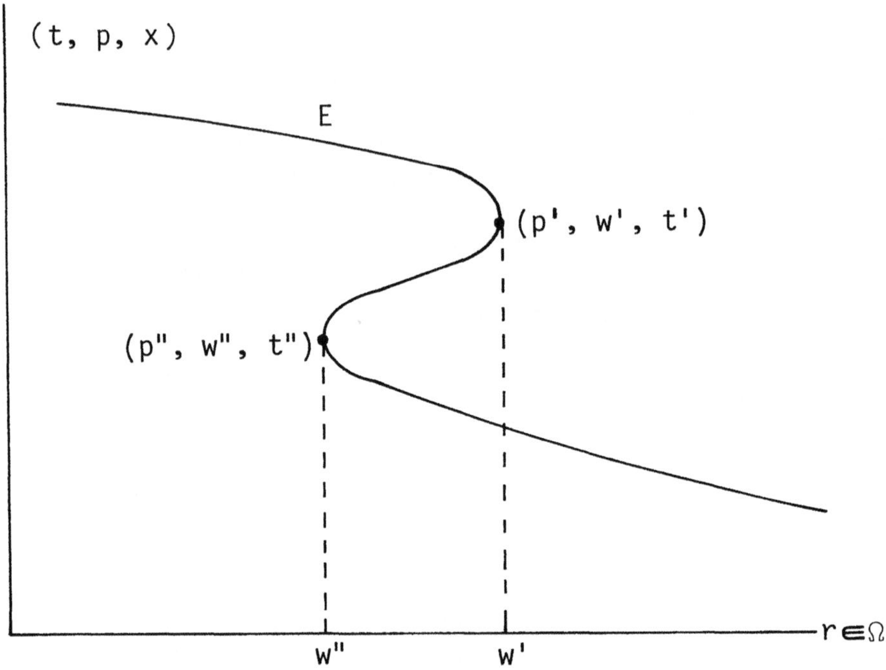

Figure 1–4. Debreu Mapping

APPENDIX: PROOF OF THE THEOREM

Before giving the proof of the theorem, we give some notations. To simplify, let the ith consumer's utility function u_i be u without suffix. By assumption (1), for any $t \in I$, there is a C^{r-1}-diffeomorphism $f^t : S_+ \times R_+ \to R^l_+$, called a demand function (see Figure 1–5), such that $f^t(p, w)$ is a maximizer of u^t in the budget set $\{x \in R^l_+ \mid p \cdot x = w\}$. Furthermore, f^t is an inverse function $\phi^t : R^l_+ \to S_+ \times R_+$ with

$$\phi^t(x) = \left(\frac{Du^t(x)}{\|Du^t(x)\|}, \frac{Du^t(x)}{\|Du^t(x)\|} \cdot x\right)$$

for any $x \in R^l_+$. Clearly $D\phi^t(x)$ is an isomorphism of R^l onto $T\phi^t(x)(S_+ \times R_+)$, where $\| \cdot \|$ is a Euclidean norm and $T_y(S_+ \times R_+)$ is a tangent space of $S_+ \times R_+$ at y. (See Smale 1974 and Debreu 1972 for details.)

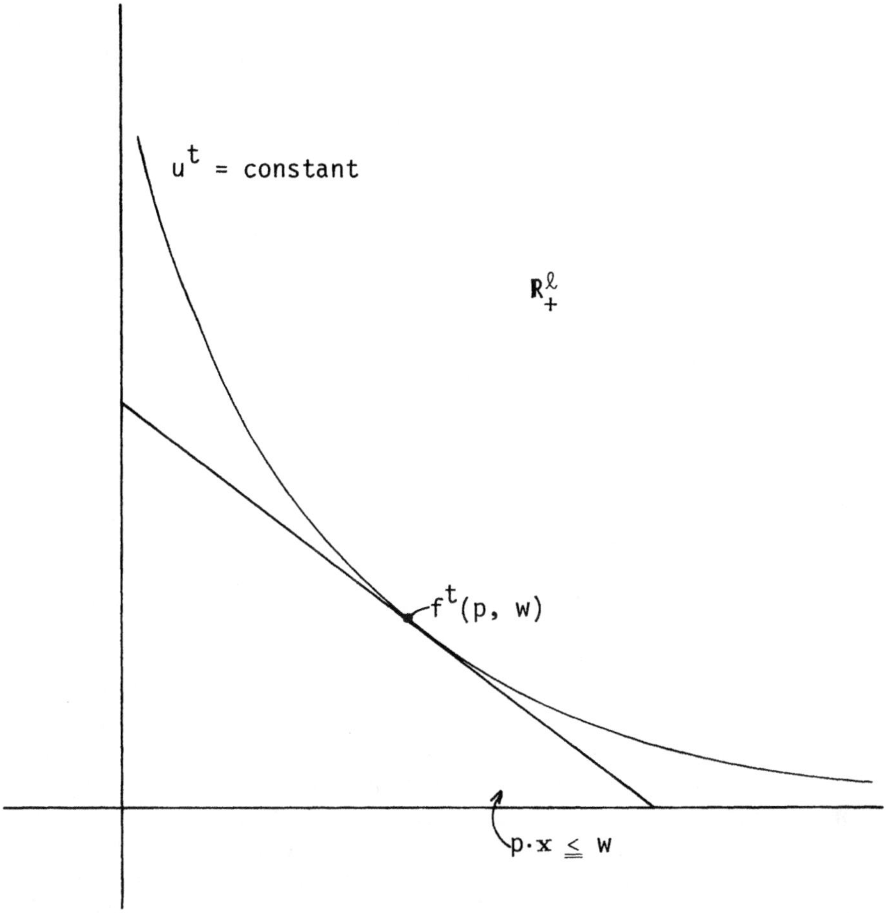

Figure 1–5. Demand Function Associated with u^t

We define a function $F : I \times S_+ \times R_+ \to I \times R^l_+$ by the formula $F(t, p, w) = [t, f^t(p, w)]$.

LEMMA 1.1. *The function F is a C^{r-1}-diffeomorphism.*

Proof. Let $G : I \times R^l_+ \to I \times S_+ \times R_+$ be a C^{r-1}-map with

$$G(t, x) = \left(t, \frac{\pi Du(t, x)}{\|\pi Du(t, x)\|}, \frac{\pi Du(t, x)}{\|\pi Du(t, x)\|} \cdot x\right),$$

where $\pi : R \times R^l \to R^l$. Clearly $G(t, x) = [t, \phi^t(x)]$. Then $F \circ G(t, x) = F[t, \phi^t(x)] = \{t, f^t[\phi^t(x)]\} = (t, x)$. Hence $F \circ G$ is the identity map on $I \times R^l_+$. Similarly, $G \circ F$ is the identity map on $I \times S_+ \times R_+$. Hence it is sufficient to show that rank $DG(t, x) = l + 1$ for any $(t, x) \in I \times R^l_+$.

$$DG(t, x) = \left[\begin{array}{c|c} 1 & 0 \\ \hline * & D\phi^t(x) \end{array}\right].$$

Since rank $D\phi^t(x)$ is l, rank $DG(t, x) = l + 1$.

Let $(t^*, x^*) \in I \times R^l_+$ be a point with $(\partial u/\partial t)(t^*, x^*) = 0$, $p^* = [\pi Du(t^*, x^*)]/[\|\pi Du(t^*, x^*)\|]$, and $V^* = V^*(t^*, x^*) = (u)^{-1}[u(t^*, x^*)]$.

LEMMA 1.2. *The set V^* is a C^r-submanifold in $I \times R^l_+$ with $T_{(t, x)}V^* =$ kernel $Du(t, x)$.*

Proof. By assumption (1), $Du^t(x) \neq 0$. Hence $Du(t, x) \neq 0$. By regular value theorem, the lemma is proved.

Let $L = \{(t, x) \in I \times R^l_+ \mid p^* \cdot x = p^* \cdot x^*\}$ (see Figure 1–6).

LEMMA 1.3. $V^* \cap L = \{(t^*, x^*)\}$.

Proof. Let $w^* = p^* \cdot x^*$. Since $f^t(p^*, w^*)$ is a point in the budget set $\{x \in R^l_+ \mid p^* \cdot x = w^*\}$ for any $t \in I$, $F(t, p^*, w^*) \in L$ for any $t \in I$. Hence we define a C^{r-1}-map $\tilde{F} : I \to L$ by $\tilde{F}(t) \doteq F(t, p^*, w^*)$ (see Figure 1–6). Clearly $(d\tilde{F}/dt)(t)$ and $(d^2\tilde{F}/dt^2)(t) \in T_a(L)$, where $a = \tilde{F}(t)$. We suppose that $(t', w') \in V^* \cap L$. Then $u \circ \tilde{F}\ (t') \geqq u(t', x')\ [= u(t^*, x^*)]$ (Figure 1–2). We may assume $t' > t^*$. We define a C^{r-1}-map $H : I \to R$ by $H(t) = u \circ \tilde{F}(t)$. Clearly $H(t') \geqq H(t^*)$. Since $(\partial u/\partial t)(t^*, x^*) = 0$, $D^2u(t^*, x^*)$ is negative definite on kernel $Du(t^*, x^*) = T_{(t^*, x^*)}V^*$ by assumption (2). Hence for (t, x) close to (t^*, x^*) in L, $u(t, x) < u(t^*, x^*)$ so that $H(t^* + \epsilon) = u \circ F(t^* + \epsilon) < u \circ F(t^*) = H(t^*)\ [\leqq H(t')]$ for small $\epsilon > 0$. Therefore there is $\alpha \in (t, t')$ such that

I. $(dH/dt)(\alpha) = 0$.
II. $(d^2H/dt^2)(\alpha) \geqq 0$.

Now $(dH/dt)(\alpha) = Du[\tilde{F}(\alpha)] \cdot (d\tilde{F}/dt)(\alpha) = (\partial u/\partial t)[\tilde{F}(\alpha)]$. By (I), $(\partial u/\partial t)[\tilde{F}(\alpha)] = 0$. Hence $D^2u[\tilde{F}(\alpha)]$ is negative definite on kernel $Du[\tilde{F}(\alpha)]$ by assumption (2) and kernel $Du[\tilde{F}(\alpha)] = T_{\tilde{F}(\alpha)}L$.

On the other hand,

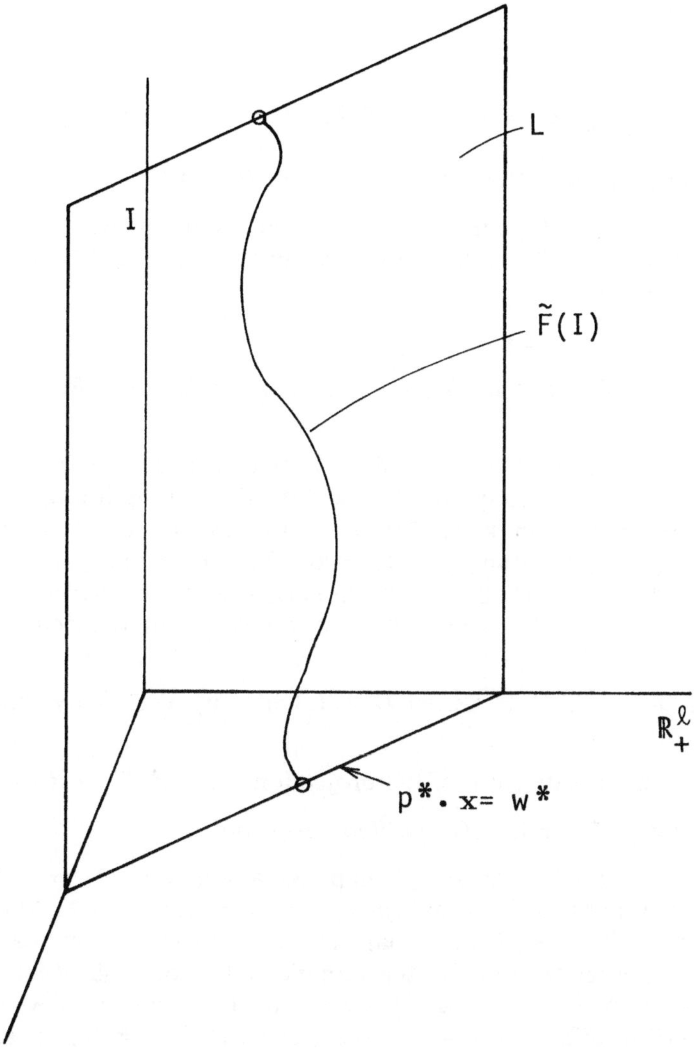

Figure 1–6. Locus of $\tilde{F}(I)$

$$\frac{d^2H}{dt^2}(\alpha) = D^2u[\tilde{F}(\alpha)]\left[\frac{d\tilde{F}}{dt}(\alpha), \frac{d\tilde{F}}{dt}(\alpha)\right] + Du[\tilde{F}(\alpha)]\frac{d^2\tilde{F}}{dt^2}(\alpha) < 0$$

since

$$\frac{d^2\tilde{F}}{dt^2}(\alpha) \text{ and } \frac{d\tilde{F}}{dt}(\alpha) \in T_{\tilde{F}(\alpha)}L = \text{kernel } Du[\tilde{F}(\alpha)].$$

This contradicts to (II). Thus $V^* \cap L = \{(t^*, x^*)\}$.

Remark. By Lemma 1.3, differential monotonicity and convexity imply u has (t^*, x^*) as maximum on the set $\{(t, x) \in I \times R^l_+ \mid p^* \cdot x \leqq p^* \cdot x^*\}$ (see Figure 1–7).

Let $\Lambda = \{(t, x) \in I \times R^l_+ \mid (\partial u/\partial t)(t, x) = 0\}$.

LEMMA 1.4. *The set Λ is a C^{r-1}-submanifold in $I \times R^l_+$ with dim $\Lambda = l$.*

Proof. Let $\Phi : I \times R^l_+ \to R$ be a map with $\Phi(t, x) = (\partial u/\partial t)(t, x)$. Clearly Φ is a C^{r-1}-map and $\Lambda = \Phi^{-1}(0)$. By assumption (2), $D^2u(t, x)$ is negative definite on kernel $Du(t, x)$ for any $(t, x) \in \Phi^{-1}(0)$. Hence $(\partial^2u/\partial t^2)(t, x) \neq 0$ for any $(t, x) \in \Phi^{-1}(0)$. For $D^2u(t, x)(e_1, e_1) = (\partial^2u/\partial t^2)(t, x) < 0$ where $e_1 = (1, 0, \ldots, 0) \in$ kernel $Du(t, x)$. Therefore, rank $D\Phi(t, x) = 1$ for any $(t, x) \in \Phi^{-1}(0)$. By regular value theorem, the lemma is proved.

Remark. $T_y(\Lambda) =$ kernel $D\,\Phi\,(y)$ for any $y \in \Lambda$ by regular value theorem.

Let $\tilde{\pi}$ be a restriction of the projection $\pi : R \times R^l \to R$ to the set Λ.

LEMMA 1.5. *$\tilde{\pi}$ is a C^{r-1}-diffeomorphism.*

Proof. Clearly $\tilde{\pi}$ is a C^{r-1}-map. By assumption (2), $\tilde{\pi}$ is 1 to 1 and onto. It suffices to show that rank $D\,\tilde{\pi}\,(y) = l$ for any $y \in \Lambda$; i.e., kernel $D\,\tilde{\pi}\,(y) = \{0\}$. Let Φ be a map, as in the proof of Lemma 1.4. Then $T_y(\Lambda) =$ kernel $D\,\Phi\,(y)$ by the remark of Lemma 1.4. Hence kernel $D\,\tilde{\pi}\,(y) = \{0\} \Leftrightarrow$ if $D\,\Phi\,(y) \in \{0\} \times R^l \Leftrightarrow$ if $(\partial^2u/\partial t^2)(y) \neq 0$. As in proof of Lemma 1.4, $(\partial^2u/\partial t^2)(y) \neq 0$ so that kernel $D\,\tilde{\pi}\,(y) = \{0\}$ for any $y \in \Lambda$.

Let $\tilde{\pi}' : F^{-1}(\Lambda) \to S_+ \times R_+$ be a restriction of the projection $\pi' : I \times S_+ \times R_+ \to S_+ \times R_+$, where F is a C^{r-1}-diffeomorphism, as in Lemma 1.1. Similarly $\tilde{\pi}'$ is a C^{r-1}-diffeomorphism of $F^{-1}(\Lambda)$ onto $S_+ \times R_+$.

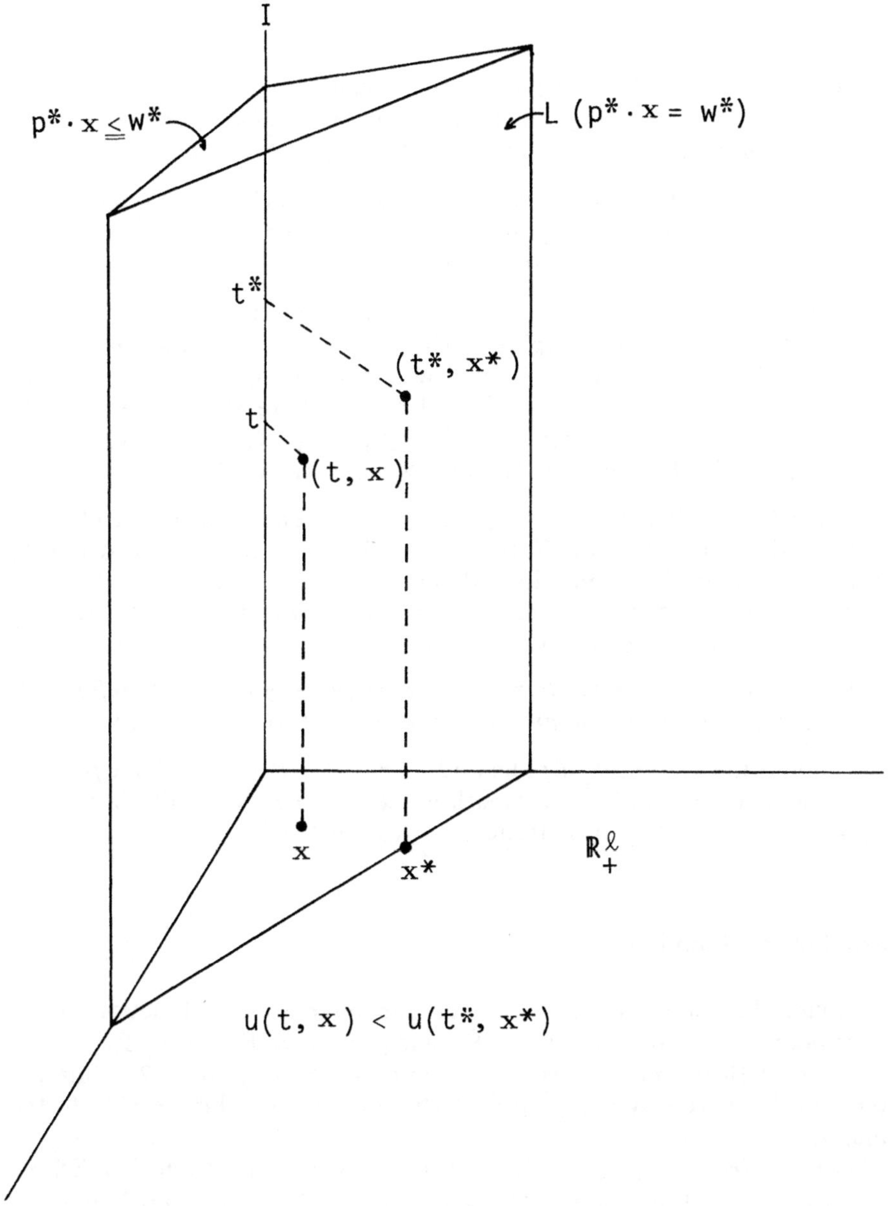

Figure 1–7. Budget Constraint

We define a map $f : S_+ \times R_+ \rightarrow R^l_+$ by the formula

$$f = \tilde{\pi} \circ F \circ (\tilde{\pi}')^{-1}.$$

Clearly f is a C^{r-1}-diffeomorphism and satisfies the Walras law [i.e., $p \cdot f(p, w) = w$] (see Figure 1–8). Note that $(\partial u/\partial t)(q) = 0$ and $[\pi Du(q)]/[\|\pi Du(q)\|] = p$, where $q = (\pi)^{-1} f(p, w)$.

LEMMA 1.6. *The map f satisfies Debreu's boundary condition — that is, (*) if the sequence (p_n, w_n) in $S_+ \times R_+$ converges to (p_0, w_0) in $\partial S_+ \times R_+$, then $\{f(p_n, w_n)\}$ converges to $+\infty$.*

Proof. We suppose that $\{f(p_n, w_n)\}$ converges to a point ω. Then $\omega \not\in \mathbf{R}^l_+$ since f is a diffeomorphism of $S_+ \times R_+ \rightarrow \mathbf{R}^l_+$. Hence $\omega \in \partial\mathbf{R}^l_+$. Let $A_n = \{(t, x) \in I \times \mathbf{R}^l_+ \mid p_n \cdot x < w_n\}$, $A = \cap_n A_n$. Then $A \neq \phi$. For A contains $A_0 = \{(t, x) \in I \times \mathbf{R}^l_+ \mid \|x\| < w\}$, where $w = \inf_n w_n$ ($w \gneqq 0$ since $w_n, w_0 \in \mathbf{R}^l_+$). Now let $x_n = (\tilde{\pi})^{-1} \circ f(p_n, w_n)$, $V_n = u^{-1}[u(x_n)]$. Then $A_n \cap V_n = \phi$ by Lemma 1.3. Hence $I \times \mathbf{R}^l_+ - \cup_n V_n \supset A$.

Let $a \in A$. Then $u(a) < u(x_n)$ for any n. Hence closure of $\cup_n V_n$ is contained in a closed set $u^{-1}[u(a), +\infty]$. Since $u^{-1}([u(a), +\infty]) \cdot \Lambda \cap \partial\mathbf{R}^l_+ \times I = \phi$ by boundary condition (1) (iii), closure of $\bigcup_n V_n \cap \partial\mathbf{R}^l_+ \times I \neq \phi$. This contradicts to the fact that $\pi(x_n) = f(p_n, w_n)$ converges to $\omega \in \partial R^l_+$. Therefore Lemma 1.6 is proved.

LEMMA 1.7. *The map f has the weak property of revealed preference; that is, if $p \cdot f(p', w') \leqq w$ and $(p, w) \neq (p', w')$, then $p' \cdot f(p, w) > w'$.*

Proof. Let $x = (\pi)^{-1} \cdot f(p, w)$ and $x' = (\pi)^{-1} \cdot f(p', w')$. Since $p \cdot f(p', w') \leqq w$, $u(x') \lneqq u(x)$ by the remark of Lemma 1.3. Similarly, if $p' \cdot f(p, w) \leqq w'$, then $u(x') \gneqq u(x)$. Hence $p' \cdot f(p, w) > w'$.

Proof of the Theorem

Applying the above notations to each consumer's utility function u_i, we may define the maps $\tilde{\pi}_i : \Lambda_i \rightarrow R^l_+$ and $f_i : S_+ \times R_+ \rightarrow R^l_+$ for $i = 1, \ldots, m$ with the properties as in Lemmas 1.5, 1.6, and 1.7. Thus the theorem is proved by applying Balasko (1975) and Debreu (1970) to the map f_i.

Let $r = (r_1, \ldots, r_m) \in \Omega$. Then there is $p^* \in S_+$ such that $\Sigma f_i(p^*, p^* \cdot r_i) = s$, by Balasko and Debreu. Let $(t^*_i, x^*_i) = (\tilde{\pi})^{-1}_i \circ f_i(p^*, p^* \cdot r_i)$, $i = 1, \ldots, m$ and $x^* = (t^*_1, x^*_1, \ldots, t^*_m, x^*_m)$. By definition of $\tilde{\pi}_i$, $(\partial u_i/\partial t)(t^*, x^*) = 0$ for all i, and $[\pi Du_i(t^*_i, x^*_i)]/[\|\pi Du_i(t^*_i, x^*_i)\|] = p^*$. By

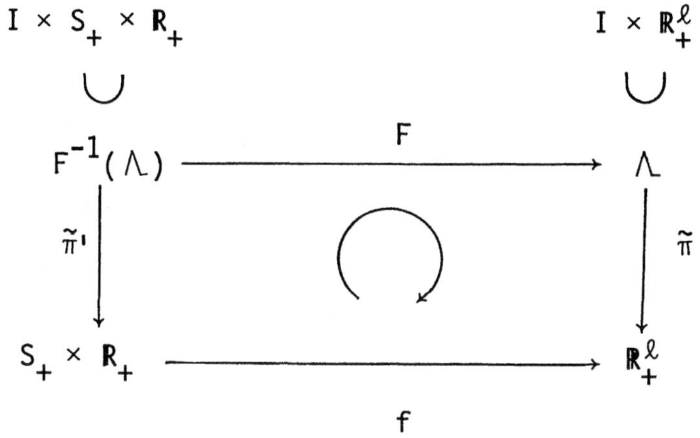

$$f = \pi \circ F \circ \tilde{\pi}'^{-1}$$

Figure 1–8. Diffeomorphism and the Walras Law

the remark of Lemma 1.3, u_i has (t_i^*, x_i^*) as maximum on the set $\{(t_i, x_i) \in I \times R^l_+ \mid p^* \cdot x_i \leqq p^* \cdot r_i\}$ for all i. Therefore, (x^*, p^*) is a Walras price equilibrium with locations for $r \in \Omega$. Similarly, the second part of the theorem is proved.

< $= \phi$ by boundary condition (1) (iii), closure of $\cup_n V_n \cap \partial \mathbf{R}^l_+ \times \quad \neq \phi$.

2 A MODEL OF THE URBANIZATION PROCESS: *An Application of Elementary Catastrophe Theory*

In Chapter 1 we examined the individual's location choice with respect to environmental quality from the viewpoint of equilibrium, based on a one-parameter family of utility functions. With this microscopic foundation, we now shift our attention to the macroscopic phenomenon of the urbanization process.

In studies of urbanization, much interest has focused on agglomeration from both theoretical and practical perspectives. In the process of urban agglomeration, economies and diseconomies of scale are apparently conflicting factors. Isard's discussion of this point, based on the presence of scale economies in urban areas, fails to account sufficiently for the diseconomies of scale (Isard 1959).

The workings of economies of scale in a location are a prime aspect of economic growth. Yet economic growth brings with it degradation of the natural environment, such as water pollution and air pollution as well as scarcity of open space. If the level of environmental degradation is expressed by a composite scale of Qej, the interrelation between Qej and economic growth is as shown in Figure 2–1.

The factors that favorably affect population growth and agglomeration

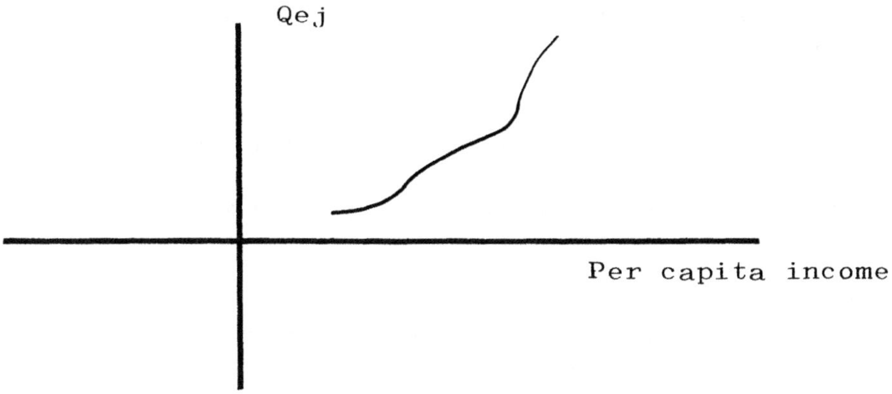

Qej: Level of Environmental Degradation

Figure 2–1. Change in Environmental Quality

are usually denoted as the attractiveness of the city. Economic theory stresses that the utility of the individual is the key concept in explaining the attractiveness of the city. The difference in utility between the locations *i* and *j* to a consumer is the decisive factor for his or her location. Except for the commuting cost, the main cause of the difference in utility is the difference in the wage rate. Wage rate differentials are attributed to the differences in productivities that are caused largely by the economies of scale achieved in the process of the production.

As is well known, location theory and land use theory are closely interrelated with respect to the phenomenon of agglomeration (Mills 1972). In theories of individual location, two explanatory factors are contained in the utility function. One is the usual factor of private goods, and the other is distance from the city center or central business district (CBD). The demand for labor is presupposed to be relatively concentrated in the CBD. The distance to the CBD for a resident has two complex meanings. One is the disutility of the commuting distance to the CBD, and the other is the housing and amenity expressed by location theory; relatively cheaper housing is traded off with commuting costs (Alonso 1964; Muth 1969). The latter point should be extended to include the amenity value or the environmental quality of the location (Schweizer, Variya, and Hartwick 1976).

The utility function in the usual location model is formulated as follows:

$$U = U(Y, t),$$

where Y denotes the vector of the private goods and t denotes the distance to the CBD.

We can rewrite the model more generally as follows:

$$U = U(Y, A),$$

where A denotes a vector, the elements of which are various indicators of the amenity level of the location. The amenity level is considered to be the result of the working of various kinds of externalities in the area. For instance, amenity might be a function of the open space of the location and, accordingly, of the tax level that is the function of the open space. Much research has been done on this point. For example: "Households may derive utility from low population density — households derive utility from 'consuming open space' at the location where they are resident. Open space is then a public good. Suppose that households can be charged with a tax for consuming this public good. This tax may depend upon location and upon household class" (Schweizer, Variya, and Hartwick 1976). Until this point was made clear, most of the land use models formulated after Alonso's work had not taken exact notice of the relation between the concepts of externality and population density; in other words, they neglected the relations between the population density and tax — namely, the real income level.

In this sense, the relationship between distance and real income and environmental quality or population density represents two conflicting factors in an individual's utility function. We attempt to explain the urbanization process on the basis of these two factors.

THE MODEL

When we consider city population as a phenomenon that is an aggregation of individuals from the city population as well as from other regions' populations, we understand the phenomenon as the result of aggregated individual behaviors. On the basis of this understanding, we can formulate a model of individual behavior. In this section we are concerned with the following two modes of individual behavior: (1) the *agglomeration movement,* in which the individual moves to the urbanized area, and (2) the *dispersion movement,* in which the individual leaves the

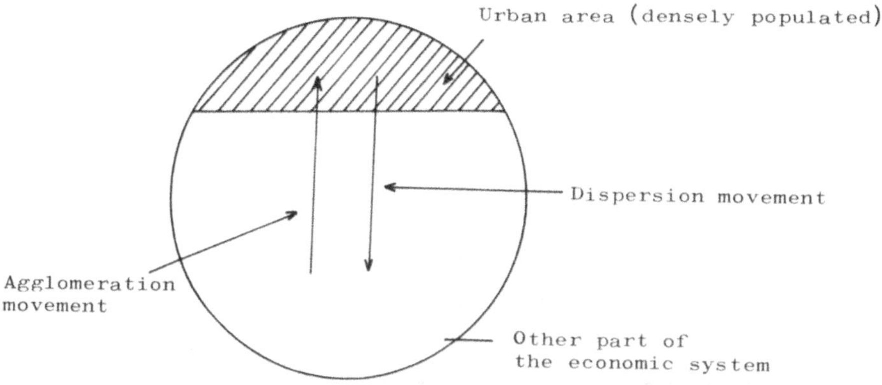

Figure 2–2. An Economic System and Population Movement

urbanized area. In Figure 2–2 we illustrate these two types of individual behavior with two arrows, one pointing toward the urban area and one pointing away from it.

We will explain the location-choice behavior by two factors. One is the difference between per capita income in the urban area and in the other area; this represents the attractiveness of the urban area. The other is the degradation of the environmental quality in the urban area, which represents the repulsion of the urban area. We note that the difference between per capita income in the city and in the other region promotes the agglomeration movement, and the degradation of the environmental quality promotes the dispersion movement. Dendrinos and Mullally (1981) presented their paper in a similar context.

We make the following assumptions:

1. For each consumer the level of the degradation of the environmental quality is supposed to be acknowledged as a composite measure of the environmental qualities of the city.
2. Individuals express their behavior over time by relocating, which might be called a Tiebout-type hypothesis (Tiebout 1956).
3. If the difference in per capita income is small and the degradation of the environmental quality is large, then the psychological tendency is unified (i.e., it has a single maximum) (Figure 2–3).
4. If the difference in per capita income is large and the degradation of the environmental quality is small, then the psychological tendency is unified, as shown in Figure 2–4.

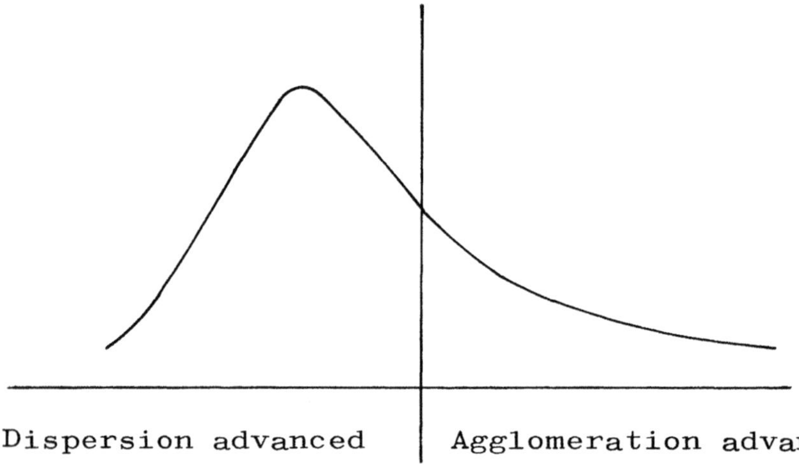

Figure 2–3. Distribution of the Psychological Tendencies: Dispersion Advanced

5. If the difference in per capita income and the degradation of the environmental quality are large, then the psychological tendency will be split between the agglomeration advanced and dispersion advanced, as in Figure 2–5.

Let C be a horizontal plane with coordinates a and b. We call C the *control space* or *parameter space*. A point $c = (a, b)$, and c is called a control point. Here, parameter a expresses the level of difference in per capita income, and b represents the level of environmental degradation in the concerned urban area.

Let X be a vertical line with coordinate x. X is called the *behavior space*. It represents the possible level of individual behavior, where level means the strength of the psychological tendency. The two modes of movement are supposed to be dependent on the individual psychological process regarding movement. The process is recognized as a potential of parameters a and b from the viewpoint of location-choice behavior, which is reflected in the utility function of the location. Thus the individual's psychological process regarding the location choice would be dominated by a dynamic that is represented by a gradient system of a potential. Suppose that the domain of the function is a one-dimensional line, R, which represents multi-dimensional psychological factors. Now the individual's psychological situation tends to maximize the potential locally so that his behavior is determined by local maxima. The function might

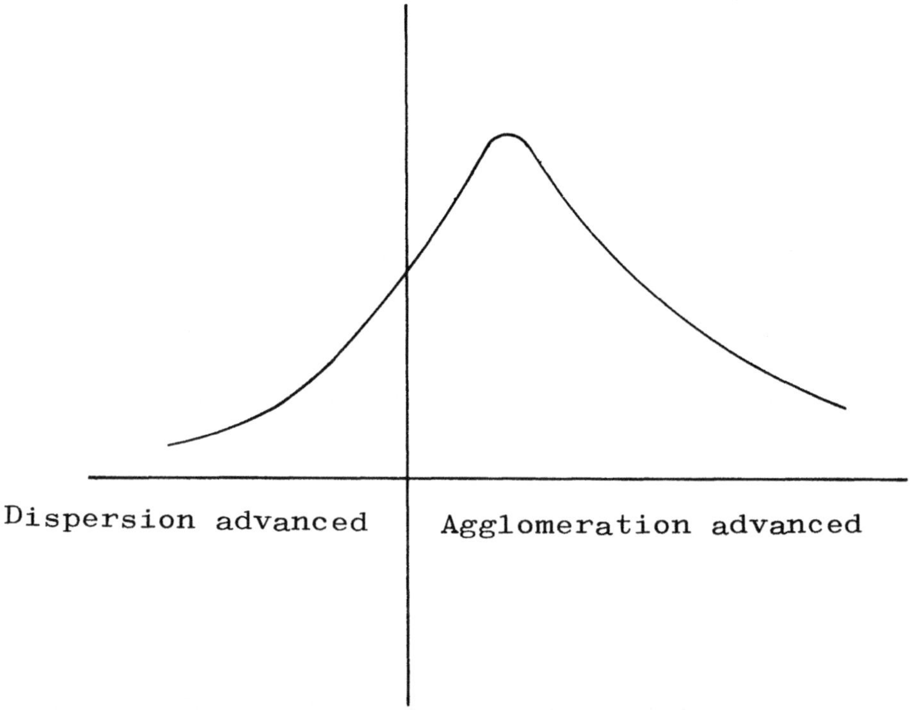

Figure 2–4. Distribution of the Psychological Tendencies: Agglomeration Advanced

in a sense be the distribution of the psychological tendency. The psychological tendency is caused by the psychological impact of different levels of attractiveness and repulsion in the urban area and in the other area.

We can summarize mathematically the background of our discussion as follows: *The control space parameterizes the distribution of the psychological tendency of the location behavior of consumers* (any particular diffeomorphism $g\colon U \to W \cap M$ is called a *parameterization* of the region $W \cap M$). In other words, each control point $c \in C$ determines a particular distribution P_c of psychological tendency X. We can incorporate the parameterized family of distributions into a single function, P, by defining

$$P\colon C \times X \to R$$

by the formula $P(c, x) = P_c(x)$.

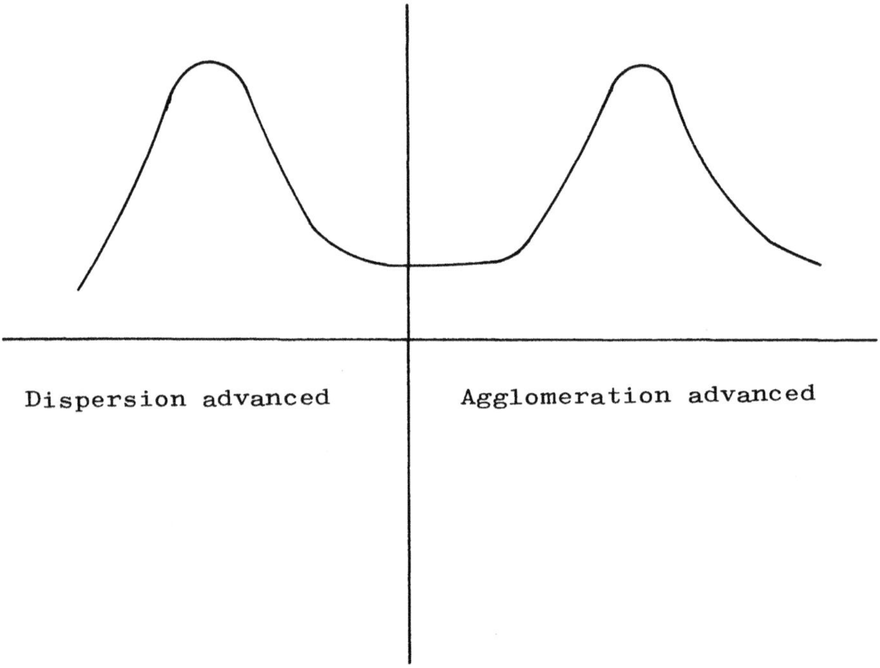

Figure 2–5. Distribution of the Psychological Tendencies: Split of the Psychological Tendencies

Let G_c denote the set of maxima of P_c. For example, if P_c is a distribution with a unique maximum at x_1, then G_c consists of the single point x_1. If, on the other hand, P_c is a distribution with two maxima at x_2, x_3, then G_c consists of the pair of points $\{x_2, x_3\}$.

Now, G_c is a function from c to x, which is sometimes single valued and sometimes double valued. Let G denote the graph of function G_c. The graph G is contained in a three-dimensional space, $C \times X = \mathbf{R}^3$, and is defined as a set of points (Zeeman and Isnard 1974):

$$G = \text{closure of } \{(c, x) : c \in C, x \in G_c\}.$$

Under this assumption, we could apply the classification theorem (Zeeman and Isnard 1974), which has been expressed as follows: Let $C = R^2$, $X = R$, P be any smooth generic function on $C \times X$, and G the resulting graph in $\mathbf{R}^3$. Then the only singularities of G are fold-curves and cusp-points. We formulate the following statement: The difference between per capita income in the city and in the other region and the rate of degradation of environmental quality are conflicting factors influencing the psychological tendency of the consumers.

If the amount of private goods increases in an economic system, achieving economic growth, and is accompanied by an increase of disamenity in the residential areas (i.e., the other region), the path that the system would follow should be drafted as such a path in the control space, as shown in Figure 2–6. Generally, when the real income of an

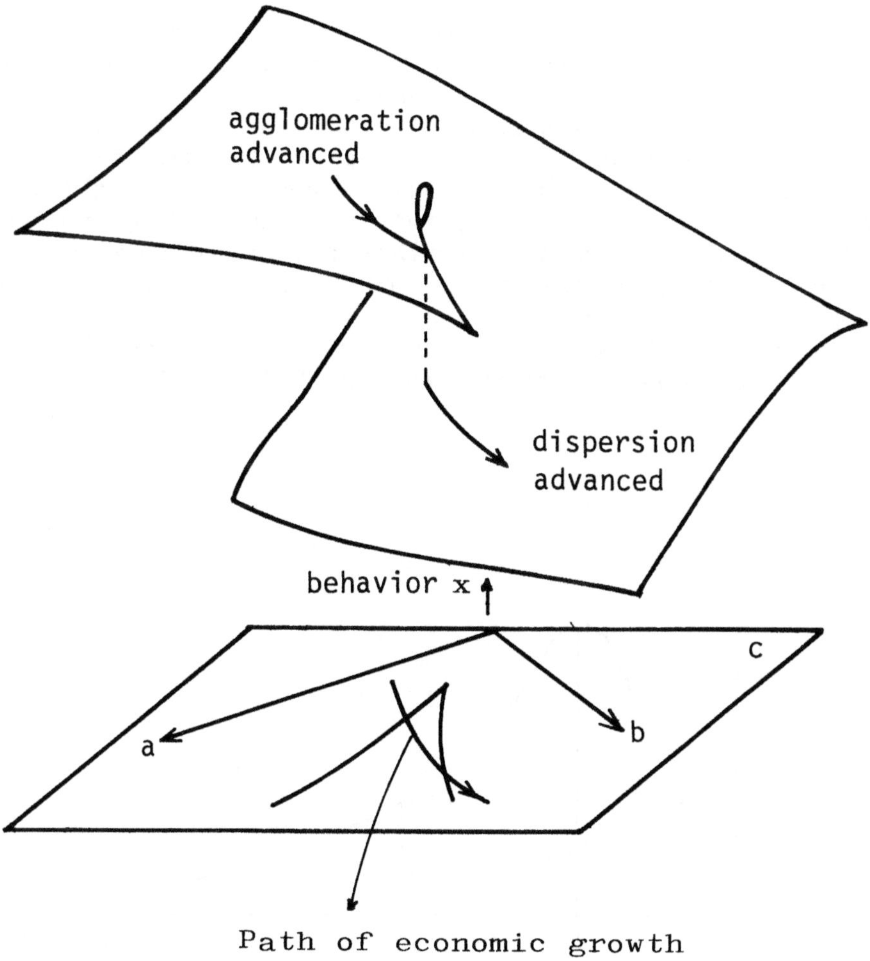

Figure 2–6. Behavior of the Consumer

economic system is small, economic growth is not associated with severe degradation of environmental quality. However, the higher the level of real income attained, the more severely the environmental quality is degraded, as shown in Figures 2–1 and 2–6. Finally, the process reaches a point *c*, a catastrophe point, and the consumer's psychological tendency changes from agglomeration advanced to dispersion advanced.

AN IMPLICATION FOR ENVIRONMENTAL POLICY

As the second step of our analysis, we relax the Tiebout assumption. Now we suppose that the consumers are able to influence policy formulation instead of always having to move.

We assume the following points: (1) Policy is influenced by the opinions of the individuals. Let $P(x)$ be the number of people who support policy x. (2) As Zeeman and Isnard (1974) suppose, the administration makes a policy decision according to Maxwell's rule (to change policy to where support is maximum) and the Delay rule (to change policy in the direction that locally increases support). We illustrate distribution of policy support in Figure 2–7.

As shown in Figure 2–8, while the administration's choice is policy x_1, it changes to policy x_2 by Maxwell's rule. In Figures 2–9 through 2–

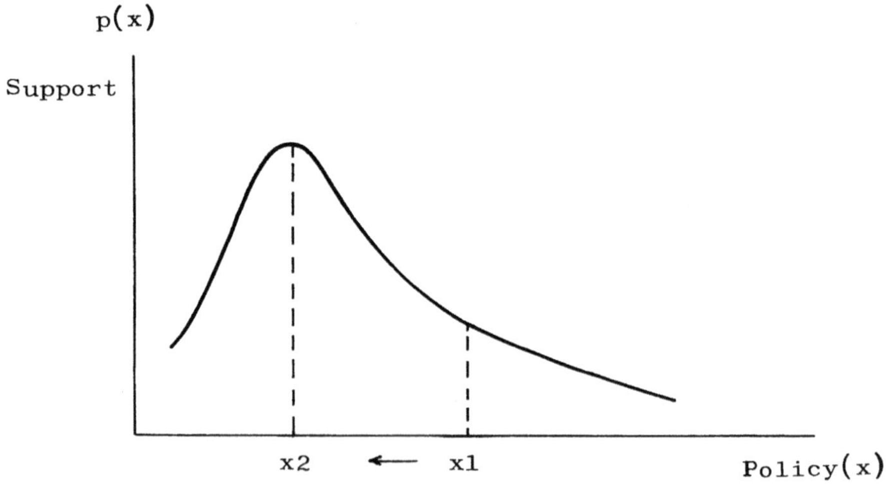

Figure 2–7. Distribution of Policy Support

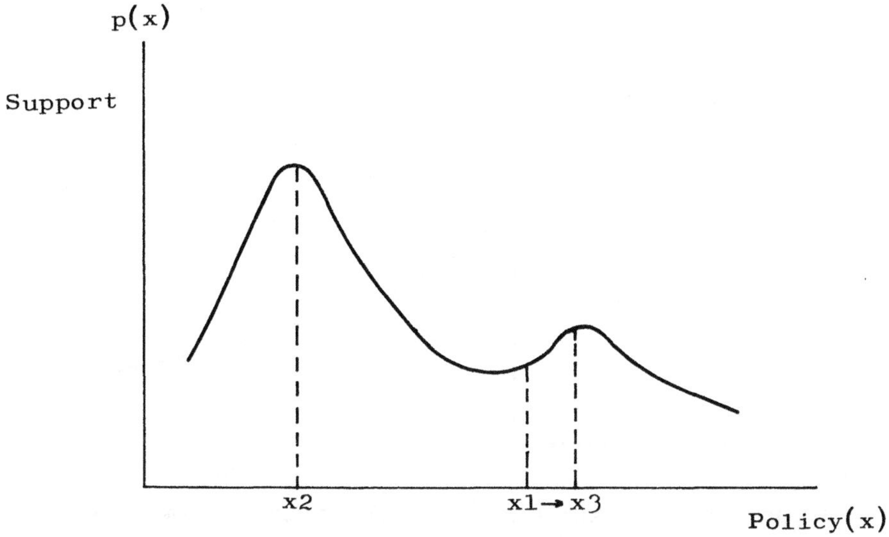

Figure 2–8. Maxwell's Rule and the Delay Rule

11, the policy is changed to x_3 by the Delay rule, in spite of lower support than for x_2. This is a result of lack of information, sociological pressure, inertia of past history, and so on (Zeeman 1977). In this model, when the consumer's psychological tendency is dispersion advanced, he will simultaneously support a policy for environmental conservation. On the other hand, the consumer will support a policy for industrial development when his tendency is agglomeration advanced. It is reasonable to set these additional assumptions: (3) If the difference in per capita income is minimal and the degradation of the environmental quality is large, then the distribution of consumer opinion has a single maximum, as shown in Figure 2–9. (4) If the difference in per capita income is large and the degradation of the environmental quality is small, then the distribution of opinion is as illustrated in Figure 2–10. (5) If the difference in per capita income and the degradation of environmental quality are both large, then opinion will be split, as shown in Figure 2–11. On the basis of the argument of the preceding section, the two factors are conflicting factors influencing the policy for industrial development and the policy for conserving environmental quality.

Now two cusps appear on the control space C (see Figure 2–12). As the economic growth path in Figure 2–12 shows, many consumers' psy-

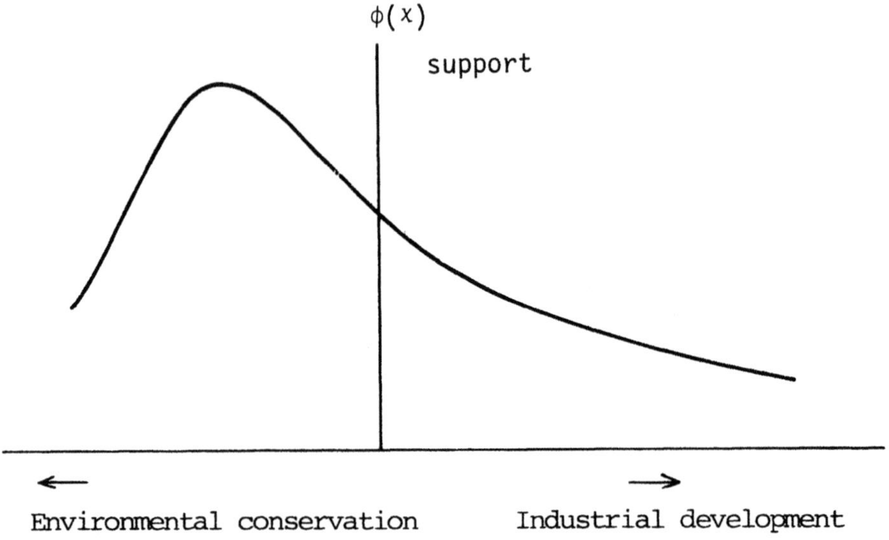

Figure 2–9. Distribution of Opinion: Environmental Conservation–Oriented

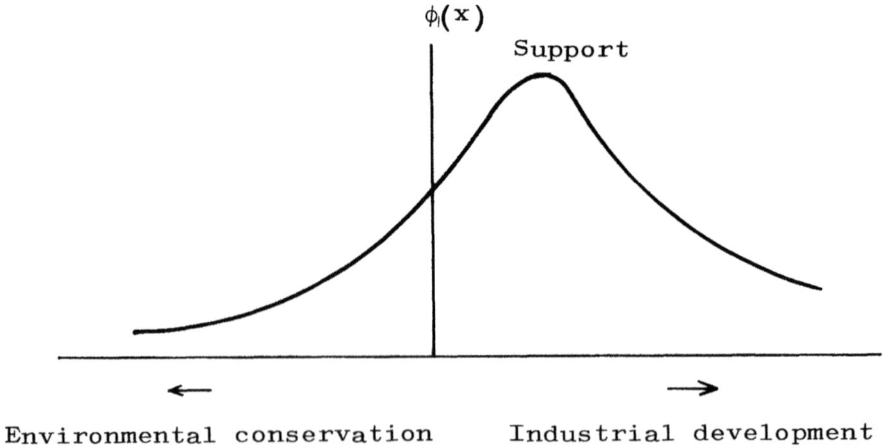

Figure 2–10. Distribution of Opinion: Industrial Development–Oriented

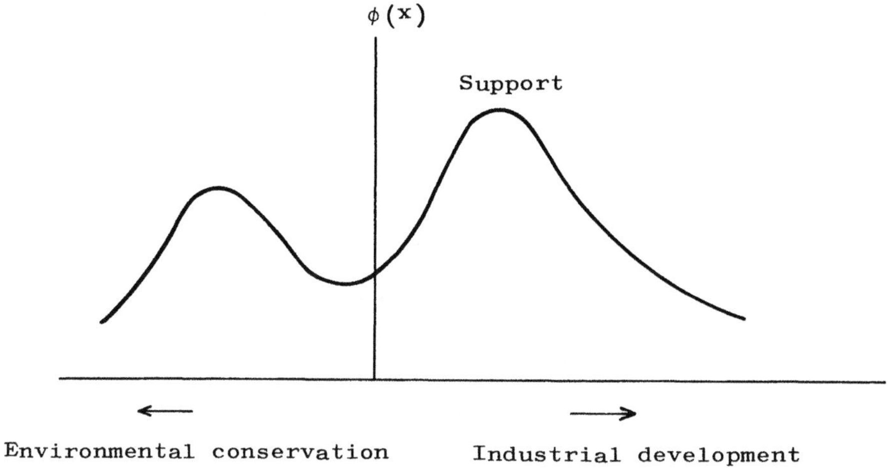

Figure 2–11. Distribution of Opinion: Split of the Support

chological tendencies jump catastrophically at c, but the government keeps the policy for industrial development. With some time delay, the policy changes from industrial development to environmental conservation at c'. Thus, if we project different kinds of folds and cusps in the same control space, we can show that the path of development of an economic system would cross various kinds of quantitatively discontinuous points.

Reviewing the process from a historical point of view, we find that consumers increasingly feel the need for the economic development and agglomeration of urban areas. As a result, the environment of urban areas is degraded — and the cost of compensating for it is expensive. Economic development necessarily entails the subsidization of rural industries and the degeneration of urban environments; in consequence, government expenses increase and become heavier for the taxpayer. Accordingly, regardless of how entrenched government policy for industrial development is, the government tends to change the policy to favor environmental conservation.

The path we have described is the type that has been followed by developed countries. The economic systems of developing countries will generally follow a similar path of industrial development. But in the case of developing countries, the escalating cost of development delays any action until the government catastrophically declares a policy of development. There might, of course, be other factors that would affect these

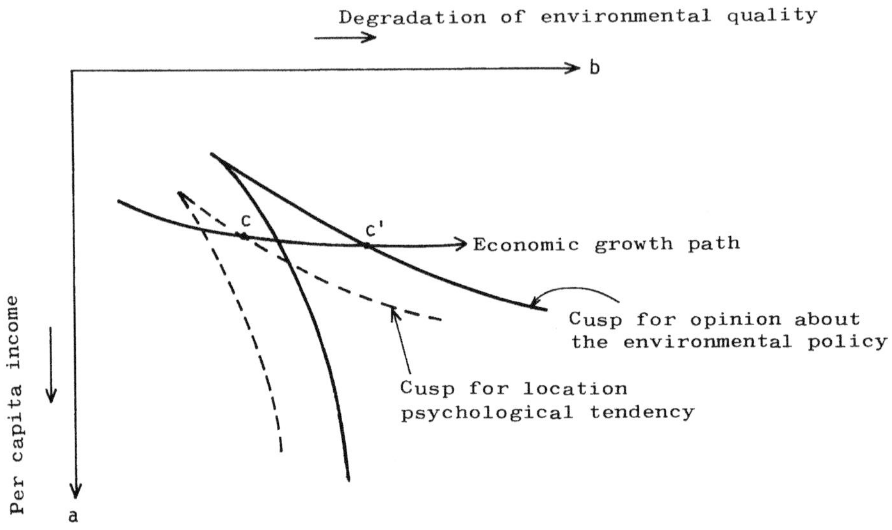

Figure 2–12. Two Cusps on the Control Space

outcomes and distributions of psychological tendency or opinion. Among these factors, the level of income should be easily recognized. In such a case, they would be parameterized by a higher-dimensional control space, so that the changes of behavior would be explained by higher — that is, "swallowtail" or "butterfly" — catastrophes.

CONCLUSION

We recognize many factors in the process of urbanization that influence the process. Simplifying greatly, we synthesized the complex factors into only two *conflicting factors*.

Although this model is but a simple application of elementary catastrophe theory to the urbanization process, it introduces a new perspective on the urbanization process made possible by recent developments in mathematics (Thom 1975). This urbanization model is a static one, which needs to be transformed within a dynamic equation system. The empirical research on this model is presented in Chapter 3. We hope to achieve a complete social, economic, and environmental representation of the dynamic urbanization process on the basis of this approach in the near future.

3 POPULATION DENSITY GRADIENT AND RENT GRADIENT

In Chapter 1 we considered the existence of location equilibrium conditions with respect to the environmental quality of each location, and in Chapter 2 we examined a model of the process of urbanization accompanied by environmental degradation. Both models make clear theoretically the motivation of individual behavior.

In this chapter we examine the changes in population distribution and in urban rent resulting from acknowledged location equilibrium conditions. Our empirical analysis focuses on the interrelationship between economic growth and the urbanization process in the intra-urban context, with respect to environmental degradation. We examine the suburbanization process by checking the shift in population density of urban areas as an index of population distribution, which gives us a typical projection of the urban land use phenomenon.

We hypothesize that the deviation between the population density gradient and the rent gradient observed in most large metropolitan areas can be explained as the result of environmental degradation in the central business district (CBD) vicinity, which renders it less desirable as a residential area. The change of the parameters of the population density gradient equation, shown later in this chapter, is consistent with our hypothesis, although we cannot completely test our hypothesis. The analysis uses time-series data for Tokyo and New York. The chapter also considers some perspectives for further study, based on dynamic systems theory. (We have already presented one suggestion for further study along these lines in Chapter 2.) Finally, since the rent gradient and population density gradient are closely related theoretically as well as empirically, additional empirical research is included in the chapter appendixes for the reader's reference.

DIFFERENCE BETWEEN THE POPULATION DENSITY GRADIENT AND THE RENT GRADIENT

In this section we indicate the difference between the rent gradient and the population density gradient and elaborate the hypothesis that environmental degradation in the CBD is a primary cause of this difference. As is well known, the population density gradient is approximated by the negative exponential function of the distance from the city center (Muth 1969; Mills 1972). This population density gradient hypothesis is reduced from a single-center city structure of the Thünen type as the first-step approximation of the urban economic structure. The Thünen-type approach has been applied in much recent research effort, since it reflects one of the most important features of the city structure. On the other hand, we find that the rent gradient hypothesis is, quite logically, also related to the negative exponential function of population density. So, theoretically, the rent gradient and the population density gradient are commonly derived from the equilibrium location of economic agents. This equilibrium condition assumes profit maximization by housing producers as well as utility maximization by consumers (Mills 1972).

The population density gradient decreases in accordance with increases in the income of the residents. Thus, it can be said that the economic growth of a country, to some degree, causes the so-called suburbanization phenomenon. Mills suggests that the suburbanization phenomenon can be attributed to a change in the marginal utility of residential space resulting from income growth (Mills 1972).

The close relationship between the population density gradient and the rent gradient has been demonstrated empirically as well as theoretically. Mills has provided strong empirical evidence showing that the size of the population and the per capita income of the city work to flatten both the population density gradient and the rent gradient.

Much empirical research on population distribution has been based on the negative exponential function of population density. Berry and Gillard

(1977) have depicted a regularity, which is a consistent decrease of the absolute value of the power number of the negative exponential function among cities of all sizes in the United States and in other developed countries. Figures 3–1 through 3–3 illustrate the remarkable change of the value in the case of Tokyo (density in these figures is shown in thousands per square kilometer; distance is in kilometers).

However, if we look in greater detail at the empirical tests made on the negative exponential population density function, some questions emerge. Certainly, in the case of urban rent or land price structure, the original negative exponential equation fits the data during the recent process of urbanization. But in the case of residential population density, the negative exponential equation hypothesis does not seem to be an explanation because, within close vicinity of the CBD, the residential population is considerably less dense than that given by the negative exponential equation, especially in the big metropolitan areas. Thus, in the neighborhood of the CBD, the gradient is not necessarily approximated by the negative exponential equation. Figure 3–4 illustrates how the negative exponential curve is appropriate for the rent gradient but not for the population density gradient. Therefore, it is incorrect for the rent gradient and the residential population density gradient to be approximated by the same functional form. Nonetheless, this contradiction has not been studied, and, as we have already mentioned, most of the models on the population density structure are typically reduced theoretically from the rent gradient. Although a formal theory to explain this contradiction is not presented here, the following remarks may offer some insights into why residential population density tends to decline in the vicinity of the CBD.

First of all, residential population density in the vicinity of the CBD may be influenced by the phenomenon called urban blight (Chapin 1965), where urban blight refers to the physical deterioration (or the existence of deficiencies in the quality) of structures and their immediate environment. More generally, in the vicinity of the CBD, the intensity of environmental degradation in terms of air, noise, and visual pollution may well represent a severe diseconomy to residential dwellers.

Second, it is important to distinguish the real concentration of business firms in the CBD from what is hypothesized by the Thünen model. Fales and Moses (1972) pose an interesting question in this regard: Why did theorists who were concerned with the internal spatial structure of cities largely ignore Weber's reasoning and turn to Thünen? They point out that Weber's theory can provide a great deal of insight into the spatial structure of cities that developed in the nineteenth century. Their approach presents a strong and reasonable alternative to the recently pop-

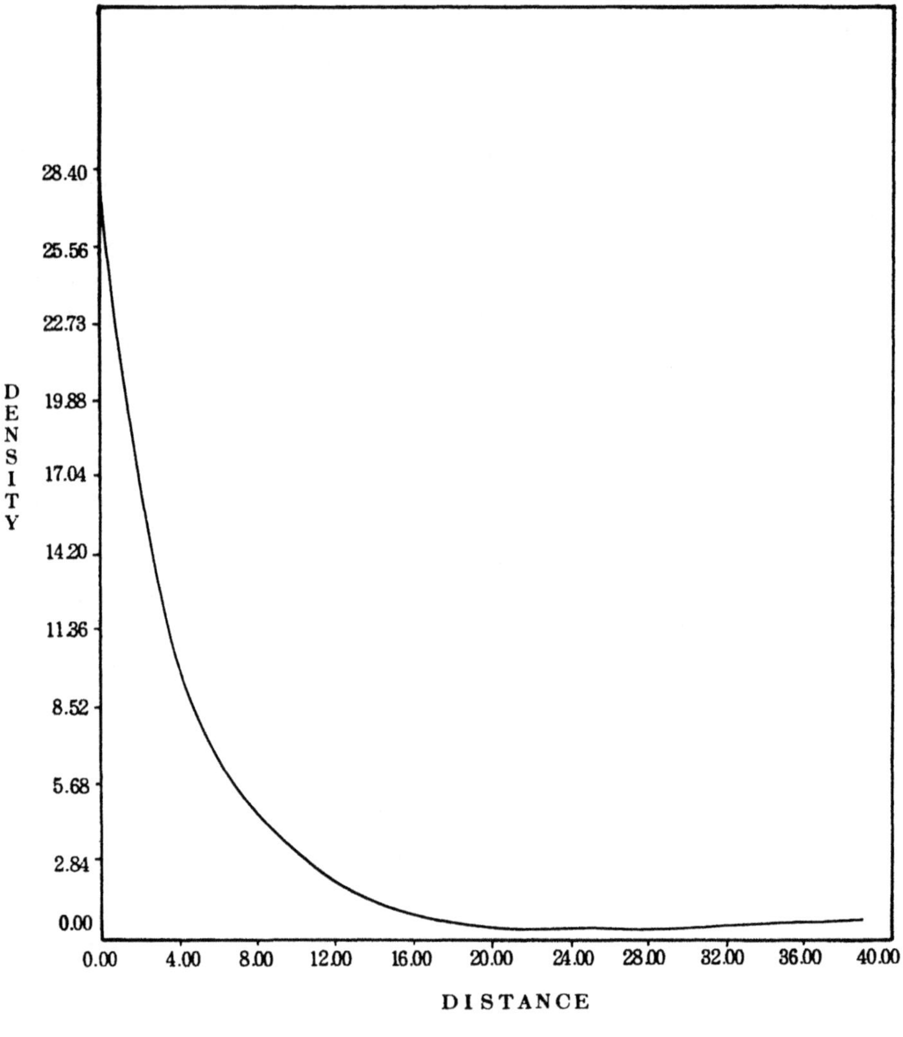

Figure 3–1. Changes in the Negative Exponential Urban Population Density Gradient, Tokyo, 1920

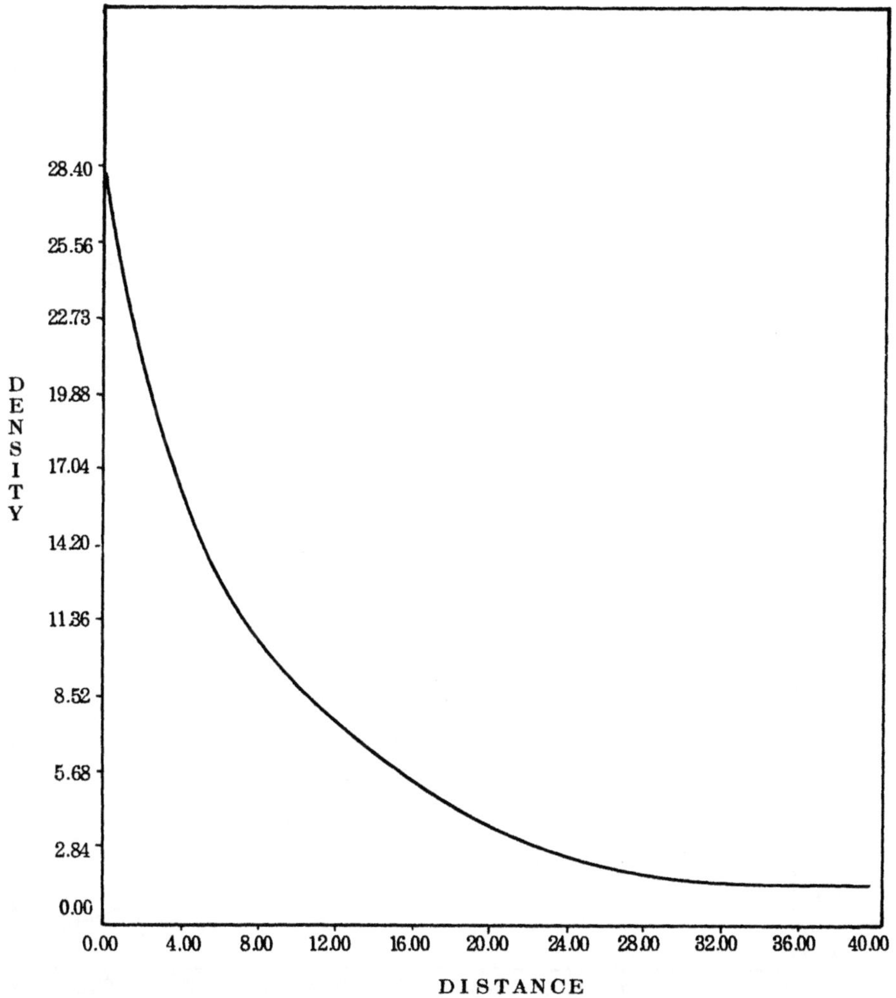

Figure 3–2. Changes in the Negative Exponential Urban Population Density Gradient, Tokyo, 1950

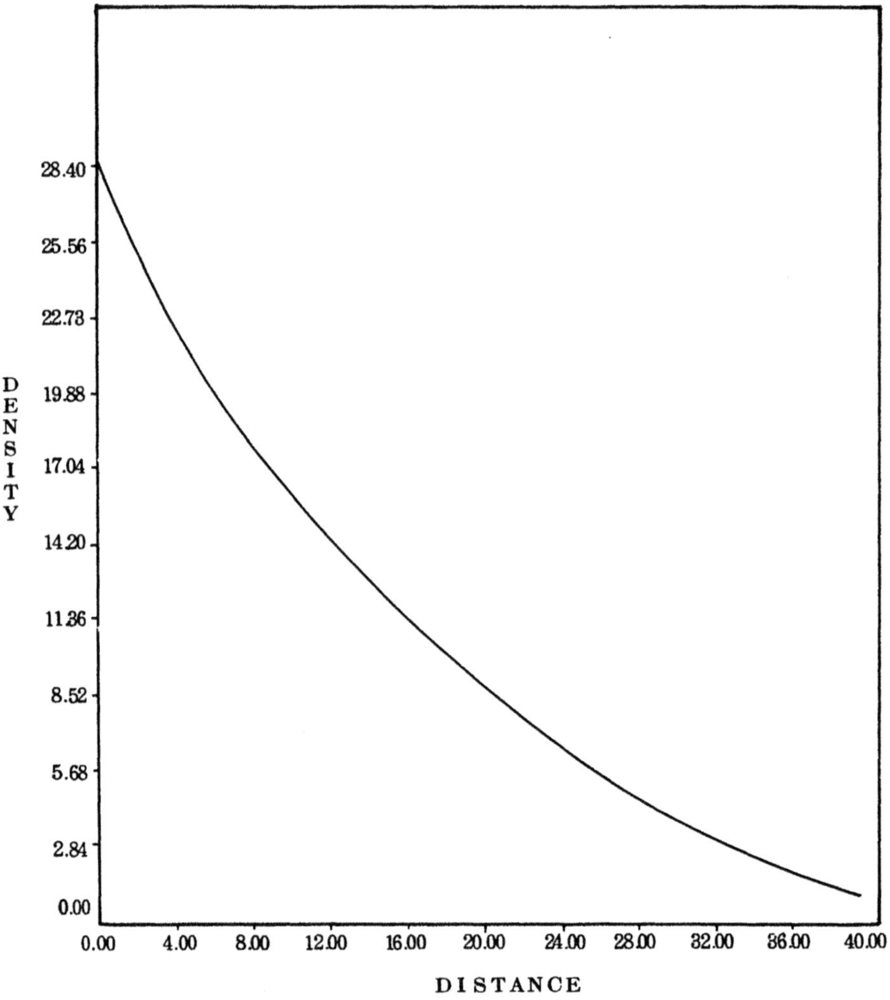

Figure 3–3. Changes in the Negative Exponential Urban Population Density Gradient, Tokyo, 1975

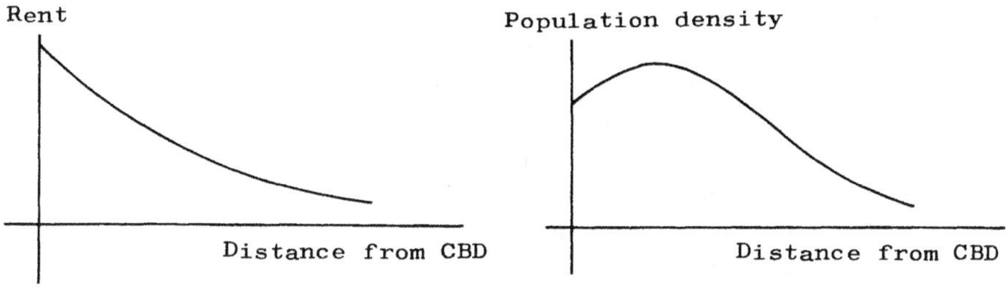

Figure 3–4. Shapes of the Rent and Population Density Gradients

ular utility-function approach in depicting features of the population distribution in urban areas.

Along these lines of reasoning, the importance of industrial structure to intracity population density is evident. An empirical test of the city of Yokohama has shown that population distribution within the city is affected by changes in industrial structure (Orishimo 1971, 1973). Specifically, whether the population density gradient becomes flatter or steeper seems to depend heavily on changes in the industrial structure (basic-nonbasic industry ratio) within parts of the city (see Andrews 1953). In the case of Yokohama, the population density gradient varied according to changes in industrial structure along the radials extending from the city center.

A general rule applies to the relationship between city size and the basic-nonbasic ratio of the industrial structure: As city size becomes large, the weight of service industries increases. Thus, since for service (or nonbasic) industries agglomeration economy works naturally in the CBD area, a high proportion of businesses are drawn to the CBD.

Here, it might be useful to consider some of the above points within a dynamic framework. Harrison and Kain (1974) have described the urbanization process as the result of the cumulative distribution of newly added dwelling units in a time period and of the location choices of economic agents in the industrialized area. This viewpoint is expressed in the following formulation:

$$D_t = \sum_{i=1}^{t} d_i u_i \Big/ \sum_{i=1}^{t} u_i,$$

where D_t = average net residential density at time period t, d_i = net residential density of the dwelling units added to the area in time period i, and u_i = number of dwelling units added to the area in time period i.

$$D(k, t) = F[X(k, t)].$$

$X(k, t)$ denotes the vector, the elements of which are the price of residential land, the price of nonland factors, the preferences of consumers for relatively more land, the per family incomes of likely purchasers, and the transportation costs incurred at location k, at time period t, which result from the spread of urban blight, physical environmental degradation, and greater concentration of the business firms in the CBD caused by the change of the industrial structure of the city. Change in $X(k, t)$ affects only incremental density.

If we look at the problem posed by the divergence between the population density gradient and the rent gradient from the dynamic point of view illustrated by Harrison and Kain's model, we might gain some insight. At an early stage of the urbanization process (Figures 3–5a and 3–6a), the shapes of the rent gradient and the population density gradient are similar. But after the urbanization process progresses to a mature stage (Figures 3–5c and 3–6c), the shape of the population gradient is different from that of the rent gradient. Figure 3–7 shows the shift of the shapes of the locus of the first quadrant of Figure 3–5.

AN EMPIRICAL TEST FROM THE DYNAMIC VIEWPOINT

In addition to the negative exponential model for the population density gradient, many other varieties of empirical models have been developed (e.g., McDonald and Bowman 1976). Among them, the following model has been formulated by Newling (1969) and tested by many researchers (e.g., Glickman 1979).

$$D(k, t) = \alpha \exp [\beta k(t) + \gamma k^2(t)], \tag{3.1}$$

where $D(k, t)$ denotes the density, k the distance from CBD, and t the time period. In this model the signs of the parameters give us the change of the shape of the locus as shown in Figure 3–8.

In this empirical research on the shift of the population density gra-

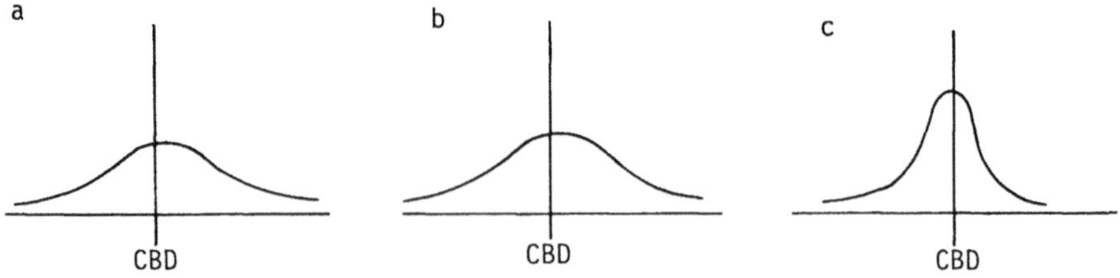

Figure 3–5. Shift of the Rent Gradient

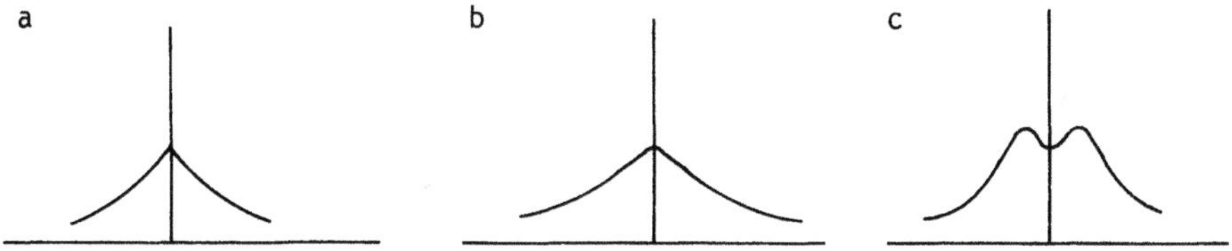

Figure 3–6. Shift of the Residential Population Density Gradient

dient, this form of the model seems to be an adequate first approximation because of the relationship between the shapes of the locuses and the signs of the parameters. In other words, this form shows us some characteristics of the process of change of the urban population density gradient. Using time-series data for population density by districts in New York and Tokyo metropolitan areas, we computed the secular changes of the parameters of equation (3.1). It is especially noteworthy that the sign of the parameter, β, has changed from minus to plus in the Tokyo area, as shown in Figure 3–9. The change of the sign of the estimated parameter corresponds to the fact that the land use characteristics of the CBD and its vicinity change drastically. The vicinity of the CBD has become a nonresidential area for several reasons — for instance, the unattractive features of the area as a residential area, such as high rent, high tax rate, environmental degradation, and urban blight. On the other hand, because of the advantages of agglomeration economy, a high concentration of business firms prevails in the CBD. Thus, rents rise exceedingly in the vicinity of the CBD, regardless of partial urban blight. Accordingly, the shapes of the population density and rent gradients become different.

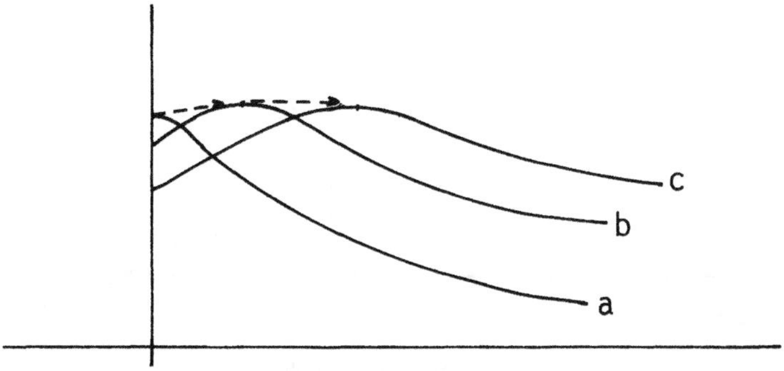

Figure 3–7. Shift of the Maximum Point of Population Density

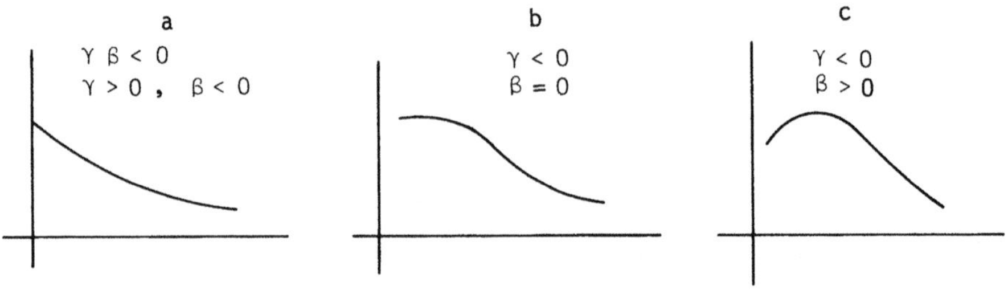

Figure 3–8. Shapes of the Population Density Gradient Locus and the Change of Parameter's Signs

Figure 3–10 shows the estimated locus of β and γ computed by the available data. This represents the typical shift of the shapes of the locus of population density illustrated in Figures 3–5 and 3–6. We estimate the parameters α and β for New York and Tokyo. The results are shown in Tables 3–1 and 3–2.

For the New York metropolitan area, Figure 3–11 shows the estimated locus of β and γ given the available data. In contrast with the case of Tokyo, the sign of β does not change. However, it is assumed that with supplemental data points for New York at prior stages of the urbanization process, the sign of β was negative, as illustrated in Figure 3–12. Nonetheless, this empirical work indicates one common feature — namely, in some time period of the urbanization process, land use changes are very rapid in the CBD and its vicinity.

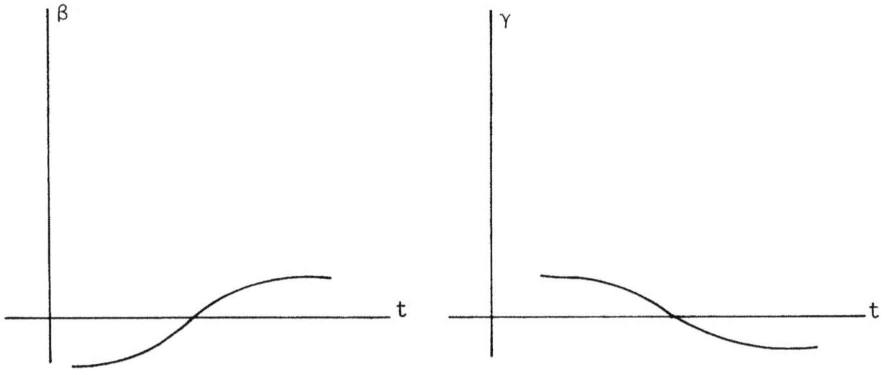

Figure 3–9. Change of the Signs of β, γ — Tokyo

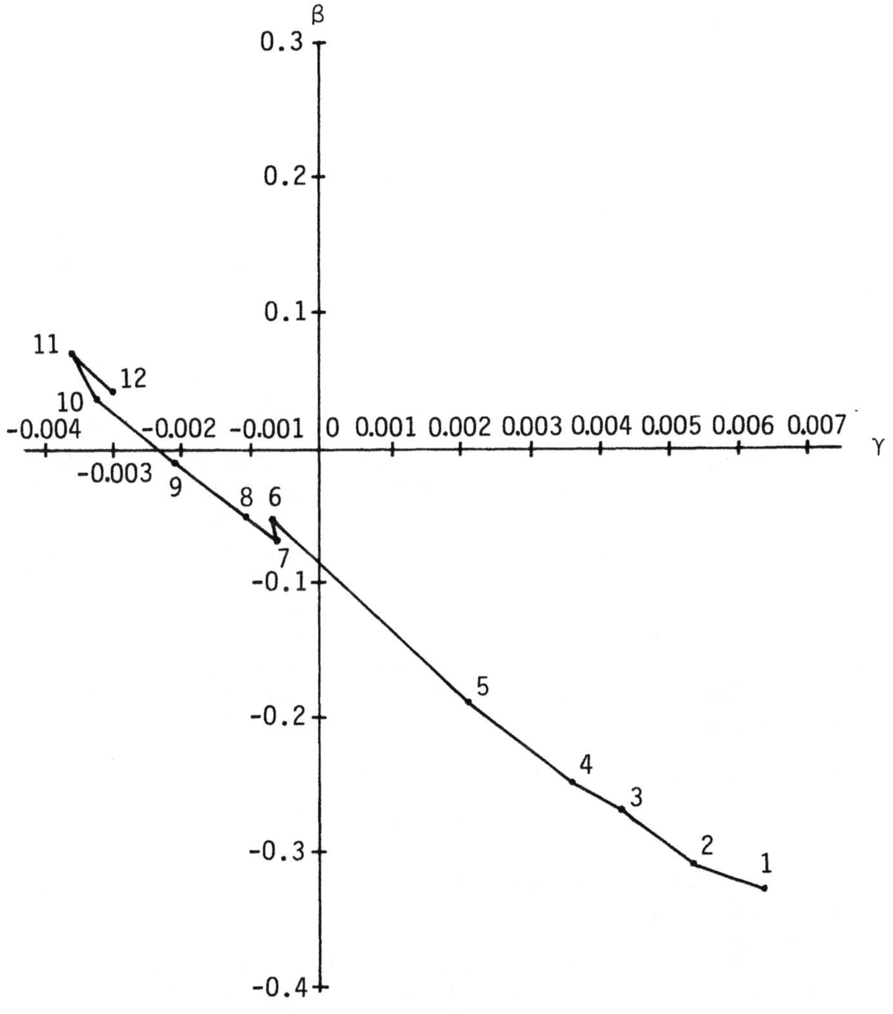

Figure 3–10. Estimated Locus of β, γ — Tokyo

Table 3–1. Estimated Values of Parameters in New York and Tokyo: $D = \alpha + \beta k + u$

New York					
Year	R^{*2}	α	β	$t\text{-}v(\alpha)$	$t\text{-}v(\beta)$
1920	0.688	63587.9	−0.136801	40.165027	−5.694259
1930	0.413	44816.7	−0.106241	23.935973	−3.173790
1940	0.333	36266.1	−0.094188	21.221210	−2.544910
1950	0.242	24042.9	−0.050315	29.026579	−1.935288

Tokyo					
Year	R^{*2}	α	β	$t\text{-}v(\alpha)$	$t\text{-}v(\beta)$
1920	0.706	4184.9	−0.084854	16.200461	−3.857546
1925	0.800	7170.3	−0.096880	19.947775	−5.094099
1930	0.854	10416.7	−0.104026	23.598456	−6.209615
1935	0.887	13686.6	−0.109700	26.918746	−7.255567
1940	0.921	17682.7	−0.109789	33.964885	−8.922154
1945	0.893	7048.0	−0.066385	42.825131	−7.508393
1950	0.939	16850.9	−0.088252	48.224994	−10.233553
1955	0.932	22701.3	−0.091663	45.348951	−9.698142
1960	0.925	28273.8	−0.093347	43.142672	−9.194613
1965	0.882	29098.2	−0.084642	36.697304	−7.071793
1970	0.829	26107.7	−0.071915	34.081768	−5.639774
1975	0.774	31030.6	−0.071736	28.887534	−4.688699

Note: The unit used is persons per square kilometer.

$$R^{*2} = 1 - \frac{\Sigma_i(Y_{li} - \alpha - \beta_l x_{li})^2/(n - l - 1)}{\Sigma_i(Y_i - \bar{Y})^2/(n - 1)},$$

where R^* is the multiple correlation coefficient adjusted for the degrees of freedom, and i denotes number of sample size.

t-v: *t*-values.

Sources: Tokyo: Statistics Bureau, Japanese Prime Minister's Office, *National Report of Census* (Tokyo: Nihon-Tokei-Kyokai, 1920–1975). Samples for area population are based on ku (ward), shi (city), and cho-son (town and village) and are arranged in a western direction from the center.

New York: See Appendix 3.3.

Table 3–2. Estimated Values of Parameters in New York and Tokyo: $D = \alpha + \beta k + \gamma k^2 + u$

New York								
Year	α	$t\text{-}v(\alpha)$	β	γ	$t\text{-}v(\beta)$	$t\text{-}v(\gamma)$	R^{*2}	*MAPE*
1920	10.0162	14.872988	0.130202	−0.0130858	0.939739	−2.000269	0.795	4.7
1930	9.35308	14.838441	0.197962	−0.0129898	1.711224	−2.714542	0.540	11.0
1940	9.28629	14.732486	0.177535	−0.0116029	1.534654	−2.424717	0.450	13.6
1950	9.75375	15.474096	0.024509	−0.0031950	0.211863	−0.667694	0.303	6.8
1960	9.09695	14.432091	0.100972	−0.0053032	0.872821	−1.108239	0.214	7.7
Tokyo								
Year	α	$t\text{-}v(\alpha)$	β	γ	$t\text{-}v(\beta)$	$t\text{-}v(\gamma)$	R^{*2}	*MAPE*
1920	9.91496	29.448714	−0.333214	0.006423	−8.591013	6.636955	0.935	5.7
1925	10.2053	30.311038	−0.306131	0.005411	−7.892751	5.591826	0.947	5.0
1930	10.3184	30.646969	−0.272240	0.004350	−7.018967	4.495215	0.945	5.0
1935	10.3982	30.883902	−0.247457	0.003562	−6.380003	3.681292	0.947	5.2
1940	10.3056	30.609005	−0.192581	0.002141	−4.965174	2.212468	0.947	5.1
1945	8.6987	25.836416	−0.040890	−0.000659	−1.054254	−0.681297	0.906	3.7
1950	9.5935	28.494157	−0.066409	−0.000564	−1.712185	−0.583724	0.945	3.8
1955	9.7540	28.970806	−0.048142	−0.001125	−1.241213	−1.163020	0.945	3.8
1960	9.7417	28.934237	−0.013286	−0.002070	−0.342556	−2.139481	0.956	3.4
1965	9.5038	28.227634	0.037446	−0.003157	0.965457	−3.262602	0.957	2.9
1970	9.2914	27.596841	0.066554	−0.003581	1.715923	−3.700367	0.952	2.9
1975	9.6057	28.530207	0.044429	−0.003004	1.145487	−3.104327	0.867	3.8

Note: The unit used is persons per square kilometer.

$$R^{*2} = 1 - \frac{\Sigma(Y_i - \alpha - \beta k_i - \gamma k_i^2)^2/(n - 2 - 1)}{\Sigma(Y_i - \overline{Y})^2/(n - 1)} .$$

MAPE: mean absolute percentage of error.

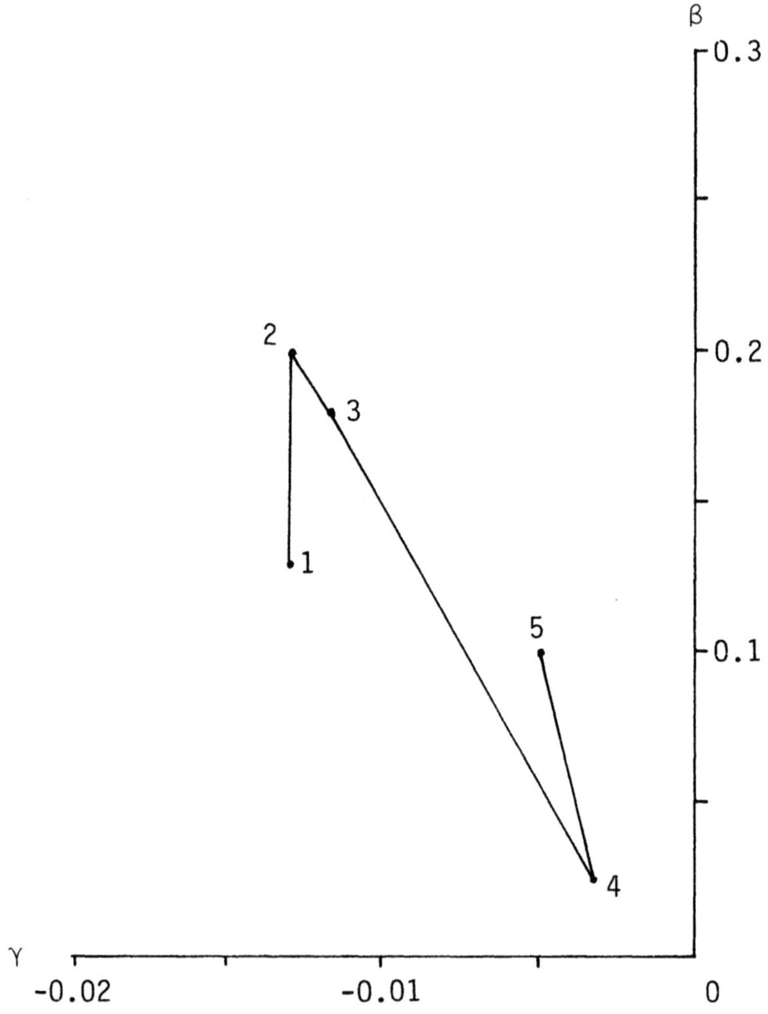

Figure 3–11. Estimated Locus of β, γ — New York

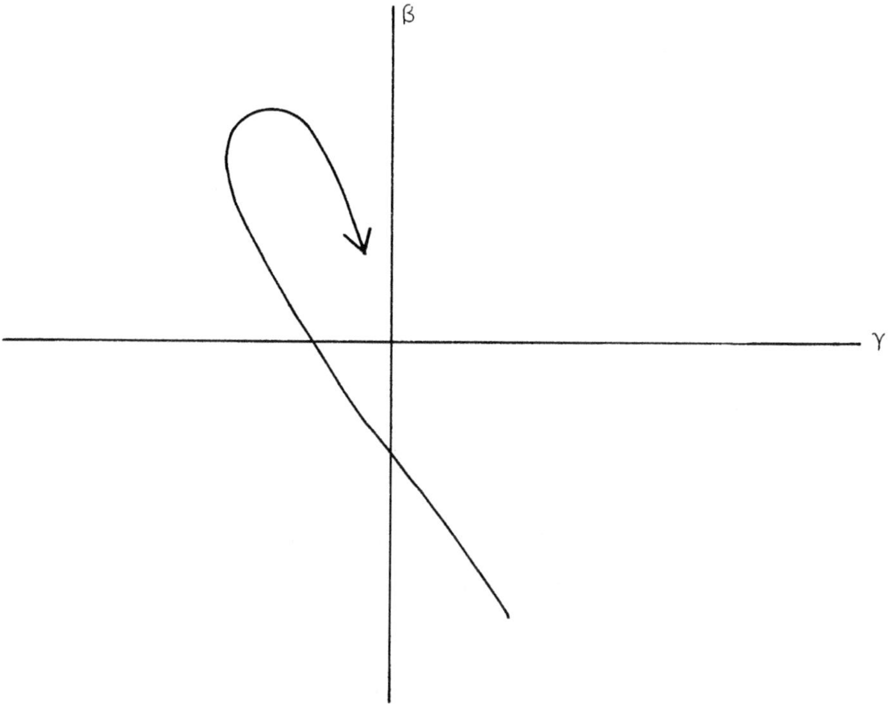

Figure 3–12. Estimated Locus of β, γ — New York

PERSPECTIVES FOR FUTURE STUDY

We have just examined the changing characteristics of demographic phenomena in urban areas on the basis of a hypothesis. Our intent was to make clear the exact characteristics of the divergence between the rent gradient and the population density gradient, using time-series data.

In Figure 3–13, which records the urbanization process, we consider the population density gradient as one dimensional; the urbanization process is expressed in the figure by the n-dimensional space $\mathbf{R}^n$. This urbanization process might be considered to be caused by economic and social elements, $Y(t)$. We can suppose that the change in the urbanization process over time is understood as a flow or vector field, $\dot{X}(t) = F(X,Y)$, such that change in the urbanization process is a function of the urbanization process itself and economic and social elements. Fundamentally,

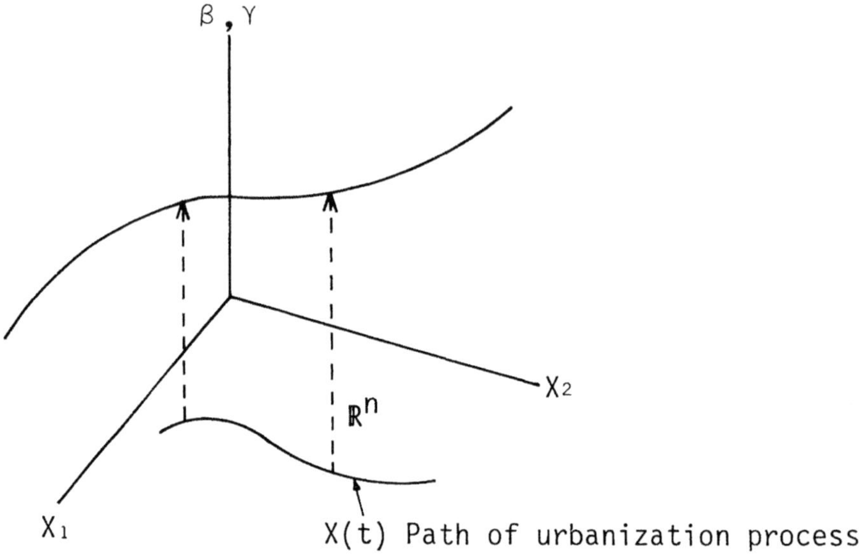

Figure 3–13. β, γ and the Urbanization Process

$$\beta, \gamma : \mathbf{R}^n \rightarrow \mathbf{R},$$

or, in words, the β and γ parameters that portray population density gradient simply represent one explanatory dimension of the urbanization process.

$$X : t \rightarrow \mathbf{R}^n.$$

X represents the more complete set of social, economic, and environmental elements that, when characterized over time, provide a multidimensional representation of the urbanization process. The flow or vector field, X, is illustrated in three-dimensional space in Figure 3–13.

If we formulate the dynamic equation system that expresses the urbanization process, we will be able to prove more clearly the hypothesized relationship between the urbanization process and environmental degradation. This formulation should be the subject of future study.

We already examined the change of the parameter's sign based on our hypothesis of Figure 3–7, as shown in Figure 3–10 on Tokyo and Figure 3–11 on New York. Also, approximated locus of the location change of the population density in New York and Tokyo since 1920 were estimated based on the real observed data as shown in Figures 3–14 to 3–21.

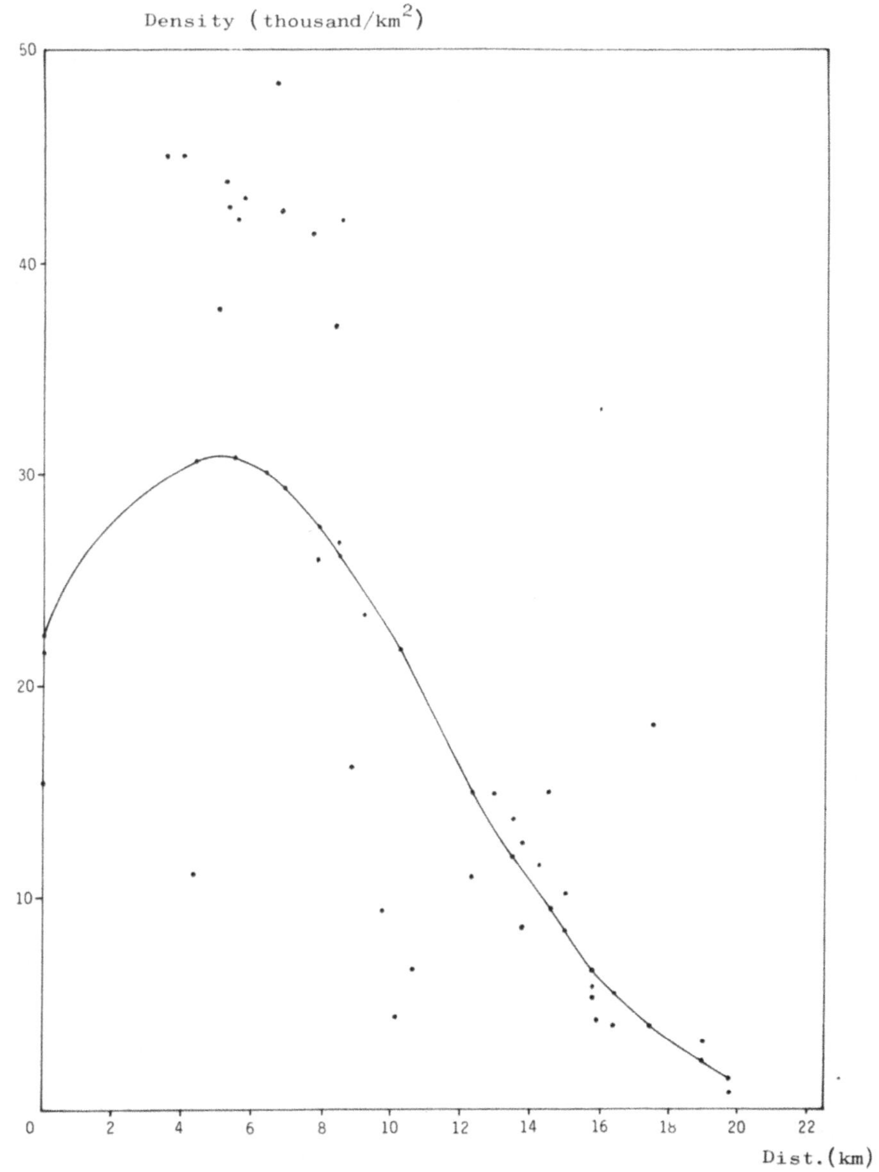

$$D = 22386 \cdot \mathrm{Exp}\,(0.1302K - 0.0130858K^2)$$

Dotted points denote actual values, and curve expresses the locus of estimated values.

Figure 3–14. New York, 1920

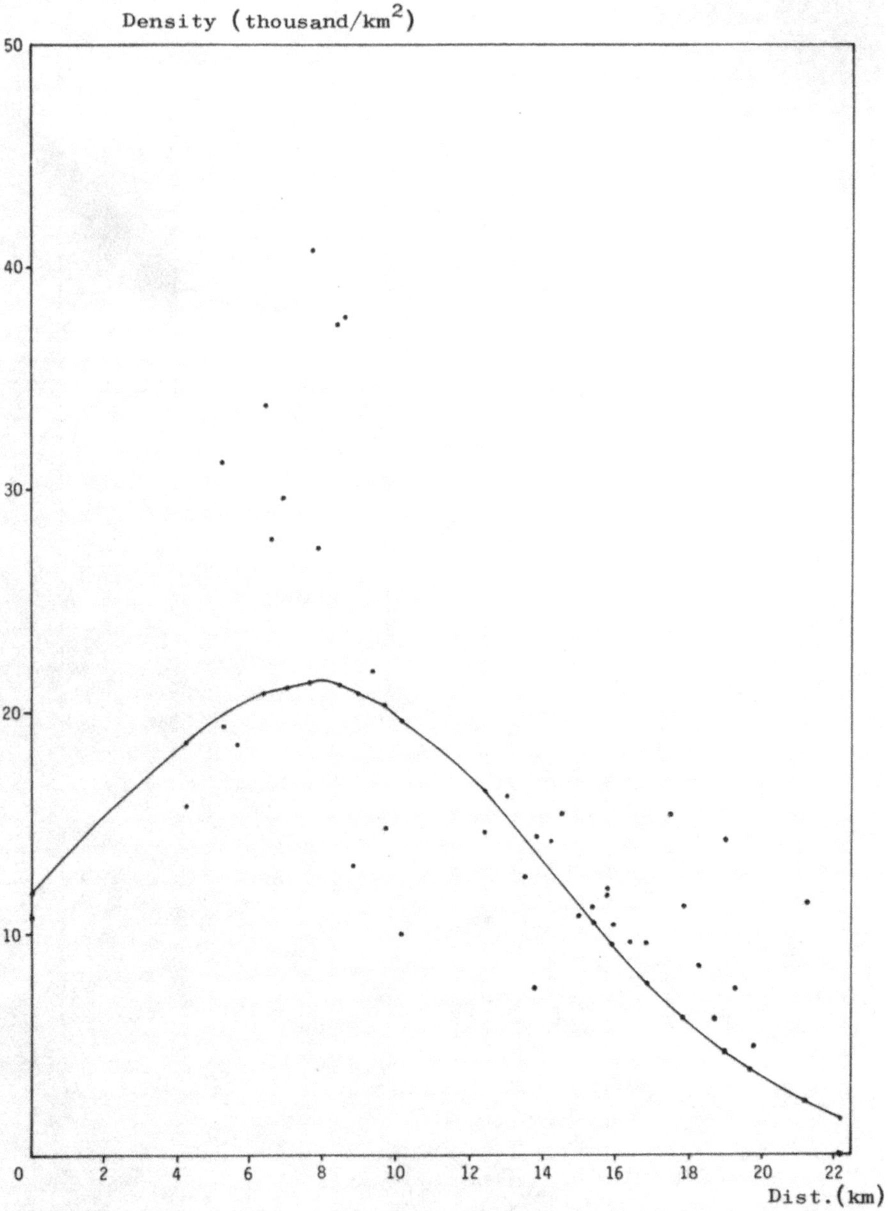

$$D = 10789 \cdot \text{Exp}\,(0.177535K - 0.011629K^2)$$

Figure 3–15. New York, 1940

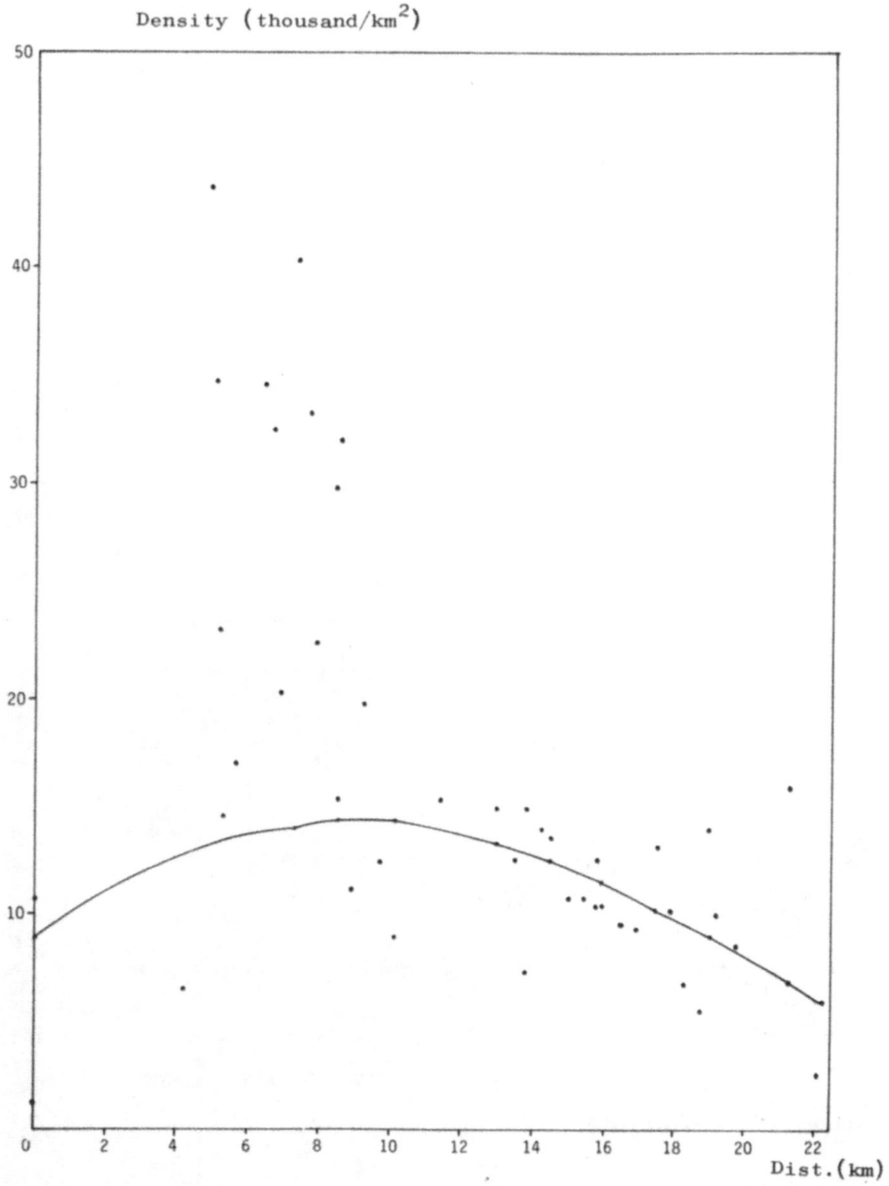

$$D = 8928 \cdot \text{Exp}\,(0.100972K - 0.00530321K^2)$$

Figure 3–16. New York, 1960

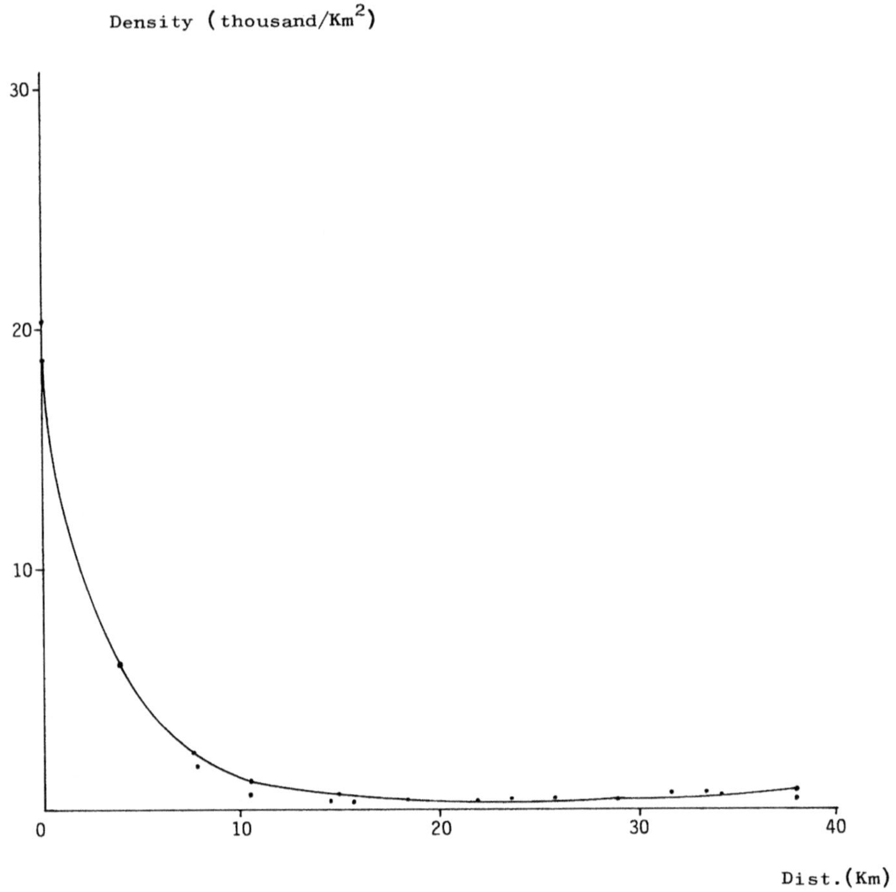

$$D = 20231 \cdot \text{Exp}\,(-0.333214K + 0.006423K^2)$$

Figure 3–17. Tokyo, 1920

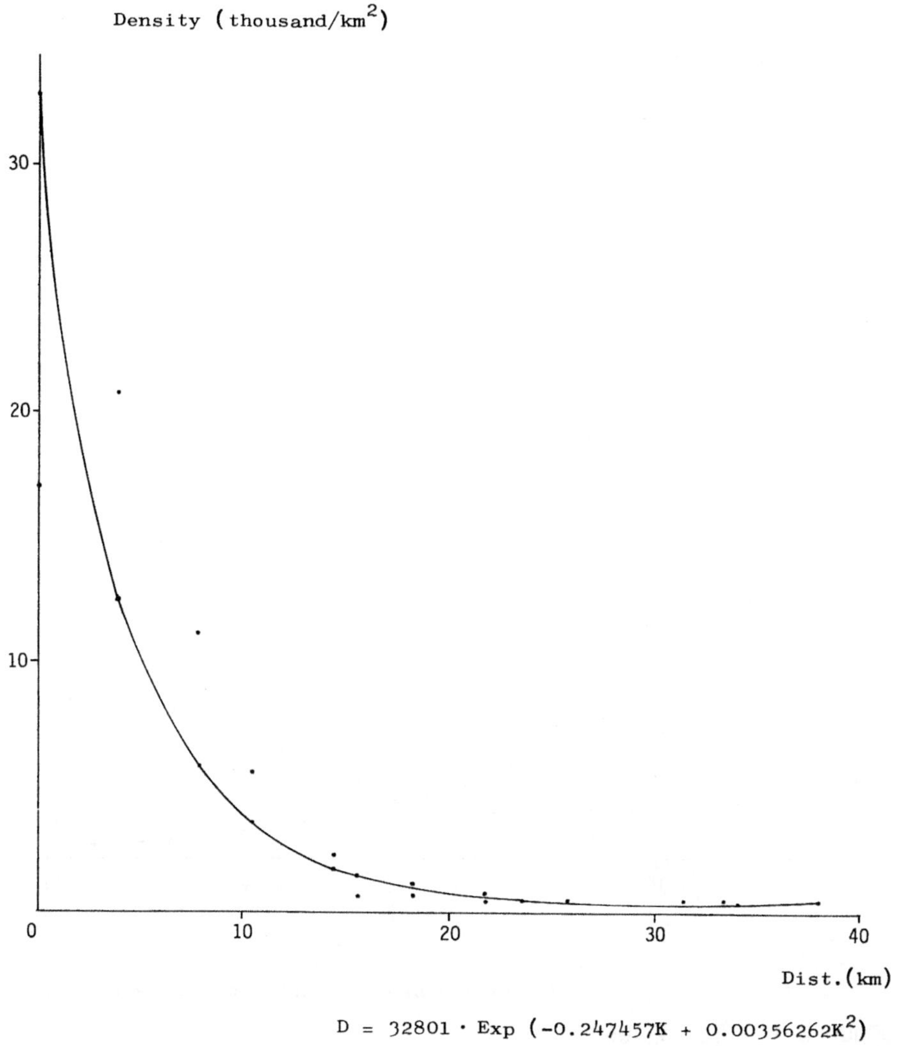

Figure 3–18. Tokyo, 1935

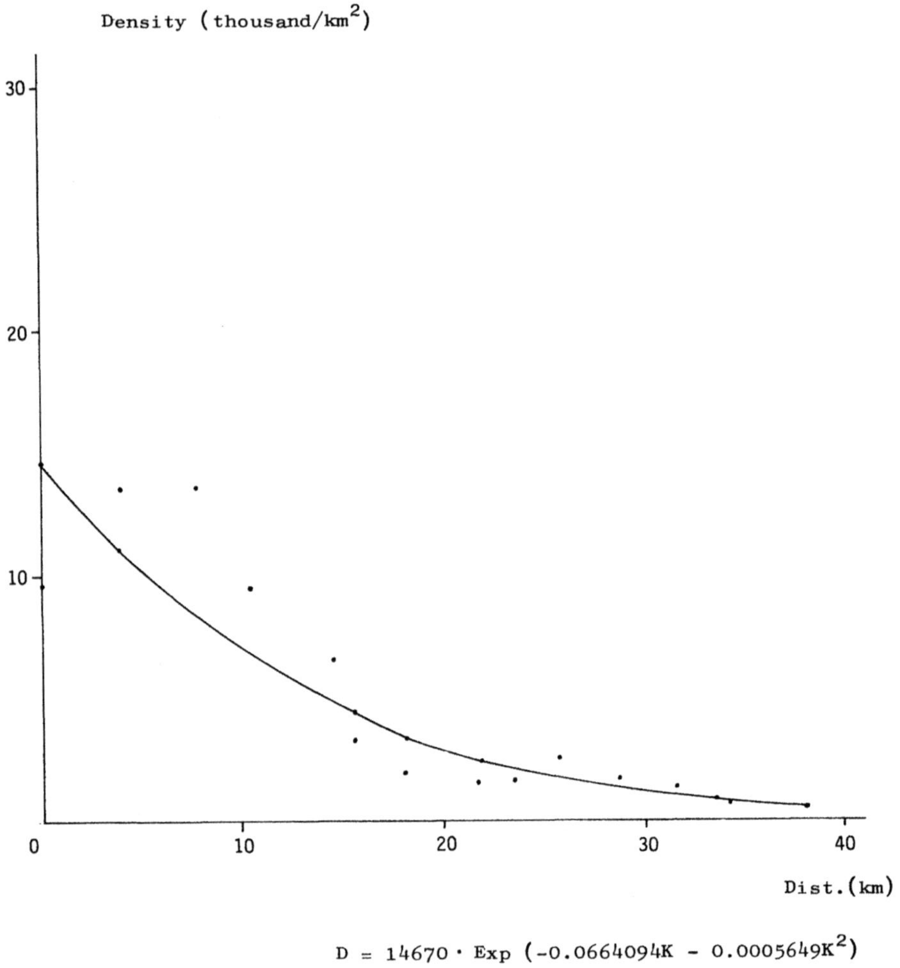

Figure 3–19. Tokyo, 1950

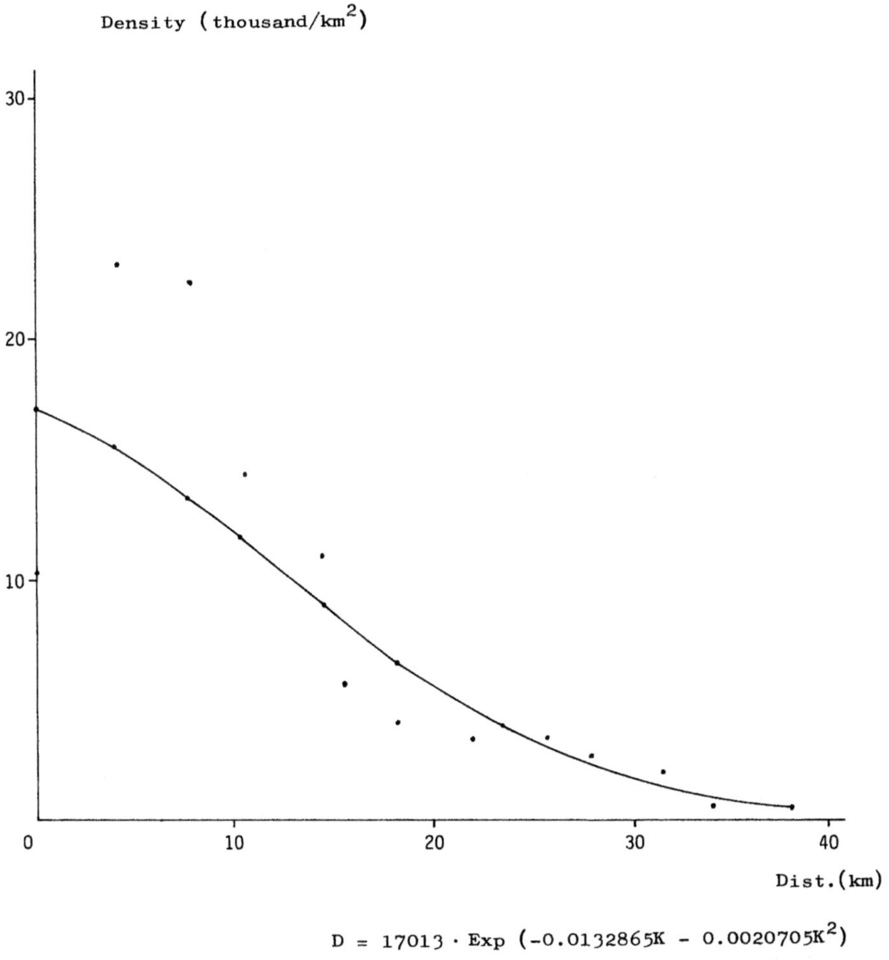

Figure 3–20. Tokyo, 1960

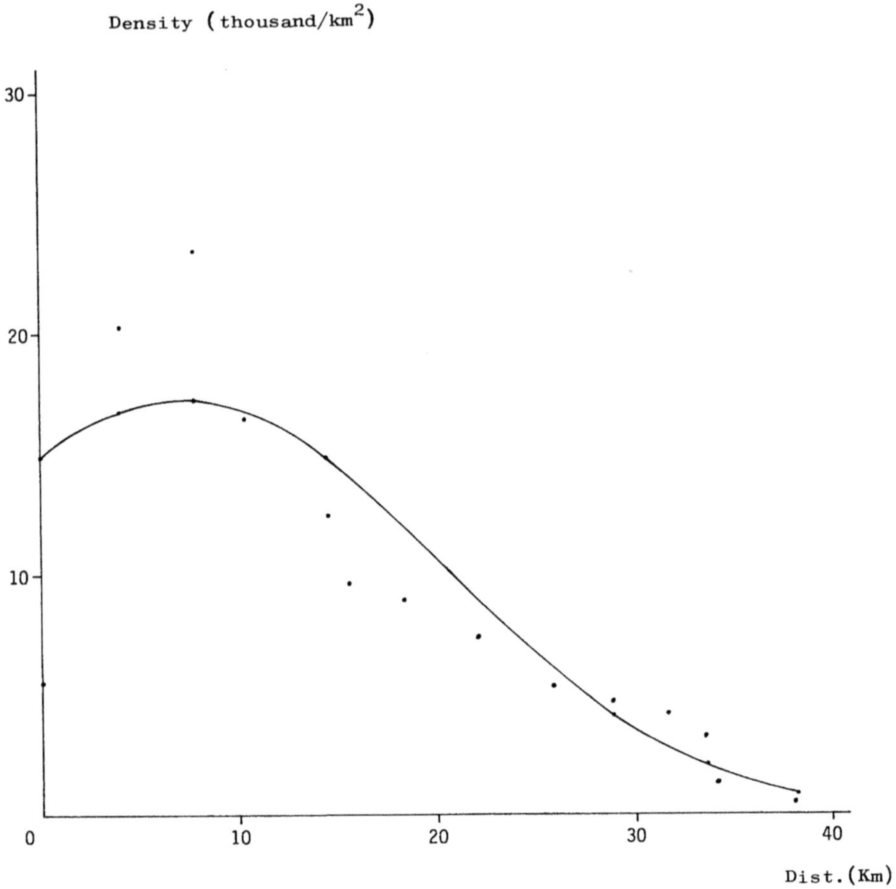

$$D = 14849 \cdot \text{Exp}\,(0.0444292K - 0.00300425K^2)$$

Figure 3–21. Tokyo, 1975

APPENDIX 3.1: SHIFT OF THE LAND PRICE GRADIENT IN THE TOKYO METROPOLITAN AREA

This appendix is based on a previous study (Orishimo 1971) and is closely related to this chapter's discussion of the population density gradient and the rent gradient.

In the previous study we measured the gradients of urban land prices in thirty-three sample cities annually from September 1959 to September 1967. The data on land prices of each city were appraised prices, and we postulated that these appraised prices were the approximate market prices. The linear distances between each site and the most highly appraised site were assumed to be the distances from the city center to each site (Brady 1967; Brigham 1965). The equation for the computation of the gradients is as follows:

$$R_{ilt} = \alpha R_{iot} \exp^{-g_{it}^{k} ilt},$$

where R_{ilt} is the appraised land prices of the lth sites in the ith city at the tth year, in yen per 3.3 m^2; R_{iot} is the highest appraised land prices in the ith city at the tth year, in yen per 3.3 m^2; and ^{k}ilt is distance between the lth site and the site of the highest appraised land in kilometers. The results of the calculation are shown in Table 3–3.

We tested the computed values of parameters, g, by a t-test and found that the only cities for which the gradients are not statistically significant at the level of 80 percent were nos. 1, 20, and 30.

We tried cross-section regression analysis on the measured gradients of cities in September 1967, using the obtainable data of economic indexes of each city as independent variables.

$$G_i = \alpha_o + \sum_j \alpha_j X_{ij} \qquad (i = 1, \ldots, 33),$$

where X_{ij} represents the jth economic index (Japan Association of City Mayors 1966), which is considered to be able to explain the gradients of the ith cities.

By a t-test, we found that the signs of the parameters of the next variables were significant. The values of the parameters are shown below:

1.2059	X_1:	public expenditure of the city;
−338.7076	X_3:	age of the city;
−1.1397	X_4:	rate of population growth between 1955 and 1965;
−0.8427	X_6:	consumption per household unit;

Table 3–3. Changing Values of Land Price Gradients by Cities

City No.	*1959*	*1960*	*1961*	*1962*	*1963*
1	0.327646 (1.02)	0.347656 (0.98)	0.401553 (1.42)	0.408216 (1.42)	0.390791 (1.35)
2	1.210520 (1.61)	1.398030 (1.82)	1.122690 (1.68)	1.163710 (1.87)	1.216930 (1.80)
3	1.298900 (2.33)	1.238150 (2.05)	1.318690 (2.06)	1.246440 (1.88)	1.238340 (1.84)
4	2.577340 (1.90)	2.617630 (1.93)	2.517690 (1.89)	2.395300 (1.67)	2.524250 (1.92)
5	1.161540 (2.20)	1.066280 (2.46)	0.999575 (2.14)	1.068770 (2.32)	1.061180 (2.32)
6	2.125590 (1.65)	1.951540 (1.53)	1.844340 (1.50)	1.693470 (1.50)	1.786740 (1.50)
7	1.816580 (2.02)	1.643140 (1.85)	1.824530 (2.18)	1.647830 (2.13)	1.631190 (2.10)
8	1.403670 (2.45)	1.831210 (2.67)	1.822650 (2.53)	1.844880 (2.55)	1.745390 (2.47)
9	1.382870 (1.78)	1.294710 (1.57)	1.364770 (1.58)	1.500360 (1.77)	1.487360 (1.73)
10	1.379150 (2.46)	1.163120 (2.15)	1.159850 (2.12)	1.167870 (2.11)	1.177760 (2.27)
11	2.741040 (1.96)	3.714610 (2.03)	3.486880 (2.01)	3.342720 (2.03)	3.342720 (2.03)
12	1.271820 (1.41)	1.097090 (1.27)	0.856681 (1.02)	0.797764 (0.95)	0.676711 (0.81)
13	0.749968 (2.35)	0.672479 (2.20)	0.685842 (2.20)	0.679135 (2.20)	0.631503 (2.20)
14	0.311624 (1.66)	0.301114 (1.56)	0.302900 (1.47)	0.306824 (1.50)	0.304886 (1.46)
15	0.760233 (1.54)	0.804084 (1.59)	0.859243 (1.65)	0.919058 (1.72)	1.151240 (2.38)

16	1.850910 (1.41)	2.031080 (1.39)	2.069120 (1.53)	1.508210 (1.98)	1.433010 (1.76)
17	0.707325 (2.13)	0.689244 (2.14)	0.582888 (2.05)	0.552158 (1.95)	0.560697 (1.90)
18	0.595244 (1.66)	0.486163 (1.48)	0.447724 (1.43)	0.458043 (1.50)	0.446800 (1.47)
19	1.003220 (2.22)	1.014120 (2.09)	0.959483 (2.18)	0.953505 (2.24)	1.010410 (2.34)
20	−0.000742 (0.00)	0.052093 (0.10)	0.007679 (0.01)	−0.018384 (0.03)	−0.032680 (0.06)
21	1.379080 (1.04)	1.452570 (1.03)	1.312620 (0.99)	1.378010 (1.02)	1.242330 (0.98)
22	0.210141 (2.03)	0.210582 (2.08)	0.211879 (2.26)	0.211016 (2.27)	0.202520 (2.20)
23	1.091980 (1.47)	0.994907 (1.43)	0.933260 (1.37)	0.878840 (1.33)	1.476470 (1.75)
24	3.080130 (2.15)	2.695600 (2.09)	2.910960 (2.06)	2.926440 (2.04)	3.336300 (1.97)
25	0.278576 (1.85)	0.253713 (1.75)	0.234188 (1.73)	0.172089 (1.38)	0.173480 (1.42)
26	0.296272 (1.50)	0.303238 (1.56)	0.273426 (1.48)	0.301172 (1.33)	0.061162 (0.48)
27	0.137394 (1.38)	0.134887 (1.40)	0.135201 (1.56)	0.124619 (1.48)	0.122219 (1.35)
28	1.660240 (2.30)	1.742890 (2.33)	1.685850 (2.19)	1.695180 (2.07)	1.471610 (1.97)
29	0.147688 (1.28)	0.132379 (1.26)	0.139014 (1.34)	0.127614 (1.45)	0.137539 (1.54)
30	0.240324 (0.83)	0.232621 (0.80)	0.249901 (0.92)	0.269576 (0.96)	0.242441 (1.13)
31	1.788760 (2.72)	1.909480 (2.64)	2.018080 (2.72)	1.924200 (2.71)	1.690630 (2.68)
32	1.090240 (1.97)	0.984120 (1.79)	1.358070 (2.34)	1.267860 (2.41)	1.157190 (2.35)
33	1.623310 (2.23)	1.610070 (2.25)	1.547360 (2.29)	1.475670 (2.28)	1.443220 (2.25)

Table 3–3. *(continued)*

City No.	*1964*	*1965*	*1966*	*1967*
1	0.415668 (1.38)	0.388142 (1.31)	0.400913 (1.31)	0.357455 (1.22)
2	1.160580 (1.73)	1.198530 (1.81)	1.171460 (1.76)	1.083120 (1.69)
3	1.165550 (1.78)	1.069600 (1.73)	1.085380 (1.74)	0.952924 (2.52)
4	2.504220 (1.90)	2.494450 (1.88)	2.473420 (1.88)	2.450820 (1.84)
5	1.044080 (2.26)	0.941649 (2.11)	0.914629 (2.14)	1.017810 (2.24)
6	1.886190 (1.53)	2.003570 (1.59)	2.119610 (1.56)	2.238180 (1.50)
7	1.633020 (2.12)	1.771690 (2.01)	1.901520 (1.96)	2.149870 (2.02)
8	1.741710 (2.45)	1.769550 (2.46)	1.828140 (2.48)	1.732930 (2.38)
9	1.378420 (1.60)	1.853830 (2.35)	1.839610 (2.32)	1.805140 (2.28)
10	1.164340 (2.26)	1.136230 (2.28)	1.176660 (2.27)	1.168180 (2.30)
11	3.328560 (2.03)	3.114930 (2.02)	3.040720 (2.05)	2.870140 (2.02)
12	0.556645 (0.68)	0.786932 (1.13)	0.918434 (1.21)	0.765150 (0.96)
13	0.578058 (2.08)	0.570012 (2.10)	0.568557 (2.09)	0.546540 (2.11)
14	0.306067 (1.43)	0.323049 (1.50)	0.329216 (1.54)	0.331046 (1.54)
15	1.264850 (2.39)	0.545369 (2.29)	0.511863 (2.18)	0.513980 (2.12)
16	1.421820 (1.73)	1.403170 (1.74)	1.365080 (1.71)	1.386350 (1.74)

17	0.642082 (1.88)	0.735033 (1.97)	0.756314 (2.00)	0.755193 (2.01)
18	0.457275 (1.55)	0.469474 (1.62)	0.476782 (1.65)	0.498517 (1.69)
19	1.003690 (2.36)	0.934257 (2.29)	1.001800 (2.31)	0.961595 (2.40)
20	−0.065360 (0.13)	−0.062138 (0.12)	0.007896 (0.01)	−0.101906 (0.20)
21	1.358400 (1.06)	1.421640 (1.09)	1.486210 (1.14)	1.477310 (1.16)
22	0.193258 (2.12)	0.190371 (2.10)	0.184839 (2.35)	0.171642 (1.87)
23	1.815750 (1.69)	1.942930 (1.61)	1.798150 (1.68)	2.088600 (1.66)
24	3.390680 (1.96)	3.375640 (2.15)	3.486380 (1.93)	3.697000 (1.87)
25	0.175925 (1.43)	0.178874 (1.43)	0.180249 (1.42)	0.178961 (1.41)
26	0.083970 (0.76)	0.125476 (1.10)	0.145003 (1.23)	0.157071 (1.33)
27	0.134183 (1.50)	0.153116 (1.64)	0.192316 (1.81)	0.198492 (1.85)
28	1.450270 (1.89)	1.397270 (1.88)	1.554990 (1.96)	1.525650 (1.95)
29	0.161798 (1.64)	0.133982 (1.38)	0.157655 (1.56)	0.176139 (1.63)
30	0.299117 (1.23)	0.288067 (1.19)	0.284956 (1.18)	0.281370 (1.15)
31	1.579420 (2.65)	1.612630 (2.66)	1.648190 (2.68)	1.307100 (2.43)
32	0.998297 (2.46)	0.986122 (2.45)	0.963878 (2.40)	0.716614 (2.51)
33	1.406630 (2.23)	1.384900 (2.19)	1.396860 (2.21)	1.451030 (2.27)

Note: Numbers in parentheses = value of t.

−0.00252	X_{8-1}:	retail sales;
460.2250	X_{8-2}:	wholesale sales;
7.8321	X_9:	rate of spread of waterworks service;
−1.5434	X_{10}:	percentage of the number of employees employed by the manufacturing industries compared to the total number of employees in the country.

Examination of the signs of the parameters showed that the variables responsible for the gentle slope of the land price of each city were X_1, X_4, X_{8-2}, and X_9. In contrast, the variables that brought about the steep slope were X_3, X_6, X_{8-1}, and X_{10}.

The minus sign of the parameter of the age of the city implied that the transportation system was not adapted to the growth of the city, as Muth (1961) reasoned on the population density gradients. The minus sign of the parameter of X_4, rate of population growth, was an outcome of the rapid growth of the population in a city, which made the price gradients less steep because the demand for land in the peripheral parts of the city had increased more rapidly and the rise in price was more remarkable. By the same reasoning, the rate of dispersion of waterworks service or general public expenditures by local government had also brought about the gentle slope of land price.

All of these estimations were, of course, subject to the limitation of static analysis of the cities concerned. Accordingly, it would be inappropriate for us to regard the results of our estimation as a definite conclusion about the determinants of the cities' land price structure under changing economic conditions.

To test the effects of economic growth on the urban land price structure (Maisel 1964), we examined the rate of change in the computed gradients of land price annually from 1959 to 1967. First, we found that the computed values of g differed by cities. By observing the trends of the gradients, we could classify the cities into three groups: one with increasing trends of gradients — that is, $dg_i/dt > 0$; another with decreasing trends of gradients — that is, $dg_i/dt < 0$; and the third with unchanging trends of gradients — that is, $dg_i/dt = 0$. The first indicates that the rise of price at the peripheral sites of the city is more rapid than in the inner part of the city, or that the demand for land is increasing more rapidly in suburban areas than in central parts of the city. The second indicates the contrary. The third shows that the changes of gradients are parallel.

We can postulate that the most important factors that determine the rates of change of land price gradients are the pattern of urban development and the way in which urban transportation systems adjust themselves to urban growth. The latter, in turn, might be determined by types and amounts of public investment. In this context, we attempted to discover by means of some statistical approximation the relationship between the rate of change of g and the pattern of urban development and the types and amounts of public investment for each city.

The data were very limited. Tentatively, regressions were run on the gradients every year by cities during 1959 and 1967, as independent variables, and the amount of public investment (on a yen basis) in roads in the city area, which was denoted as I_G (Ministry of Construction 1978). In tests of the calculated value of the parameter, the signs of the significant parameters were almost minus. Only nine out of thirty sample cities had plus signs, but the levels of significance of these parameters were very low, on the basis of the values of standard errors. This shows us that the amount of public investment in roads, as expected, was negatively related to the absolute value of the gradient of the city in general.

Next, we proposed an economic index, N^2it/N^3it, which would show us the pattern of urban development of the city, where N^2it represents the number of employees in the secondary industries and N^3it represents the number of employees in the tertiary industries of the ith city at the tth year. The upward trend of the value of N^2it/N^3it means that the pattern of development of the city is industrial, and the downward trend of this value means that the pattern of the city's development is commercial. In other words, $[d(N^2it/N^3it)]/dt$ being λ in the case of $\lambda_i > 0$, the ith city had an increasing number of employees in the manufacturing industries compared with the service industries during the period of our research. In contrast, in the case of $\lambda_i < 0$, the ith city had a decrease in the number of employees in commercial industries compared with the manufacturing industries.

We assumed that the pattern of urban development by industrialization might extend the peripheral boundary of the city, increasing the demand for land more in the peripheral than in the inner part and resulting in a gradual decrease of the gradient of the land price of the city. Accordingly, in the case of $\lambda_i > 0$, we can expect that the sign of the parameter of N^2it/N^3it may be minus, and in the case of $\lambda_i < 0$, the sign may be plus.

The signs of the computed parameters were as we had expected. In most of the cities posited as industrially developed, with $\lambda > 0$, we found the gradient of land prices decreasing — that is, $dg/dt < 0$ — and the rise of land prices was more marked. In contrast, in the cities hypothesized as commercially developed, with $\lambda < 0$, we found the gradient of land prices increasing — that is, $dg/dt > 0$. There were a few exceptions, in which we found special features of the cities that explained the deviation. In the third group, where $dg/dt = 0$, the signs of the parameters were not necessarily significant.

Furthermore, the causes that affect the fluctuation of the gradients may be not only the types and amounts of public investments or pattern of urban development, but also the rate of growth or mode of distribution of the urban population. This was shown by analysis of cross-section data, in which one of the determinants of the gradients by cities turned out to be the rate of growth of population. Growth is defined as an increase in the demand for sites, which leads to a more intensive and extensive use of the sites. Obvious determinants of increased demand are a rise in population or income, a shift in consumer preferences, or a combination of these and other factors (Seyfried 1963).

The determinants affecting the land price structure of the city may consist of various other factors. Clark (1951) and Muth (1960) suggested that the causes of changes in population density were increases in income, in costs of commuting, and so on. The determinants of the land price may contain the causes of change, such as appreciated value of time or change of taste. According to the change of level of income, the restrictions in consumer behavior may change from time to income, or from income to time, by respective classes of income (Wingo 1962).

The determinants of the location of the firm may be more complex than those of residential location, since firm location is dependent on other factors, such as economies of scale and agglomeration economies. Thus, in a sense, the firm's derived demand for land by location may actually be more complex.

Demand for land and equilibrium land prices induced by firms and consumers may contain a complex of causes and results. This research is an approach to these chains of cause and effect, which brings us to a focus on the pattern of development and the effect of public investment. The pattern of regional development or its expected direction would be one of the most important factors that influence the main trends of fluctuations in the land prices of an area. Similarly, the effect of the growth of population or public investment on land price depends mainly on the pattern of development. An attempt to analyze closely the pattern of urban development in this sense would be helpful to any effective planning for land use because it considers a change in the land price structure.

APPENDIX 3.2: TRANSPORTATION MODAL CHOICE — A STUDY USING PROBIT ANALYSIS

An individual's economic behavior changes discontinuously at a certain point of time. The discontinuity is observed in various behavioral realms over time, during which the objective variables surrounding the individual change continuously.

We consider here the choice of transportation mode as an example of individual behavior. The choice is reflected in the transportation demand by mode, which affects the characteristics of the urbanization process.

Theoretically, travel demand by mode is derived from the consumer's utility function. In recent studies on transportation demand by mode based on the utility function, the independent variables of the utility function are considered to be a composite of system characteristics and of user's characteristics. Environmental quality or crowding parameters apparently belong to system characteristics.

In order to study the transportation modal choice, we applied logit and probit analyses as well as linear probability analysis. Originally logit and probit analyses were developed to analyze discontinuous phenomena statistically. We hope that in the near future we will be able to apply this approach to the location choice behavior mentioned in the previous chapters by the same statistical analyses.

Quandt and Baumol's (1966) analysis of transportation demand is not formulated in terms of the demand for each travel directly by mode. The so-called abstract mode is an indirect measure of each mode, which is characterized by the values of several variables that affect the desirability of the mode's services to the public — namely, speed, frequency of service, comfort, and cost. Although the *abstract mode model* has some inherent shortcomings, it was the first model that tried to explain human choice behavior by several continuous variables.

Reichman and Stopher's (1971) *behavioral modal-choice model* clarified the nature of various kinds of variables by identifying their respective characteristics. Specifically, the variables were classified by their characteristics as follows: System variables are travel cost, time, and so on; user characteristics are income, sex, stage in the family life cycle, car availability, and so on; trip characteristics are based on the derived demand of the activity that will be carried out at the end of the trip; the values of system characteristics are objective estimation; and the environmental characteristic is the time of day.

McGillivray's (1970) *discrimination-classification model* was based on a simplified utility function. It was intended to clarify the nature of the variables: the long-run decision of how much to spend on car, urban travel, and land-residential space, and the short-run decision of mode of travel.

Finally, Domencich and McFadden (1975) formulated the range of transport-related decisions made by consumers as a *rational choice behavior model* based on the following variables: the location of residence and job; sales of labor and purchases of commodities, including vehicles; frequency of work, shopping, recreation, and other trips; destination of trips; time of day; and mode of travel. Although Domencich and McFadden say that their description of the economic consumer is within the framework of the Court-Griliches-Becker-Lancaster consumption-activity household-production model, the frameworks of these models are not necessarily closely related. Their ideas seem to originate from different points of view. Among them, Lancaster's (1966) household production model includes the important point that "the most important aspects of consumer behavior relevant to a complex economy as that of the United States are those of consumer reactions to new commodities and to quality variations." Here, new commodities and quality variations are considered as travel mode (Houthakker 1952; Muellbauer 1974).

We could consider that, within Lancaster's framework, each trip-mode possesses two characteristics — convenience for the traveler and comfort. Convenience is understood as an exogenous system property reflecting the extent of impediments to travel and measurable by the uncertainty or perceived unreliability of the system. Comfort is a main endogenous system variable, which may be treated by carrying out a cross-comparison of comfort characteristics among mode alternatives. The characteristics to be examined would include the space for each passenger, shock and vibration, noise, privacy, and other variables relating to the physiological and psychological characteristics of movement systems. Safety might be yet another important characteristic. As Lancaster (1966) stresses, the objective nature of the goods-characteristics relationship is very important in the analysis. We can distinguish between objective and private reactions to such things as changes in relative price.

We can reformulate the traveler's rational choice behavior model based on the goods-characteristics relationship as follows: A consumption activity is assumed to be a finite vector, Y, which is contained in a universe Ω. Elements of the activity vector are composed from the choice of travel mode, and time is separated into lifetime terms. Z represents the characteristics that show us the want satisfaction levels. M is a linear operator that transforms the activity vector space to the characteristics vector space. N is also a linear operator, which transforms the activity vector space to the commodity vector space X.

$$U = U(Z). \tag{3.2}$$

$$Z = MY. \tag{3.3}$$

$$X = NY. \tag{3.4}$$

Therefore

$$U = U(MN^{-1}X) = U(X). \tag{3.5}$$

$$pX = k \quad x \geqq 0, \tag{3.6}$$

where k is total lifetime income.

$$Y = (y_{11}, \ldots, y_{1L}, y_{21}, \ldots, y_{2L}, \ldots, y_{H1}, \ldots, y_{HL}),$$

$$M = \begin{bmatrix} m_{11}^1, \ldots, m_{1L}^1, m_{21}^1, \ldots, m_{2L}^1, \ldots, m_{H1}^1, \ldots, m_{HL}^1 \\ m_{11}^2, \ldots, m_{1L}^2, m_{21}^2, \ldots, m_{2L}^2, \ldots, m_{H1}^2, \ldots, m_{HL}^2 \\ \cdots\cdots\cdots\cdots\cdots\cdots\cdots\cdots\cdots\cdots \\ m_{11}^r, \ldots, m_{1L}^r, m_{21}^r, \ldots, m_{2L}^r, \ldots, m_{H1}^r, \ldots, m_{HL}^r \end{bmatrix},$$

$$r \times (L \times H),$$

where r = number of characteristics, L = number of modes, and H = number of lifetime separations.

$$N = \begin{bmatrix} n_{11}^1, \ldots, n_{1L}^1, n_{21}^1, \ldots, n_{2L}^1, \ldots, n_{H1}^1, \ldots, n_{HL}^1 \\ n_{11}^2, \ldots, n_{1L}^2, n_{21}^2, \ldots, n_{2L}^2, \ldots, n_{H1}^2, \ldots, n_{HL}^2 \\ \cdots\cdots\cdots\cdots\cdots\cdots\cdots\cdots\cdots\cdots \\ n_{11}^s, \ldots, n_{1L}^s, n_{21}^s, \ldots, n_{2L}^s, \ldots, n_{H1}^s, \ldots, n_{HL}^s \end{bmatrix},$$

$$s \times (L \times H),$$

where s = number of commodities.

From the viewpoint of this model, we can synthesize the various kinds of characteristics, such as identification of system variables (travel cost, travel time), user characteristics (income, age, sex, stage of family life cycle, car availability), trip characteristics, values of system characteristics (objective and subjective estimation), and environmental characteristics (time of day) named by Reichman and Stopher (1971). According to Lancaster (1966), these characteristics are classified into two kinds of choices: (1) an efficiency choice, determining the characteristics frontier and associated efficient goods collection (travel cost, travel time, car availability, time of day, and income may be included as the variables that determine the efficiency choice) and (2) a private choice, determining which point of the characteristics frontier is preferred by the user (Anderson and Crocker 1972). Age, sex, and stage in the family life cycle on subjective estimation belong to the decision variables of private choice.

As shown by Domencich and McFadden (1975), in the long run the consumer's decision on the modal choice and auto ownership are strongly interrelated, but in the short run automobiles are treated as a fixed durable by the consumer, with mode choice made conditional on automobile possession. From this point of view, the model we discussed above is a general long-run equilibrium model, which would include all of the socioeconomic characteristics. In a short-run decision model, we must include some socioeconomic variables, such as age, sex, income, and so forth. The usual cross-section data contain the factors of both the short-run and the long-run decision (Koopman, Diamond, and Williamson 1964).

Needless to say, the demand function by mode is derived from the utility function. We reviewed the characteristics of the utility function regarding transportation modal choice in order to consider the results of the empirical test of travel demand by mode. In this brief survey, we concentrate our attention on the goods-characteristics approach to the transportation modal choice of the consumer, since this approach gives us some perspective on the travel demand by mode, from both the viewpoints of user characteristics and system characteristics as well as from long-term and short-term viewpoints.

We studied the data of the Tokyo metropolitan area collected by the Advanced Study Group for Transportation of Toyota Motor Sales Co., Ltd. The field survey was made in July 1975 by interviewing drivers at eight sample districts within the Tokyo metropolitan area. Sample districts had been selected from the CBD and from districts at thirty-, sixty-, and 90-minutes distance from Tokyo's CBD. Samples were selected randomly among drivers who owned cars at the time of the research. Given this sampling method, this research is confined to car owners and is a short-run analysis, as defined in the previous section. The sample size was 3,800. The items of the questionnaire are composed of the actual trip mode, the alternative mode, and the attributes of travelers.

Three types of models were used for the estimation. One is the linear probability model, which is estimated by usual regression analysis, and the other two are the binomial choice logit model and the probit model, which are estimated by the maximum likelihood methods.

The items of the questionnaire — user's characteristics, system characteristics, short-term characteristics, and long-term characteristics — are complex. Based on consideration of the characteristics of the utility function, the independent variables for travel demand by mode and the notations are as follows:

CARU:	1 if own car is used, and 0 if not;
CCST:	the estimated cost for car trip (¥);
TCST:	the estimated cost for mass transit trip (¥);
TOTC:	CCST less TCST;
CTME:	the necessary time for car trip (minutes);
TTME:	the necessary time for mass transit trip (minutes);
TOTT:	CTME less TTME;
RUSH:	1 if trip is made at rush hour, and 0 if trip is made at another time;
DRK:	1 if driver has a plan for a drink, and 0 if not;
PARK:	1 if driver has to pay a parking fee, and 0 if not;
LUG:	1 if driver has heavy luggage, and 0 if he has not;
WALK:	walking time to the nearest station from driver's house (minutes);
SEX:	1 if the driver is male, and 0 if the driver is female;
HOUS:	1 if a homeowner, and 0 if not;
INCOM:	income (million ¥).

The characteristics of the independent variables are as follows: CCST, TCST, CTME, TTME, RUSH, DRK, and PARK are system variables; CARU and WALK are long-term variables; and LUG, SEX, and INCOM are user's variables.

We divided the samples into five groups according to the object of the trip: commuting, going to school, business, shopping, and leisure. The sample sizes of each group were, respectively, 1,130; 58; 1,140; 430; and 420 (the mean values and standard deviations of the variables by each group of sample are shown in Table 3–4). To examine these subgroups more closely, we reviewed the values of the constant terms, which are 0.67482, 0.80460, 0.86089, and 0.81857. The constant term for shopping is the largest; people use their cars more often than in the other cases. The results of the estimation follow.

Table 3–4. Mean Values and Standard Deviations of the Independent Variables

	Commuting		*Going to School*		*Business*		*Shopping*		*Leisure*	
TOTC	345.03	(694.48)	228.79	(715.77)	243.46	(635.96)	32.581	(384.52)	39.714	(1286.9)
TOTT	−7.2310	(37.292)	−1.6552	(45.304)	−1.0149	(42.945)	−5.6628	(28.870)	−4.0667	(42.658)
RUSH	0.81327	(0.38986)	0.56897	(0.49955)	0.31228	(0.46362)	0.16744	(0.37380)	0.32619	(0.46937)
DRK	−0.02035	(0.14127)	0.06896	(0.25561)	0.02280	(0.14935)	0.02093	(0.14332)	0.12143	(0.32701)
LUG	0.03185	(0.17569)	0.06896	(0.25561)	0.21754	(0.41275)	0.07674	(0.26648)	0.18810	(0.39124)
PARK	0.11239	(0.31597)	0.08620	(0.28312)	0.04210	(0.20091)	0.20233	(0.40219)	0.09761	(0.29715)
WALK	6.2929	(6.8237)	5.5862	(5.7462)	4.2421	(8.5227)	7.7558	(14.121)	6.5405	(0.10589)
AGE	34.345	(10.055)	26.466	(8.6353)	34.610	(9.5479)	34.686	(10.137)	32.452	(10.250)
SEX	0.96460	(0.18486)	0.89655	(0.30720)	0.95439	(0.20873)	0.81628	(0.38771)	0.89286	(0.30966)
HOUS	0.68319	(0.46543)	0.74138	(0.44170)	0.65789	(0.47462)	0.70233	(0.45777)	0.69048	(0.46284)
INCOM	3.2841	(1.9180)	3.8103	(2.4040)	3.3877	(2.0892)	3.6849	(2.0541)	2.1936	(2.1936)
CARU	0.68142	(0.46613)	0.65517	(0.47946)	0.79561	(0.40342)	0.86512	(0.34199)	0.38344	(0.38344)
CCST	419.04	(669.91)	423.62	(626.22)	347.22	(595.14)	211.79	(297.20)		
TCST	74.009	(196.74)	194.83	(434.26)	103.75	(340.34)	179.21	(314.32)		
CTME	41.675	(29.268)	44.603	(62.516)	54.487	(70.763)	24.786	(21.271)		
TTME	48.906	(42.393)	46.259	(24.710)	55.502	(66.272)	30.449	(29.155)		

Note: Numbers in parentheses in Tables 3–4 through 3–7 are the standard errors of the coefficients.

Commuting

We first computed the multiple correlation using all of the independent variables based on the linear probability model, binomial logit model, and binomial probit model (see Table 3–5). According to the results by the levels of significance based on *t*-values, TOTC, TOTT, RUSH, and DRK are significant at the 95 percent level. Parameters have correct signs in all models. Auto-operating cost less transit fares affects the choice of trip mode by 12 percent per thousand yen (about four dollars). Auto time less transit line-haul time affects the choice of trip-mode 12.3 percent per 100 minutes.

In rush hour people seem to choose mass transit more often — about 11.7 percent more than at other times. If a driver plans on drinking alcohol, he chooses the car trip 42 percent less than in other cases. If he has heavy luggage, he will use the car about 15 percent more than in other cases.

With the binomial logit model, we can compare the magnitudes of the parameters with the results calculated by Domencich and McFadden in the United States. The TOTC parameter is −0.186 dollars in Japan and −2.24 dollars in the United States. Also, the value of the parameter of TOTT is −0.01352 (minutes) in Japan and −0.0411 in the United States. The results show us that these differences are more important in choosing the mode in the United States than in Japan. We could estimate that this is in accordance with the differences in road conditions and wage levels in the two countries.

We can show the following computed results: In the case of Model 1, the results of the regression analysis are that the multiple correlation coefficient = 0.31216, the coefficient of determination = 0.097445, and the standard error of dependent variables = 0.44501. Also similar calculated values

$$R^2 = 1 - \frac{\Sigma(y_i - \hat{y}_i)^2}{\Sigma y_i^2}$$

in the case of the logit model and the probit model, by the Newton-Raphson method, are as follows: the coefficients of determination are, respectively, 0.12137 and 0.10579.

In the case of Model 2, the results of regression analysis are that the multiple correlation coefficient = 0.39196, the coefficient of determination = 0.15363, and the standard error of dependent variables = 0.43036. In the case of the logit model and the probit model, similar calculation gives

Table 3–5. Estimation by Probability, Logit, and Probit Models in the Case of Commuting Modal Choice

	Model 1			
	Linear Probability Model		*Binomial Logit Model*	*Binomial Probit Model*
Variables	*Coefficients*	*t-values*	*Coefficients*	*Coefficients*
TOTC	−0.00012 (0.00002)	−5.50291	−0.00062 (0.00013)	−0.00039 (0.00007)
TOTT	−0.00142 (0.00037)	−3.84089	−0.01352 (0.00341)	−0.00419 (0.00111)
RUSH	−0.11024 (0.03430)	−3.21412	−0.57652 (0.18901)	−0.34751 (0.10949)
DRK	−0.41323 (0.09478)	−4.35995	−2.01433 (0.52822)	−1.21150 (0.29921)
LUG	0.14911 (0.07565)	1.97103	0.82782 (0.46740)	0.49553 (0.25958)
PARK	−0.06111 (0.05071)	−1.20512	−0.23395 (0.25126)	−0.12093 (0.15116)
WALK	−0.00082 (0.00202)	−0.40848	−0.00619 (0.01126)	−0.00191 (0.00612)
AGE	0.00190 (0.00137)	1.38207	0.00869 (0.00705)	0.00556 (0.00417)
SEX	−0.02128 (0.07244)	−0.29380	−0.19101 (0.37840)	−0.07967 (0.22120)
HOUS	−0.03497 (0.02956)	−1.18307	−0.16775 (0.15315)	−0.11505 (0.09040)
INCOM	−0.00538 (0.00750)	−0.71718	−0.02562 (0.03780)	−0.01750 (0.02270)
CONST	0.81700 (0.08829)	9.25306	1.57717 (0.46999)	0.94182 (0.27340)

Model 2

Variables	*Linear Probability Model* *Coefficients*	*t-values*	*Binomial Logit Model* *Coefficients*	*Binomial Probit Model* *Coefficients*
CCST	−0.00002 (0.00002)	−0.86521	−0.00010 (0.00013)	−0.00007 (0.00008)
TCST	0.00028 (0.00006)	4.44092	0.00305 (0.00071)	0.00105 (0.00025)
CTME	−0.00497 (0.00054)	−9.12959	−0.02574 (0.00321)	−0.01520 (0.00181)
TTME	0.00076 (0.00035)	2.15425	0.00416 (0.00200)	0.00266 (0.00116)
RUSH	−0.13660 (0.03298)	−4.14193	−0.78011 (0.19797)	−0.45542 (0.11218)
DRK	−0.41826 (0.09134)	−4.57882	−2.09535 (0.51244)	−1.23742 (0.29326)
LUG	0.15974 (0.07300)	2.18806	0.91615 (0.47231)	0.51678 (0.25932)
PARK	−0.17602 (0.05061)	−3.47782	−0.84695 (0.26132)	−0.49827 (0.15853)
CONST	0.97355 (0.03689)	26.38694	2.32057 (0.23239)	1.41064 (0.12886)

us the following results: coefficients of determination are, respectively, 0.17935 and 0.16828.

By stepwise programming, in which if the value exceeded the 95 percent significance level, the variables were included and, if lower than that level, the variables were excluded, the results of the computation are as follows:

$$P = \underset{(0.01531)}{0.72463} - \underset{(0.00001)}{0.00015}\ \text{TOTC} - \underset{(0.00036)}{0.00123}\ \text{TOTT}.$$

$$P = \underset{(0.03150)}{0.82053} - \underset{(0.00001)}{0.00014}\ \text{TOTC} - \underset{(0.00035)}{0.00139}\ \text{TOTT} - \underset{(0.03397)}{0.11728}\ \text{RUSH}$$
$$- \underset{(0.09438)}{0.42412}\ \text{DRK} + \underset{(0.07537)}{0.14828}\ \text{LUG}.$$

In the case of the probability model, the value of the coefficient of determination does not have the usual meaning as a measure of the fitness of the model because of its binary choice nature. If we exclude the constant term from any equation, the value of the coefficient of determination apparently approaches remarkably close to 1. In the following sections, we do not present the values of the coefficients of determination of each equation.

Going to School

In the case of the linear probability model, the significance levels of the parameters are the highest in the following model:

$$P = \underset{(0.06538)}{0.67482} - \underset{(0.00008)}{0.00009}\ \text{TOTC} - \underset{(0.00138)}{0.00194}\ \text{TOTT}.$$

In the other two models — the logit model and the probit model — the computation did not converge. We could not discover the exact reason, but, in the estimation of these models, the sample size is small and the data is insufficient.

Business

The computations of all of the models are shown in Table 3–6. The linear probability models, similarly computed, are as follows:

Table 3–6. Estimation by Probability, Logit, and Probit Models in the Case of Business Modal Choice

	Model 1			
Vari-ables	Linear Probability Model		Logit Model	Probit Model
	Coefficients	t-values	Coefficients	Coefficients
TOTC	−0.00003 (0.00001)	−1.86691	−0.00021 (0.00011)	−0.00013 (0.00006)
TOTT	−0.00025 (0.00028)	−0.91495	−0.00172 (0.00179)	−0.00080 (0.00095)
RUSH	0.03744 (0.02555)	1.46549	0.21312 (0.16732)	0.11964 (0.09510)
DRK	−0.19655 (0.07943)	−2.47434	−0.95474 (0.41860)	−0.56947 (0.25786)
LUG	0.05272 (0.02911)	1.81075	0.37055 (0.19687)	0.21156 (0.11088)
PARK	−0.01036 (0.05994)	−0.17286	−0.09412 (0.36646)	−0.03376 (0.21479)
WALK	0.00415 (0.00140)	2.96272	0.05135 (0.01580)	0.02785 (0.00841)
AGE	0.00342 (0.00127)	2.69347	0.02353 (0.00856)	0.01289 (0.00477)
SEX	−0.11834 (0.05686)	−2.08120	−1.08198 (0.53122)	−0.53146 (0.25899)
HOUS	0.02067 (0.02608)	0.79255	0.12807 (0.16344)	0.07385 (0.09427)
INCOM	−0.00745 (0.00597)	−1.24627	−0.04871 (0.03784)	−0.02920 (0.02205)
CONST	0.77418 (0.07401)	10.46051	1.47070 (0.61111)	0.82817 (0.31591)

Table 3–6. *(continued)*

	Model 2			
	Linear Probability Model		*Logit Model*	*Probit Model*
Vari-ables	*Coefficients*	*t-values*	*Coefficients*	*Coefficients*
CCST	−0.00001 (0.00002)	−0.82250	−0.00011 (0.00013)	−0.00006 (0.00007)
TCST	0.00003 (0.00003)	1.11715	0.00029 (0.00027)	0.00017 (0.00014)
CTME	−0.00052 (0.00029)	−1.76155	−0.00280 (0.00172)	−0.00158 (0.00096)
TTME	0.00015 (0.00030)	0.51027	0.00084 (0.00184)	0.00038 (0.00098)
RUSH	0.03897 (0.02573)	1.51437	0.24775 (0.16519)	0.14069 (0.09373)
DRK	−0.20026 (0.08004)	−2.50199	−0.96246 (0.41320)	−0.58030 (0.25547)
LUG	0.04896 (0.02901)	1.68760	0.33003 (0.19301)	0.18673 (0.10793)
PART	−0.01421 (0.06091)	−0.23338	−0.09106 (0.36339)	−0.04730 (0.21305)
CONST	0.80045 (0.01865)	42.91555	1.37621 (0.11431)	0.84110 (0.06562)

$$P = \underset{(0.01280)}{0.80460} - \underset{(0.00001)}{0.00003}\ \text{TOTC} - \underset{(0.00028)}{0.00039}\ \text{TOTT}.$$

$$P = \underset{(0.07131)}{0.77343} - \underset{(0.00001)}{0.0003}\ \text{TOTC} - \underset{(0.00027)}{0.00027}\ \text{TOTT} - \underset{(0.07938)}{0.19311}\ \text{DRK}$$
$$+ \underset{(0.02885)}{0.05852}\ \text{LUG} + \underset{(0.00139)}{0.00425}\ \text{WALK} + \underset{(0.00124)}{0.00323}\ \text{AGE}$$
$$- \underset{(0.05669)}{0.11307}\ \text{SEX}.$$

In the case of business trips, it is reasonable that the magnitudes of the parameters of the variables TOTC and TOTT are smaller than in the case of commuting.

Shopping

We calculated two types of models, shown in Table 3–7. In this case the conditions of the signs of the parameters are apparently not reasonable, and the significance levels are not so high.

In the following linear probability models, the signs of the parameters are not so unreasonable, and the significance levels are higher than in the other case. The magnitude of the absolute value of the parameter of PARK shows us the importance of the parking fee for shoppers.

$$P = \underset{(0.01686)}{0.86089} - \underset{(0.00004)}{0.00001}\ \text{TOTC} - \underset{(0.00057)}{0.00080}\ \text{TOTT}.$$

$$P = \underset{(0.01881)}{0.88686} - \underset{(0.00004)}{0.00004}\ \text{TOTC} - \underset{(0.00056)}{0.00068}\ \text{TOTT}$$
$$- \underset{(0.04474)}{0.13430}\ \text{PARK}.$$

Leisure

Generally, the significance levels are low, except for the parameter of TOTT in the first model and of DRK in the second model. The directions of the signs of each parameter seem to be correct, especially in the second model, and the magnitude of the parameter of DRK is remarkable.

$$P = \underset{(0.01873)}{0.81857} - \underset{(0.00001)}{0.00001}\ \text{TOTC} - \underset{(0.00043)}{0.00084}\ \text{TOTT}.$$

Table 3–7. Estimation by Probability and Logit Models in the Case of Shopping

	Linear Probability Model			*Binomial Logit Model*	
Variables	*Coefficients*		*t-values*	*Coefficients*	
CCST	0.00007	(0.00007)	0.98899	0.00045	(0.00069)
TCST	−0.00003	(0.00005)	−0.65753	−0.0036	(0.00045)
CTME	−0.00039	(0.00088)	−0.44701	−0.00978	(0.00876)
TTME	0.00077	(0.00061)	1.26987	0.02387	(0.01334)
RUSH	0.04112	(0.04396)	0.93535	0.40765	(0.43456)
DRK	−0.31232	(0.11452)	−2.72724	−1.76265	(0.71704)
LUG	0.05458	(0.06126)	0.89097	0.57247	(0.63728)
PARK	−0.14090	(0.05011)	−2.81153	−1.03735	(0.40980)
CONST	0.86597	(0.02984)	29.01593	1.64097	(0.31391)

$$P = \underset{(0.01815)}{0.87723} - \underset{(0.00001)}{0.00005}\ \text{TOTC} - \underset{(0.00040)}{0.00092}\ \text{TOTT} - \underset{(0.05203)}{0.48858}\ \text{DRK}.$$

From the viewpoint of statistical testing, only the analyses of commuting and business are meaningful. This limitation on validity results primarily from the limited sample size. We cannot specify the effect of continuously changing such individual variables as income. But system variables, such as time, cost, schedule of drinking, and rush hour, significantly affect modal choice. Probit or logit analysis applied to modal choice could be effectively applied to other behavior, such as the psychological location tendency in the urbanization process that we examined in previous chapters.

APPENDIX 3.3: A NOTE ON THE DATA

Walter Laidlaw made up census tracts and used them to take censuses from 1905 through 1930. The government used his census tracts in 1940, but they were changed in 1950, 1960, and 1970.

Using the census tracts given in Walter Laidlaw's *Population of the City of New York 1890–1930,* each assembly district for the census years 1900–1970 was matched with a set of census tracts. The acreage of these census tracts was given by Laidlaw (1932). We found the total acreage for each of these sets of census tracts and used this as the area of the assembly district. This is an approximation, since the boundaries of assembly districts do not exactly coincide with census tract boundaries.

Since the 1940 U.S. Census used the same census tracts as Laidlaw, very clear census tract maps were available. Assembly district boundaries were obtained from the *Brooklyn Daily Eagle Almanac* for 1900 and 1910 (written descriptions). The *Searchlight* of the Citizen's Union contained assembly district maps for 1920, 1930, and 1940. Written descriptions of boundaries for 1950 assembly districts were in the New York State secretary's *Manual for the Use of the Legislature*. The *Voter's Directory* of the Citizen's Union contained assembly district maps for 1960 and 1970.

Groupings of census tracts along the layout from Lower Manhattan are the smallest possible; as a result, exact census tract boundaries could include exactly the same region from 1900 to 1960. Comparability between 1960 and 1970 census tracts proved to be possible only in a very inexact manner.

4 SYSTEMS OF CITIES: *An Approach to Central Place Theory*

Our concern in this chapter is with research on the optimal distribution of cities by size. We review the theory of the hierarchical distribution of cities, or central place theory, from the viewpoint of intercity commodity flows and environmental degradation.

Theoretically, the system of cities is expressed as a linear transformation, based on a matrix that represents the efficiency of transportation and different grades of environmental qualities among cities. Using this model, we prove that the distribution of cities depends not only on the transportation network, but also on differences in per capita income or in the productivity of each city, and accordingly on the degree of the degradation of environmental quality — in the context mentioned in Chapters 2 and 3 — and on the demands of the rural area and of foreign trade. On the basis of this model, by trying simulations on the various city systems, we can clarify the nature of the city system.

The classical works on the hierarchical distribution of cities have been those of Christaller (1933) and Lösch (1954). Following the earlier work, Zipf (1941) developed the well-known rank-size rule that views the city system as a kind of organism. From the viewpoint of so-called social physics, Stewart (1950) suggested that rural population can be treated as a gas and cities as condensations of "human molecules."

Beckmann subsequently introduced the principle of allometric growth theory into the social phenomenon of urbanization, and he has presented a theoretically generalized hierarchy model with analytical solutions for population in centers and in complementary areas at all levels of the hierarchy (1958, 1970). Bos (1965), also a contributor in this field, makes clear one of the important spheres of the interrelation between the types and systems of centers and transportation costs of product flows. On the other hand, to relate industrial structure and size of population, Isard, Kavesh, and Kuenne (1953) developed the theory of basic-nonbasic ratio analysis.

The model explained here is a simple variation of the input-output model consisting of the intercity commodities flows. The model is based on the following assumptions: The quantity of commodity flows should depend principally on the agglomeration points of the population — that is, on city size. City size will be considered to represent various kinds of local economic activities. Commodity flows will depend on a matrix, to be denoted as T, that expresses the efficiency of the commodity flows between cities. As the concept of centrality was originally represented in central place theory (Christaller 1933) and in later related theories by the size of the population of a location, these assumptions are reasonable in a presentation of central place theory.

THE MODEL

To consider the system of cities with "centralization as a principle of order" (Christaller 1933) and "the equilibrium of locations" (Lösch 1954), we confine our attention to the industrial commodity flows between the centers in the model. In original central place theory, various kinds of commodities and services were said to be produced by some "combined economic effort of the inhabitants" of each size city (Christaller 1933, p. 18) and were distributed over some economic distance in order to meet the range of demand for goods in the various regions. The range of demand for the products of a city is considered to be more extensive the larger the city or the higher its rank. In our model the commodity flows within the system of cities are expressed as linear transformations based on a matrix that represents the efficiency of transportation among the cities in a country and on the vector composed of each city size or agglomeration of population.

The other assumptions are as follows: (1) The cities are to be arranged according to their size order, which is measured by population, where the nth largest city is to be named as the nth-rank city and the ith number is appended to the ith-rank city according to city size. In this model only one city is assigned respectively to each rank. (2) According to the assumptions of the rank-size approach, we follow the hypothesis explicitly described by Bos: "Centres of the lowest rank consist of one production unit of the lowest-ranking industry only. They export part of their production to the agricultural area and have to import all other products from centres of higher rank and from agricultural areas"; and "The production unit of the highest-ranking industry exports to all lower centres and to the agricultural area" (Christaller 1933). In our model ${}_nT_n$ might be expressed as a lower triangular matrix, and the element $t_{ij} \geqq 0$ ($j \leqq i$).

The principal notation is as follows:

s = total products;
d = total demand for commodities and services;
l = number of laborers;
α = average rate of laborers per population;
x = average productivity per laborer;
p = population;
y = average income per capita;
d_f = demand for the foreign trade;
t_{ij} = quantity of the commodities and services flow from the ith city to the jth city induced by unit of income in the jth city ($t_{ij} \geqq 0$);
i = suffix denoting the ith city of the system;
r = suffix denoting the rural area;
S, D, L, X, P, and D_f denote n (= number of cities) column vectors of s_i, d_i, l_i, x_i, p_i, and d_f, respectively.

The total demand for the products of the ith city is expressed as follows:

$$d_i = \sum_j t_{ij} \cdot p_j \cdot y_j + t_{ir} p_r \cdot y_r + d_{if}, \tag{4.1}$$

and $\Sigma_i p_i + p_r = \overline{P}$, where $\overline{P}$ denotes the total population of the country.

If we suppose that the y_j are the same in all cities, we can rewrite (4.1) as (4.1′):

$$d_i = y \sum_j t_{ij} p_j + t_{ir} y_r p_r + d_{if}. \tag{4.1′}$$

Similarly, production in the ith city may be expressed as follows:

$$\begin{aligned} s_i &= x_i l_i \\ &= x_i \alpha_i p_i. \end{aligned} \tag{4.2}$$

If we suppose that the α_i are the same in all cities, we can rewrite (4.2) as follows:

$$s_i = \alpha x_i p_i. \tag{4.2'}$$

Accordingly, the condition of equilibrium may be expressed by a system of equations as follows:

$$\alpha \cdot x \cdot P = y \cdot TP + T_r p_r y_r + D_f. \tag{4.3}$$

If we set $(1/y)(T_r p_r Y_r + D_f) = c$, we can rewrite (4.3) as follows:

$$\left(\frac{\alpha \cdot x}{y}\right) P - TP = c. \tag{4.4}$$

Setting $\alpha x/y = \rho$,

$$(\rho I - T)P = c$$
$$P = (\rho I - T)^{-1}c. \tag{4.4'}$$

If the matrix, T, is given and the Hawkins-Simons condition is satisfied, then for any $c \geqq 0$, we get the solution P from (4.4.). Namely, for special value of ρ, a solution vector P does exist. Then, as is well known, $(\rho I - T)^{-1} = (1/\rho)\Sigma_{\nu=0}^{\infty} T^{\nu\rho-\nu}$ (Courant and Hilbert 1953, p. 9).

Here, c and ρ are composite variables. The former is composed from αx, T_r, P_r, Y_r, and D_f. Needless to say, c is increasing with respect to T_r, P_r, Y_r, and D_f. The latter, ρ, is increasing according to α, x and decreasing with respect to y.

If x is not common among the cities, set

$$\begin{bmatrix} x_1 & & & \\ & x_2 & & \\ & & \ddots & \\ & & & x_n \end{bmatrix} = I_x.$$

Similarly, $P = (\alpha/yI_x - T)^{-1}c$.

Next, if c is supposed to be expressed by some fraction of the products of the ith city,

$$yc_i = g_i\alpha_i x_i p_i.$$

Also, if g_i, α_i, x_i are the same among the cities and are denoted as g ($1 > g > 0$), we can rewrite (4.4) as follows:

$$\frac{1}{y}(1 - g)\alpha x P = TP. \tag{4.5}$$

Substitute λ for $(1 - g)\rho$,

$$\lambda P = TP. \tag{4.6}$$

$$(\lambda I - T)P = 0. \tag{4.6'}$$

In this case we can think of the model as closed in the sense defined by Gale (1960, p. 261). Also, if T is given and $P > 0$, then λ is the solution of the characteristic equation:

$$\phi(\lambda) = \det(\lambda I - T) = 0, P > 0$$

and for each $\lambda \geqq 0$, there is a characteristic vector $P > 0$. Only for the special value $\bar{\lambda} = (1 - \bar{g})\bar{p}$ does a solution vector $\bar{P}$ exist.

Then, the largest of real roots of equation $\phi(\lambda) = 0$ is called Frobenious root, $\lambda(T)$. $\lambda(T)$ is a monotone increasing function of T — that is (Debreu and Herstein 1953, p. 598; Nikaido 1959, p. 120),

$$\lambda(T_1) \geqq \lambda(T_2) \qquad \text{if } T_1 \geqq T_2.$$

IMPLICATIONS OF THE MODEL

In this model the characteristic vector of T plays a most important role, and thus we need to consider T in more detail. In the usual gravity model, demographic force, F, is expressed as $F = G(P_iP_j/r_{ij})$, where the population of cities i and j is designated by P_i, P_j, respectively, r_{ij} is the distance between cities i and j, and G is a constant. We can consider the elements of T as a kind of demographic force. However, in our model, p_i and p_j are treated as dependent variables. Thus, elements of T may depend only on economic distance between the cities, and it is reasonable to call this matrix an efficiency matrix of the commodity flows between the cities.

Then, in our model, p_i and p_j are considered to be some measure of agglomerated production points. In other words, we are using P as a measure so that it expresses the distribution of the other resources (e.g., capital). Accordingly, it also expresses indirectly the economies of scale in each production point. In addition, it expresses one kind of industrial composite at the production point. Thus, the variety of the bundle of commodities and the production cost are considered to be represented implicitly in the elements of P.

We have $p_iy_i/q_i \leqq \Sigma_j t_{ji} p_i y_i$. Let q_i be the price of the composite commodity. Thus $\Sigma_j t_{ji} \geqq q_i^{-1}$ — that is, the level of the price in the ith city affects inversely the quantity of commodity flow into the city induced by the income level of the city.

If t_{ij} depends on the $r_{ij}^{-\gamma}$, we can interpret T as derived from a system of transportation. In fact, T may depend on the various kinds of public investment, especially on the investment in transportation facilities as well as on the industrial composition and environmental quality of each city.

Hitherto, government investment has been said to decrease the value of $|\gamma|$ and to promote the dispersion of the population because $|\gamma|$ is considered to be the decreasing function of the investment in transportation. However, in the model presented here, T is certainly one of the factors on which the distribution of population may depend, and it is a decreasing function of the investment in the transportation system. Also, λ plays an important role in deciding the distribution of population, and the value of λ may fluctuate with economic conditions, as measured by economic indicators, and even with social structure.

Next, we would like to make clear the interrelation between this model and previously developed central place theory models. Among the central place theory models, we selected one formulated by Beckmann (1972) and compared it with our model. Beckmann's model may be shown briefly as follows:

$c = k(r + c)$ or $c = r \cdot k/(1 - k)$;
c = the city size;
r = rural population in the market area of the cities of the first order;
k = the proportionality factor.

$k/(1 - k)$ is called the "urban multiplier."

Size, p_m, of cities of each order m is expressed as follows:

p_m: population served by these cities;
S: number of satellites per city.

$$p_m = \frac{kS^{m-1}r}{(1-k)^m} \cdot$$

We are able to reformulate matrix T in accordance with Beckmann's model as follows:

$$T = \begin{bmatrix} k & & & & & 0 \\ as & k & & & & \\ as^2 & as & k & & & \\ \cdot & \cdot & \cdot & \cdot & & \\ \cdot & \cdot & \cdot & & \cdot & \\ \cdot & \cdot & \cdot & & & \cdot \\ as^{n-1} & as^{n-2} & \cdot & \cdot & \cdot & \cdot \; k \end{bmatrix}$$

In our model the input-output relation between the each rank cities might be expressed as follows:

	1	2	.	.	.	n
1	$yt_{11}p_1$					
2	$yt_{21}p_1$	$yt_{22}p_2$			0	
.	.	.	.			
.	.	.		.		
.	.	.			.	
n	$yt_{n1}p_1$	$yt_{n2}p_2$	.	.	.	$yt_{nn}p_n$

In equation (4.4), $p = (\rho I - T)^{-1}c$; if c, ρ, and T are given, p is determined in the above input-output table.

Here, we can explain the rank-size model more explicitly by means of the gravity model in the following cases. We denote the distance between a city, rank i, and a city, rank j, $j < i$, as r_{ij}.

1. In the simplest case a measure of r_{ij} may be expressed as follows (see also Figure 4–1):

$$r_{ij} = b(a^i + a^{1+l} + \ldots + a^{j-1}) \quad a > 1.$$

$$r_{ij} = b\,\frac{a^j - a^i}{a - 1}\,.$$

Under the other assumption, the measure of t_{ij} may be expressed as follows:

$$t_{ij} = \frac{c}{r_{ij}}\, i \neq j, \qquad t_{ij} = d, \qquad i = j.$$

We can consider this expression as one revised type of gravity model. Substituting for r_{ij},

$$t_{ij} = \frac{c(a^1 - 1)}{b} \cdot \frac{1}{a^j - a^i} \qquad j > i.$$

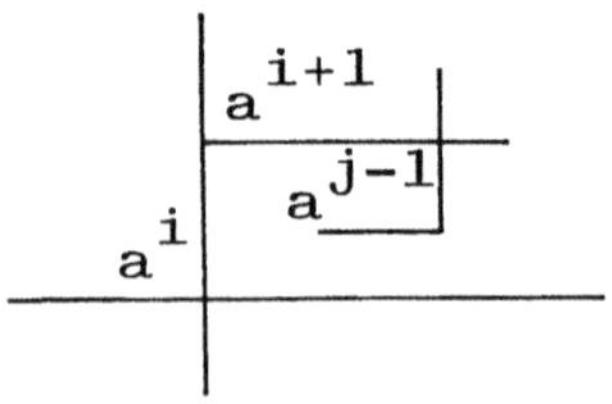

Figure 4–1. An Example of Central Place Theory

If we set $c(a^1 - 1)/b = R$,

$$T = \begin{matrix} d & \dfrac{R}{a^2 - a^1} & \dfrac{R}{a^3 - a^1} & \cdots & \dfrac{R}{a^j - a^1} \\ \dfrac{R}{a^1 - a^2} & d & \dfrac{R}{a^3 - a^2} & \cdots & \dfrac{R}{a^j - a^2} \\ & & d & & \vdots \\ & & & \ddots & \vdots \\ \dfrac{R}{a^1 - a^n} & \cdots & \cdots & \cdots & d \end{matrix},$$

where $d = t[b/c(a - 1)]$. The size of the city of rank r may be determined.

In the case of $R = 3$, if we set $d = 0$ and $R = 1$ for simplicity, we can write:

$$\begin{pmatrix} 0 & \dfrac{1}{a^2 - a} & \dfrac{1}{a^3 - a} \\ \dfrac{1}{a^2 - a} & 0 & \dfrac{1}{a^3 - a^2} \\ \dfrac{1}{a^3 - a} & \dfrac{1}{a^3 - a^2} & 0 \end{pmatrix} \cdot \begin{pmatrix} s_1 \\ s_2 \\ s_3 \end{pmatrix} = \lambda \begin{pmatrix} s_1 \\ s_2 \\ s_3 \end{pmatrix}.$$

The eigenvectors are real since T is symmetric. We set $s_1 = 1$, $s_2 = s$, and $s_3 = S$.

$$\frac{s}{(a^2 - a)} + \frac{1}{(a^3 - a)} S = \lambda,$$

$$\frac{1}{a^2 - a} + \frac{1}{(a^3 - a^2)} S = \lambda s,$$

$$\frac{1}{a^3 - a} + \frac{1}{a^3 - a^2} s = \lambda S.$$

λ is determined by

$$\det \begin{vmatrix} -\lambda & \dfrac{1}{a^2 - a} & \dfrac{1}{a^3 - a} \\ \dfrac{1}{a^2 - a} & -\lambda & \dfrac{1}{a^3 - a^2} \\ \dfrac{1}{a^3 - a} & \dfrac{1}{a^3 - a^2} & -\lambda \end{vmatrix} = 0$$

$$-\lambda^3 + \lambda\left(\frac{1}{a^3 - a^2}\cdot\frac{1}{a^3 - a^2}\right) - \frac{1}{a^2 - a}\left(\frac{-\lambda}{a^2 - a} - \frac{1}{a^3 - a^2}\frac{1}{a^3 - a}\right)$$
$$+ \frac{1}{a^3 - a}\left(\frac{1}{a^2 - a}\cdot\frac{1}{a^3 - a^2} + \frac{\lambda}{a^3 - a}\right) = 0$$

$$\lambda^3 - \left[\frac{1}{(a^2 - a)^2} + \frac{1}{(a^3 - a)^2} + \frac{1}{(a^3 - a^2)^2}\right]$$

$$\lambda - \frac{1}{(a^2 - a)(a^3 - a)(a^3 - a^2)} = 0.$$

Write $(a^2 - a)^{-1} = a_3$, $(a^3 - a)^{-1} = a_2$, $(a^3 - a^2)^{-1} = a_1$,

$$\begin{cases} a_3 s + a_2 S = \lambda, \\ a_3 + a_1 S = \lambda s, \\ a_2 + a_1 s = \lambda S, \qquad S = \dfrac{a_3 s^2 - a_3}{a_1 - a_2 s}, \end{cases}$$

$$a_2 + a_1 s = \frac{a_3^2 s(s^2 - 1)}{a_1 - a_2 s} + a_2 \frac{a_3^2 (s^2 - 1)^2}{(a_1 - a_2 s)^2}\,.$$

From the above, we can find the solution values as for s and S.

2. As the other simplified form of t_{ij}, we can consider the following special case:

$$t_{ij} = \begin{cases} e^{-\alpha(j-i)} = a^{j-i} & j > i \\ e^{-\beta(i-j)} = b^{i-j} & j < i \\ e^{-\gamma} = c & j = i \end{cases} \qquad 0 < c < b < a < 1.$$

The corresponding integral equation is

$$\lambda s(x) = \int_0^x s(t)e^{-\alpha(x-t)}dt + \int_x^1 s(t)e^{-\alpha(t-x)}dt.$$

If no trade with higher central places occurs, then

$$t_{ij} = 0 \qquad j > i.$$

$$T = \begin{pmatrix} 1 & & & & 0 \\ e^{-\alpha} & 1 & & & \\ e^{-2\alpha} & e^{-\alpha} & 1 & & \\ & & & \ddots & \\ e^{-R\alpha} & e^{-(R-1)\alpha} & \cdots & e^{-\alpha} & 1 \end{pmatrix}$$

The integral equation is

$$\lambda s(x) = \int_0^x s(t)\, e^{-\alpha(x-t)} dt,$$

$$\lambda s(x) e^{\alpha x} = \int_0^x s(t)\, e^{\alpha t} dt.$$

If we set $s(x)e^{\alpha x} = u(x)$,

$$\lambda u(x) = \int_0^x u(t) dt$$

$$u = \lambda u'$$

$$\frac{u'}{u} = \frac{1}{\lambda}$$

$$u = u(0)\, e^{(1/\lambda)x} .$$

$$s(i) = s(0) \cdot e^{i/\lambda}$$

$$= s(0)(e^{1/\lambda})^i$$

$$= s(0)\, g^i. \tag{4.7}$$

In the case of discrete,

$$\lambda s(i) = \sum_{j=0}^{i} e^{-\alpha(i-j)} s(j),$$

$$\lambda s(i)\, e^{\alpha i} = \sum_{j=0}^{i} e^{\alpha j} s(j).$$

Write $s(i)\, e^{\alpha i} = u_i$,

$$\lambda u_i = \sum_{j=0}^{i} u_j.$$

Taking the differences between i and $i - 1$, we get,

$$u_i = \lambda(u_i - u_{i-1}),$$

$$u_i = \frac{\lambda}{\lambda - 1} u_{i-1},$$

$$u_i = \left(\frac{\lambda}{\lambda - 1}\right)^i u_0. \tag{4.8}$$

The result in (4.7) or (4.8) expresses the rank-size rule itself.

CONCLUSION

Considering our model more generally, we can reformulate the model of the system of cities and postulate the continuous geographical distribution of population or some Hilbert vector space composed of the consumption and production points. After all, if we divide the area of the city into smaller and smaller communities, we finally get a virtually continuous distribution of population (Lösch 1954).

The cities or communities are numbered from the largest to the smallest and arranged pointwise in the domain

$$1 < q < k, \quad 1 < p < k.$$

We postulate the following relationship:

$f(p)$: function of the final demand for industrial products;
$\phi(p)$: production function;
$K(p, q)$: function of the intermediate demand in the qth city for the industrial products that are produced in the pth city.

$$f(p) = \phi(p) - \lambda \int K(p,q)\phi(q)\, dq. \tag{4.9}$$

For a certain value of λ, the equation possesses one and only one continuous solution, $\phi(p)$, for each arbitrary continuous function, $f(p)$ (Courant and Hilbert 1953).

We can consider a theoretical meaning of λ, as in the preceding section, or λ may be derived as some index that represents flow efficiency between the separate production points. Our new formulation is in some sense more general than that of the preceding section.

We can almost similarly add the same set theoretical explanation to the above formulation as the one developed by Arrow and Debreu (1954). In addition, we can consider the dynamic sphere of the systems of cities on the basis of our model. The dynamic model that may be developed is somewhat different from the usual I.O. model in the following respects: (1) The intermediate demand and final demand are not distinguished. (2) There is only one set of commodities and services (Holley 1952).

This model's principal characteristic is to try to separate the elements of the usual gravity model and to formulate the equilibrium model as a linear transformation based on a matrix that expresses the efficiency of transportation between the cities in order to make clear one aspect of central place theory. This model has been developed in the context of a general equilibrium model on the location problem. The reasoning in the second section of Chapter 5, together with the model of the urbanization process described in Chapter 2, will give us a perspective on the recent changing characteristics of the macro-location situation. As this chapter's appendix shows, we can empirically compare the changing behavior of the systems of cities among the developed as well as among the developing countries on the basis of the theory.

APPENDIX: CHANGING OF THE PARAMETER OF THE RANK-SIZE RULE EQUATION

In this appendix we measure the changing parameters of rank-size rule equations, setting constant the number of sample U.S. and Japanese cities throughout the years to be studied. We compare the changing behavior of these parameters in both countries. Then we review historically the economic development of both countries in order to look for idiosyncratic reasons that explain the differences.

Changing the Value of the Parameter

Here, in order to describe the rank-size structure of cities and to make clear its dynamic character, we can suppose that each city of the rank expresses a different industrial composite. The growth rate of the economic system composed of the cities depends on differences in productivity because each city expresses a different industrial composite productivity, which allows each city to attract either positively or negatively the resources of labor on the basis of the weight of its wage rate.

To clarify the meaning of the rank-size rule, we can rewrite the rank-size rule model as follows:

$$P \cdot \alpha_1 R(P) = A,$$
$$\log P = \log A - \alpha_1 \log R(P),$$

where P = population size, $R(P)$ = rank of the city, and A, constant = the largest city's population. Rank, $R(P)$, shows us the rank position occupied by the city within the system of cities. Population shows us the economic potential of the city in terms of labor resources as well as accumulated final demand. Accordingly, α_1 expresses the relation between the potential and the rank and shows us the elasticity of the potential of the city in the economic system with respect to the rank. The rank of the city expresses the order of magnitude of economic activity, which might be explained as a gravity center or as the potential of the city. It reflects the variety of the products or the area of the market of the products, the condition of the transportation network, and international trade.

Thus the parameter of the rank-size rule equation is an indicator of the hierarchical structure of the system of cities. It shows us the correspondence of the arrangement to the order of the potential of the cities. In other words, if the magnitude of the parameter is large, the pyramid of the hierarchical structure of the cities is sharp; the opposite gives a flat pyramid. We will examine the meaning of the shift of the parameter related to the economy in greater detail.

In this model we limited the number of cities or SMSAs to a constant of the upper ranks. The situation is therefore different from the case Vining (1977) considered. Vining assumed that "cities are continually 'born' at the minimum size and expand at a constant rate of growth, *g*. The rate of such births being a constant, *r*, the number of cities likewise expands exponentially" (1977, pp. 16–17). Our model is substantially different from Vining's, which is why the hypothesis in this chapter is remarkably different from his conclusion. It is noteworthy that an identical rank-size rule approach will achieve a different result if the sample size is allowed to vary.

Drawing from the rank-size rule equation, we calculated the parameter α_1 in the United States from the earliest usable data (i.e., since 1790 for the United States). We can estimate the parameters with high reliability. The results are shown in Tables 4–1 and 4–2.

Table 4–1. Parameters of the Rank-Size Rule Equation: U.S. Cities

Year		*U.S. Cities*	*t-statistic*	R^2
1790	α_0	4.3613	11.0756	0.8274
	α_1	−1.5485	−7.8945	
1800	α_0	5.1612	11.0970	0.8087
	α_1	−1.7948	−8.7217	
1810	α_0	5.3757	18.9486	0.8892
	α_1	−1.5670	−13.5872	
1820	α_0	5.5432	27.9380	0.9352
	α_1	−1.5001	−19.3745	
1830	α_0	5.5991	58.3678	0.9766
	α_1	−1.2497	−34.2006	
1840	α_0	5.8609	58.4247	0.9699
	α_1	−1.1482	−30.0481	

Table 4–1. *(continued)*

Year		*U.S. Cities*	*t-statistic*	R^2
1850	α_0	5.9815	80.3079	0.9669
	α_1	−0.8137	−28.5843	
1860	α_0	6.9617	90.9808	0.9813
	α_1	−1.1170	−38.3233	
1870	α_0	7.2667	106.6420	0.9834
	α_1	−1.0581	−40.7655	
1880	α_0	7.9506	122.1960	0.9876
	α_1	−1.1156	−47.1467	
1890	α_0	7.7087	117.6280	0.9830
	α_1	−0.9316	−37.2070	
1900	α_0	7.9972	113.8650	0.9780
	α_1	−0.9439	−35.2796	
1910	α_0	8.1457	104.1990	0.9684
	α_1	−0.8742	−29.3577	
1920	α_0	8.3956	139.1060	0.9814
	α_1	−0.8831	−38.4139	
1930	α_0	8.6463	189.1330	0.9899
	α_1	−0.9115	−52.3445	
1940	α_0	8.8634	163.0400	0.9862
	α_1	−0.9083	−44.7710	
1950	α_0	8.7029	127.7740	0.9750
	α_1	−0.8564	−33.0091	
1960	α_0	8.6189	103.5880	0.9567
	α_1	−0.7881	−24.8665	
1970	α_0	8.6081	100.4850	0.9520
	α_1	−0.7687	−23.5564	
1973	α_0	8.5790	104.1170	0.9549
	α_1	−0.7644	−24.3543	
1975	α_0	8.5632	104.7590	0.9554
	α_1	−0.7624	−24.4860	

Note: Sample size is Rank 1 to 30 for all years except 1820 (Rank 1 to 28); 1810 (Rank 1 to 25); 1800 (Rank 1 to 20); and 1790 (Rank 1 to 15).

Source: U.S. Bureau of the Census, *U.S. Census of Population: 1970,* Vol. 1, Part A, Tables 28 and 29, and *County and City Data Book, A Statistical Abstract Supplement, 1975 and 1977* (Washington, D.C.: Government Printing Office, 1970, 1975, 1977); see Statistical Appendix, Table A–1.

Table 4–2. Parameters of the Rank-Size Rule Equation: U.S. SMSAs

Year		*U.S. SMSAs*	*t-statistic*	R^2
1929	α_0	4.3283	(93.4285)	(0.9016)
	α_1	−1.1082	(−48.5236)	
1940	α_0	4.3150	(111.6172)	(0.9248)
	α_1	−1.0717	(−56.2362)	
1950	α_0	4.3463	(140.9430)	(0.9472)
	α_1	−1.0326	(−67.9277)	
1959	α_0	4.4283	(165.2668)	(0.9588)
	α_1	−1.0197	(−77.2976)	
1962	α_0	4.4502	(168.4044)	(0.9597)
	α_1	−1.0175	(−78.2079)	
1965	α_0	4.4775	(169.8926)	(0.9601)
	α_1	−1.0203	(−78.6419)	

Source: See Statistical Appendix, Table A–2.

Figure 4–2 indicates changing trends in the hierarchical structure of cities in the United States over time. On the vertical axis the slope of the rank-size rule equation (RSRE) measures the degree of skewness of city size distribution, or in other words, the degree of population size uniformity in the urban system and differences in the potential of cities within the urban system. As mentioned above, for example, when the slope of RSRE (absolute value) is high, the urban hierarchy is skewed, usually in favor of a large primate city, and considerable differences exist in the size of the next largest city, and so on down the line. Conversely, a low slope of RSRE corresponds to a relatively uniform city-size distribution.

In the case of the United States, we can recognize clearly the regularity of the decreasing trends of the parameters of RSRE in both SMSAs and cities (see Figure 4–2). Comparing the parameters for SMSAs with those of cities for the years in which we have data for SMSAs, the rate of decrease is smaller in the case of SMSAs than in cities (see Tables 4–1 and 4–2). One of the reasons for this might be that the more rapid deterioration in the quality of environment and the more rapid growth of the tax rate are pushing the people to suburban areas. This movement of population is not reflected in the more aggregate SMSA figures.

Figure 4–2 reveals that the skewness of city-size distribution in the United States has been decreasing during the nineteenth and twentieth centuries. We find that the number of cities with populations greater than 100,000 grew from nine to fifty from 1860 to 1910 (U.S. Bureau of the

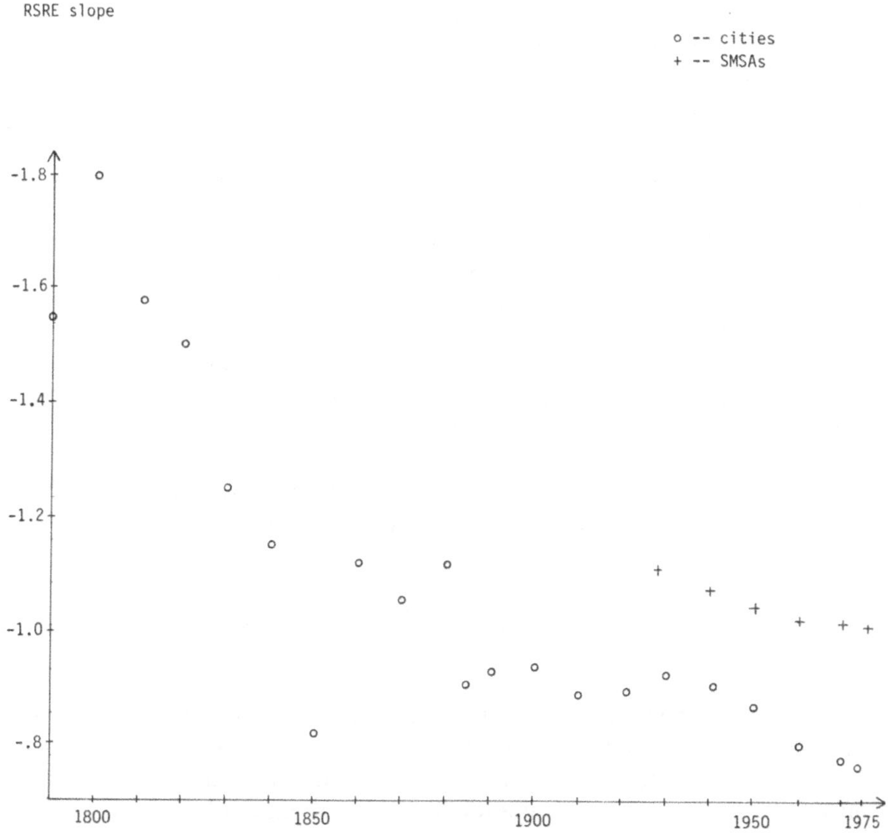

Figure 4–2. Rank-Size Rule Equation Parameters for the United States
Source: See Table 4–1.

Census 1970). America's urban structure expanded during this period because of the simultaneous rise of new factory towns, of towns based on natural resource exploitation, and of strategic regional service centers. Just under 2,000 new urban centers evolved from 1860 to 1910. By and large, this process was fueled by the tremendous supply of immigrant labor.

Since 1910 related factors widening the urban base (i.e., decreasing the slope of RSRE) were the increased use of petroleum and natural gas energy, advances in the petrochemical and communications industries, and the development of long-distance road and air transportation. To some extent these developments strongly influenced selective metropolitan growth; however, in many respects they tended to equalize differences in the economic development rates of the cities.

The stability in rank of the major metropolitan areas over the past sixty years appears to lend partial support for this suggestion. The mobility of labor and goods brought on by the pervasive rise of automotive transport in America in the 1920s through the 1940s certainly adds to this thesis; the decrease in the RSRE slope over this period must be partially attributed to the increasing mobility of Americans.

Since 1950 the RSRE slope has shown considerable stability. Most American cities have experienced growth roughly proportional to that of the nation as a whole — largely on the basis of the relative growth of existing industries. There has been, however, an explosive growth of metropolitan areas in the Southwest and West, primarily due to the growth of "footloose" industries (e.g., final processing, service sectors, and R&D industry) and to an overall rise in real incomes, which induced a change in values related to the discovery of new amenity resources (i.e., environmental air quality, open space, and so on) (Clark 1968; Berry and Gillard 1977).

Comparative Study of the Change: The United States and Japan

The primary purpose of this section is to account roughly for the remarkable differences between the United States and Japan in urbanization and evolution of city-size distribution over the past 100 years. We contrast the trends of the parameters of the rank-size rule equations and other economic trends in both countries.

In the past, Japan experienced a pattern of increasing skewness of city-size distribution, drastically severed into two distinct time periods by World War II (see Figure 4–3 and Table 4–3), while the United States registered a decreasing RSRE slope (an increasingly more even city-size distribution). However, in Japan, the pattern of increase was not constant in that the country experienced two exceptional periods.

From 1918 to 1920 a small setback in the trend toward increasing the top-heavy nature of the urban hierarchy is explained by the depression of 1919. Similarly, the decrease between 1920 and 1925 would have been larger but for the Great Earthquake of 1923, in which an estimated 100,000 people were killed and some urban outmigration occurred.

The enormous drop in the RSRE slope from 1940 to 1945 is obviously explained by World War II. Japan's urban population declined from 37.9 percent to 27.9 percent of total population during this period, and the

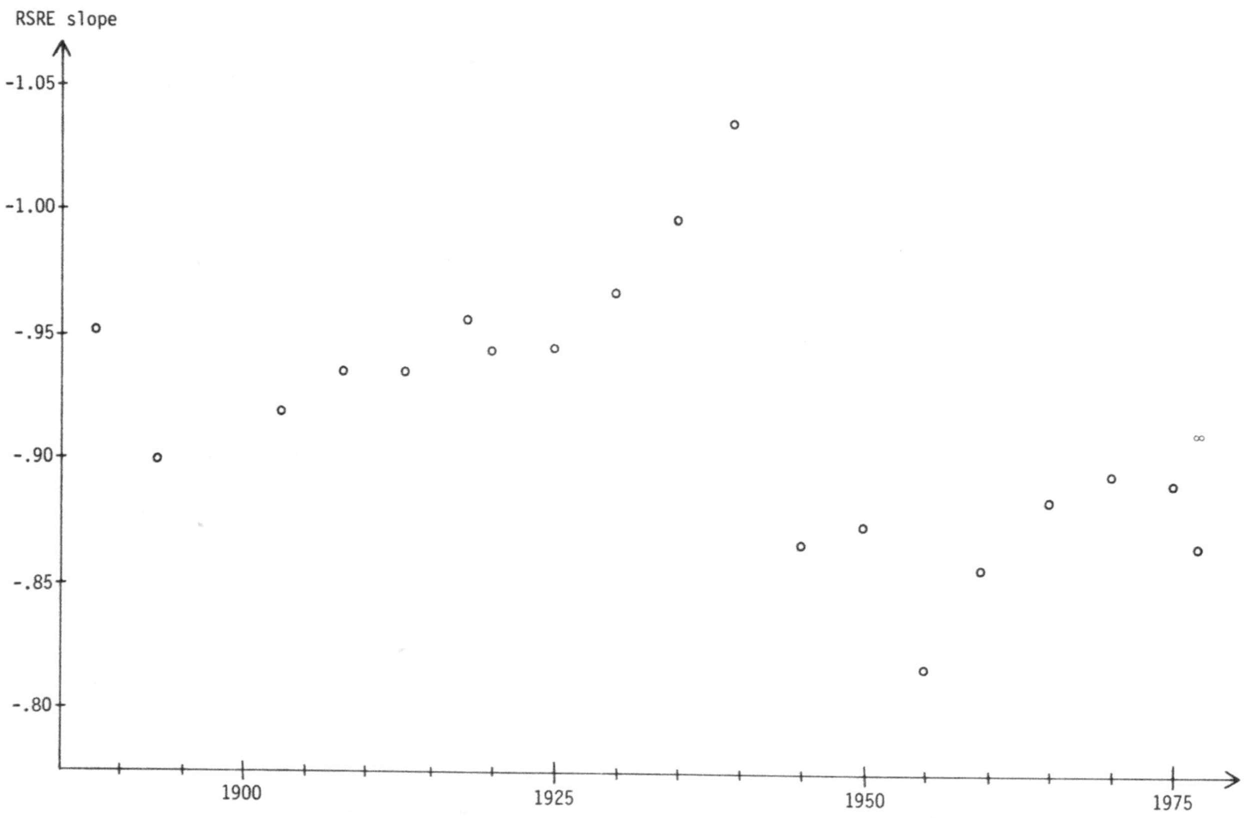

Figure 4–3. Rank-Size Rule Equation Parameters for Japan
Source: See Table 4–3.

Table 4–3. Parameters of the Rank-Size Rule Equation: Japanese Cities

Year		*Japanese Cities*	*t-statistic*	R^2
1888	α_0	2.8539	118.91	0.9801
	α_1	−0.9491	−60.07	
1893	α_0	2.8506	95.66	0.9663
	α_1	−0.8995	−45.89	
1903	α_0	3.0218	82.11	0.9538
	α_1	−0.9218	−38.89	
1908	α_0	3.1067	91.37	0.9619
	α_1	−0.9342	−43.05	
1913	α_0	3.1618	92.99	0.9624
	α_1	−0.9365	−43.36	
1918	α_0	3.2510	97.34	0.9657
	α_1	−0.9588	−45.44	
1920	α_0	3.3186	106.37	0.9693
	α_1	−0.9432	−48.12	
1925	α_0	3.3851	106.16	0.9679
	α_1	−0.9463	−47.08	
1930	α_0	3.4688	105.43	0.9675
	α_1	−0.9673	−46.73	
1935	α_0	3.5625	109.62	0.9704
	α_1	−1.9959	−49.06	
1940	α_0	3.6610	114.57	0.9736
	α_1	−1.0360	−52.06	
1945	α_0	3.4500	123.21	0.9705
	α_1	−0.8660	−49.20	
1950	α_0	3.5023	115.97	0.9665
	α_1	−0.8738	−45.99	
1955	α_0	3.5500	117.94	0.9621
	α_1	−0.8178	−43.04	
1960	α_0	3.6495	124.56	0.9674
	α_1	−0.8590	−46.68	
1965	α_0	3.7343	127.02	0.9682
	α_1	−0.8822	−47.18	
1970	α_0	3.7892	116.59	0.9623
	α_1	−0.8952	−43.25	
1975	α_0	3.8210	119.41	0.9632
	α_1	−0.8918	−43.72	
1977	α_0	6.9285	630.18	0.9826
	α_1	−0.8680	−190.72	

Note: Data of Table A–7 in the Statistical Appendix are used for estimation.

greater part of this decline occurred through the casualties and evacuations from June 1944 to August 1945. Japan's largest cities incurred the greatest share of the total urban loss (Wilkenson 1968). As a result, city-size distribution became more even.

The evolution of the urban systems in the United States and Japan shows some similarities with respect to the overall pattern of urbanization, but it exhibits striking differences regarding when and how fast the urbanization process occurred. A look at historical trends in the United States and Japan yields some insight regarding the differences in development of the respective urban hierarchies. That the United States underwent its industrial revolution almost a century before Japan is clearly a dominant explanatory factor. To explain the causes of the similarity and differences in the trends of urbanization in both countries, we can use both the historical and Weberian approaches.

The decisive points of the historical approach are (1) the time lag of industrialization, including the time lag of turning points of changes in industrial structure, and (2) the time differences in the extension of the national transport network. Correspondingly, the critical aspects of the Weberian approach that we focus upon in this comparative analysis include (1) the differences in resource availability and spatial distribution of resources and, with respect to human resources, differences in the pattern of immigration, and (2) differences of market structures in terms of international market orientation.

The economic growth rate offers one basis for explaining the differences shown in Table 4–4, since the economic growth rate is reflected,

Table 4–4. Change of the RSRE Slope

	RSRE Slope	
	U.S.	*Japan*
1890		−.90
1900	−1.36	−.92
1910	−1.19	−.93
1920	−1.10	−.94
1930	−1.01	−.97
1940	−.97	−1.02
1950	−.94	−.88
1960	−.86	−.86
1970	−.82	−.90

at least in theory, in the RSRE slope measure. As a reasonable hypothesis we can suppose that if the RSRE slope is large, a rapid economic growth rate is implied, since the differences in city size within the hierarchy are great. Apparently, relatively similar economic growth patterns brought different trends in the RSRE slope, decreasing in the United States and increasing in Japan. As is well known, Japan's rate of economic growth in the 1970s was low as compared with the rate that nation experienced from the end of World War II through the 1960s. This lower rate of economic growth is probably reflected in the gentle RSRE slope.

In contrast with the United States, Japan experienced a much later industrialization. The 1920s and 1930s introduced a new era of urbanization for Japan, driven by rapid industrialization especially in heavy industries — coal mining, iron and steel processing, and shipbuilding. To a certain extent, industrial concentration was further promoted by the collapse of the silk market following the worldwide depression in the 1930s, when displaced agricultural workers migrated into urban areas (Wilkenson 1968).

After World War II Japan mounted an intensive drive toward recovery and rapid economic and industrial growth. The increase in the RSRE slope from 1950 to 1970 is strongly associated with the concentration and rapid growth of heavy industry within the major urban centers and their satellites, significant rural-urban migration, and the assimilation of some 5 million returning soldiers and expatriates from former colonies. During the 1950s the shipbuilding industry in Japan became the world's largest; similarly, steel, petroleum refining, and chemicals were fast-growing heavy industries. Other key growth industries included the manufacture of motorcycles, which boomed in the late 1950s; the automobile industry, which experienced such a takeoff in the early 1960s that it was second only to the United States automobile industry by the early 1970s; and the electrical appliances industry (Dennison and Chung 1976). This wave of industrialization not only resulted in increasing concentration of industrial activity in the large cities but also led to creation of new, industrially specialized satellite cities within the spheres of influence of the great cities.

The downturn in the RSRE slope from 1970 to 1975 appears to be largely attributable to urban decentralization, but it is obviously a complex issue. Rapid population and employment movement out of the major cities themselves occurred apparently as a result of increasing per capita incomes and increased mobility. Industries become more footloose as labor becomes relatively homogenous, and capital, information, and communications become increasingly accessible. Furthermore, levels of urban pollution coupled with urban amenity value changes are undoubtedly linked with this process of urban decentralization.

Highlights of Historical Trends

The historical trends of urbanization and development of urban structure in both Japan and the United States highlight some of the principle factors that led to significantly different evolutions of urban hierarchy and systems of cities. From the 1840s onward, urban increases in the United States were partly supported by the beginnings of large-scale foreign immigration. Immigrants converged on cities whose industrial and commercial prospects had already attracted 25,000 or more residents. As a result, they promoted the rapid growth of both the manufacturing cities of median size and the great metropolises. New England and the Middle Atlantic states had the largest proportions of urban populations and attracted most of the new immigrants, but increasing numbers were moving west. By 1880 immigrants and their American-born children accounted for two-thirds or more of the population of cities in the industrial center of the economy (Ward 1971). Cities with the largest proportion of immigrants were ports of arrival, supply and export centers in the North Central states, and specialized manufacturing and mining centers that demanded large amounts of cheap and unskilled labor.

Urbanization and industrialization were mutually reinforced by the influx of immigrants who provided a supply of cheap labor, expanded the market, and supplied much of the enterprise. Rapid industrialization was promoted as the shoe, textile, and other industries boomed with mechanization and the employment of this cheap labor. The textile industry quickly replaced earlier native-born labor with Irish and other immigrant groups. Successive surges of new immigrants — Polish, French, Canadian, and Portuguese — enabled industrialists to fight off union demands for higher wages, which permitted urban agglomeration and expansion to occur.

The broadening base of city-size distribution in the United States must also be attributed to the widespread development of cities stimulated by availability of local natural resources. Rich endowments of mineral resources secured the industrial future of some cities throughout the country, such as Pittsburgh and Toledo; however, only where abundant supplies of coal and other fuels were found was manufacturing encouraged and urban growth maintained. Copper-, gold-, and silver-mining towns seldom became major cities. Generally, though, nearby commercial and manufacturing towns supplied various services to the mining districts and strengthened their claim to regional leadership (Denver and San Francisco, for example). The exploitation of rich mineral deposits and other natural resources provided manufacturing bases and added tremendously to the flow of commerce by which many cities prospered and grew. Once the railroad extended to the West, the presence of abundant resources greatly influenced local urbanization, the most rapid growth occurring on the West Coast where resources were most plentiful (San Francisco, Los Angeles, Portland, and Seattle, for example). In the fertile plains of the Midwest, cities prospered as processors of regional farm products (for example, Minneapolis — wheat, Kansas City — meat processing and packaging, and Milwaukee — brewing).

Conversely, in the early phases of Japanese urbanization, the major impetus to urbanization was the rapid development of international trade after Japan was opened to international contact. To a lesser extent, exploitation of mineral resources stimulated city growth.

From 1890 to 1903, Osaka, Nagasaki, Yokohama, and Kobe grew quickly, predominantly as export centers for Japan's thriving textile industry and as exclusive trading ports for Japan with the outside world. Silk and cotton production and processing were the primary basis for international trade, silk alone comprising over 25 percent of total exports from 1890 to 1914 (Wilkenson 1968). However, until the twentieth century, when Japan imported cotton-processing machinery, the textile industry remained predominantly a rural-oriented handicraft industry and did not add to the urbanization process directly. The intrigue of contact with the outside world attracted considerable interest and migration to these ports. Also, during Japan's initial urbanization phase, mineral resource exploitation led to the rapid expansion of Sapporo and Hakodate in Hokkaido and Niigata (Wilkenson 1968). From 1908 to 1920, the urbanization rate slowed considerably, even though these mineral resource centers experienced sustained growth. From 1890 to 1920, urbanization occurred slowly, but the initial pattern for the urbanization process and evolution of the urban system was established. Concentration of population in a few major urban centers began. This is shown by the increase in the RSRE slope for the period in Figure 4–3. Furthermore, the scarcity of extensive mineral resources for the most part made unnecessary any major shifts away from traditional settlement areas.

This trend of industrialization in the urban areas is related to the pattern of Japanese internal migration. As in the West, the rural population was the major source of urban expansion; however, with the exception of the period during the 1930s when the silk industry collapsed, the flow of rural-to-urban migration was relatively slow and orderly until the 1950s. Japan's rural population remained extremely stable, varying between 5.4 and 5.7 million rural households between 1872 and 1946 and rising to over 6 million in 1949 and 1951 (Wilkenson 1968). As a result, there was little expansionary pressure on urban areas in general; such pressure occurred only when there was a demand for labor. Therefore, smaller urban areas, ancillary to the major industrial centers, had little impetus for expansion. This reinforced the predominance of the major centers and further population concentration there.

In contrast to the situation in Japan, the significance of foreign trade as an impetus to urbanization during the nineteenth and twentieth centuries in the United States was small — rendered so by the tremendous growth of America's internal market. Foreign trade was extremely important in the earlier stage of America's development during the eighteenth and nineteenth centuries.

Conclusion

Historically, industrial developments in Japan and the United States have had time lags, especially with respect to the period of development of light industry, heavy industry, petrochemical and other highly developed technical industry, and the associated transportation networks. The timing of the development of transportation networks in terms of its effect on the location of economic activities has influenced their dispersion.

From the Weberian point of view, in the United States, abundant natural resources are dispersed all over the country, and the market is also quite dispersed internally. Waves of immigrants from the old continents generated a new supply of labor, which dispersed over the nation. On the other hand, Japan had to depend on overseas markets for its products as well as for its supply of materials. Thus major port cities functioned as supply points for materials as well as nodal points for the marketing of products. In Japan's case, gradual dissolution of the rural communities constituted the supply of labor. These factors induced the Japanese urbanization process to be concentrated in the traditional coastal cities.

At current levels of per capita income, after considerable slowing down of the economic growth rate, Japan already shows a decreasing pattern of the parameters of systems of cities similar to that of the United

States, regardless of their differences in economic development. According to our hypothesis, this decreasing trend of the parameters in Japan should continue.

Regardless of the idiosyncratic differences in historical trends in the United States and Japan, there should be an expected regularity of the urbanization processes, viewed through the changing behavior of the values of the RSRE parameter. In addition, we expect that these kinds of comparative studies will contribute to analysis of the urbanization process in other countries and imply more generalized regularities.

5 CITY SIZE AND ENVIRONMENTAL QUALITY

Distribution of population can be interpreted in an economic sense as the distribution of the labor force resulting from industrial agglomeration or economies of scale. The general tendencies toward concentration of population have important ramifications with respect to the various kinds of externalities that are created and are most severe in the big metropolitan areas. Notwithstanding, at least in the big metropolitan areas of developed countries, after population has reached a certain critical level of concentration, a subsequent decline in population has been observed (Berry and Gillard 1977). Environmental degradation and the costs of controlling environmental quality may be significant contributory factors in this population decline. Although metropolitan governments are in charge of policy for the conservation and improvement of environmental qualities in their areas, the effectiveness of public expenditure for environmental quality seems to be decreasing with respect to the improvement of environmental quality (Hoch 1972). In this chapter we explore the relative influence of two elements — agglomeration economies and external diseconomies of environmental quality — as they relate to individual location choice, local government, and, more generally, city size.

This chapter is divided into four sections. The first presents a theoretical framework that models intercity population movement with respect to differences among cities' environmental quality and environmental quality control expenditures, using a general equilibrium, utility function approach. The second section provides a brief survey of the empirical studies on environmental quality and urban scale, and in the third and the fourth sections, empirical analyses of the relation between environmental quality and public expenditures and on the relationship between city size and environmental quality are presented.

THEORETICAL FRAMEWORK

We first consider the relative effects of change of income and price on individuals. Assume a world in which there are two individuals and two commodities, one of which is a composite measure of all typical commodities, Q_1, and the other of which is a measure of the quality level of the environment, Q_e. The total amount of Q_1 is limited by $\tilde{Q}_1$. The aggregate of Q_e^{ij} is limited by $\tilde{Q}_e$, where i and j denote the individual and the location, respectively.

We assume that there are prices, p_1 and p_e, respectively, for the usual commodity basket and for environmental quality. The two persons reside in different locations; p_e might be different for each person. The incomes of the two individuals are respectively y_1 and y_2.

The utility functions are as follows (Baumol and Oates 1975; Mills 1978):

$$U_1 = U_1(Q_1^1, Q_e^1),$$
$$U_2 = U_2(Q_1^2, Q_e^2), \tag{5.1}$$

or

$$V_1 = V_1(p_1, p_e^1, y_1),$$
$$V_2 = V_2(p_1, p_e^2, y_2). \tag{5.2}$$

The upper suffix denotes the locations of different jurisdictions — that is, according to the notation above, the first person resides in the first location and the second lives in the second location. The constraints are as follows:

$$Y_1 = p_1\, Q_1^1 + p_e^1 Q_e^1;\; Q_1^1 + Q_1^2 = \tilde{Q}_1,$$
$$Y_2 = p_1\, Q_1^2 + p_e^2 Q_e^2;\; Q_e^1 + Q_e^2 = \tilde{Q}_e.$$

The mechanics of this simplified relationship can be considered on the basis of the following notations: E_i = public expenditure of the ith government; T_i = tax revenue of the ith government; $i = 1, 2$; and $Q_e = Q_e(E_i)$. Constraining this function, suppose that

$$\frac{dQe}{dE} > 0, \frac{d^2Qe}{dE^2} < 0. \tag{5.3}$$

$$E_i = T_i,$$
$$T_i = T_i(Y_i).$$

Now, if the income of an area increases, the revenue of the government and public expenditure also increase; subsequently, public expenditure for environmental quality control increases, and the quality of the environment increases but at a decreasing rate, by supposition (5.3). In this case the relative price of environmental quality becomes higher for the higher-income person.

Then, in this two-person, two–local government world, as a person's income rises, there is a resulting increase in the price of environmental quality. At first we supposed that the first person lives at the first location and second at the second location. But if, say, y_1 changes and as a result, T_1 and E_1 increase, then Q_e^1 will increase. Also, p_e^1, which might be supposed to be the function of Q_e, and E_1 should increase. Thus the usual equilibrium illustrated by the Edgeworth box becomes a very complex one.

In the above model, we considered the effects of changes in residents' income on public sector expenditures and hence on the degree of environmental quality, due to its increasing marginal cost. Since the aggregate measure of environmental quality, the slope of the budget line, and even the location of each person would change, we have to consider a much more complex situation than the usual equilibrium condition.

Here we would like to adhere more closely to the real world. We consider a system of cities that is composed of various agglomeration rates. The assumptions are as follows:

1. In each city, there is a different level of environmental quality.
2. The environmental quality is a Samuelsonian pure public good for the residents of the city.
3. People can choose to move among the cities.
4. Accordingly, for each individual, environmental quality is recognized as a permutation of a pure public good and the Tiebout type of world.

5. The individual's options are limited to one incremental step along the spectrum of cities' environmental quality; when environmental quality declines beyond a personal threshold of endurance, the individual will move to a city of slightly higher environmental quality. (This assumption could be broadened to include migration motivation factors other than simply the environmental quality level. In fact, intercity adjustment is caused by a combination of endogenously determined factors: inter alia differences in wage rates, differences in land value, and differences in environmental quality. In the long run, movement of capital or relocation of firms is important, but here we confine our attention to the relationship of the quality of the physical environment and movement of population.)
6. The prices of all other goods are the same in every city in the system.
7. The independent variables of the utility function are composed of environmental quality (as presented above) and all other private goods.
8. There is a shadow price for the environment in terms of all other goods in each city.
9. Over time the environmental quality of each city is going to decline in the absence of control measures. To compensate for this, increased public expenditures are required, and citizens of each city have to pay its price — increased taxes.
10. As city size increases, the relative income of residents becomes higher at the same time as the relative price of environmental quality becomes higher.
11. The adjustment process does not work instantaneously; it is a long-term adjustment process with unbalanced elements at any given time.

In examining the characteristics of the price, or marginal cost, of environmental quality with respect to the public expenditure of the city, we consider two categories of environmental quality. The first, $Q_{e\mathrm{I}}$, is improved by public investment — for instance, in a sewage treatment plant or solid waste disposal facility. The second, $Q_{e\mathrm{II}}$, is assigned with respect to city size; for instance, one of the criteria might be the amount of open space or, more generally, the ecological synthesis of the physical environment of an area. $Q_{e\mathrm{I}}$ is a stronger case of a pure public good than is $Q_{e\mathrm{II}}$.

Figure 5–1a assumes that with a given public expenditure for a pure

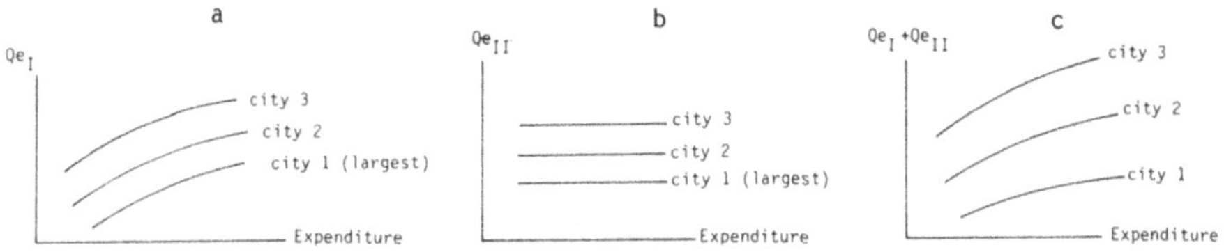

Figure 5–1. City Size and Public Expenditure for the Environment

public good, the larger city has a lower quality level. Also, there is a decreasing marginal effectiveness of expenditures on the pure public "environmental quality" good. Figure 5–1b illustrates that the overall physical quality of the environment — including open space, noise, and air quality — is determined by city size and is insensitive to expenditures. Figure 5–1c is a combination of the two types of environmental qualities and represents the overall effect of environmental quality control expenditure on environmental quality.

Finally, we assume that per capita public expenditure increases with city size (see Figure 5–2). Accordingly, the characteristics of the price of environmental quality considered above are applicable not only to public expenditure but also to city size. The following propositions on the relation between environmental quality and city size are based on these assumptions:

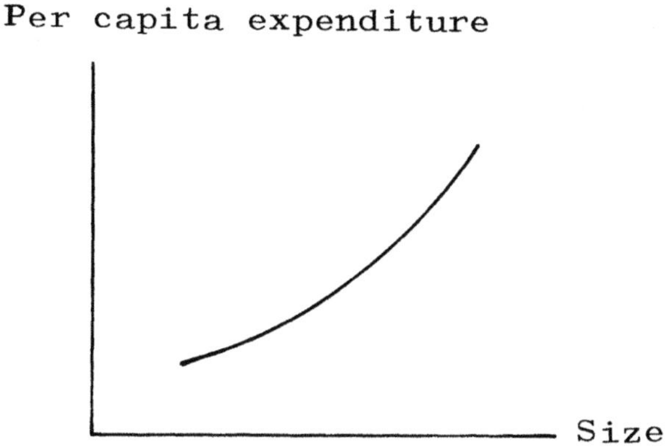

Figure 5–2. City Size and Per Capita Public Expenditure

Proposition 1. The slope of the budget line for the individual in each city expresses the relative price level of environmental quality for that city (see Figure 5–3).

Proposition 2. The slope of the budget line will shift in a clockwise direction with economic growth. The shift would have the following characteristics:

$$\frac{dp_e}{dt} \Big/ \frac{dN}{dt} > 0,$$

where N = population.

Proposition 3. There is a threshold level of city size beyond which residents find the next slightly smaller city more attractive from the point of view of environmental quality. In Figure 5–4, the first and second cities should reach their thresholds at t_a and t_b, respectively. On the basis of the situation shown in Figure 5–4, the shift of utility maximization points over time would be shown as in Figure 5–5.

A BRIEF SURVEY OF THE PROBLEM

Although the above propositions rely on a series of assumptions, most of the assumptions are considered closely parallel to the real world. Central to our discussion is the assumption relating environmental quality to city size. We first surveyed the empirical research pertaining to this

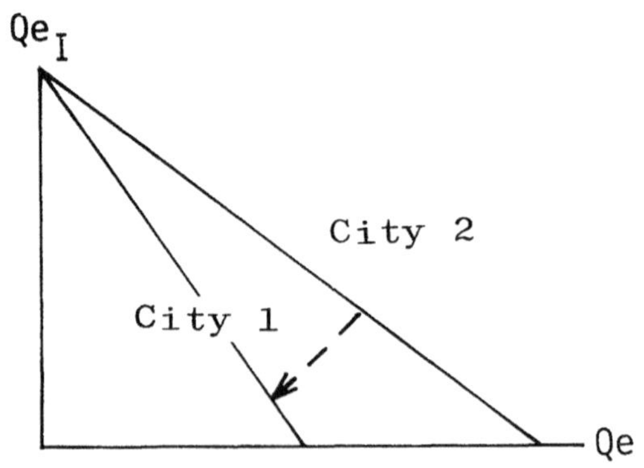

Figure 5–3. Difference of Budget Line Slope

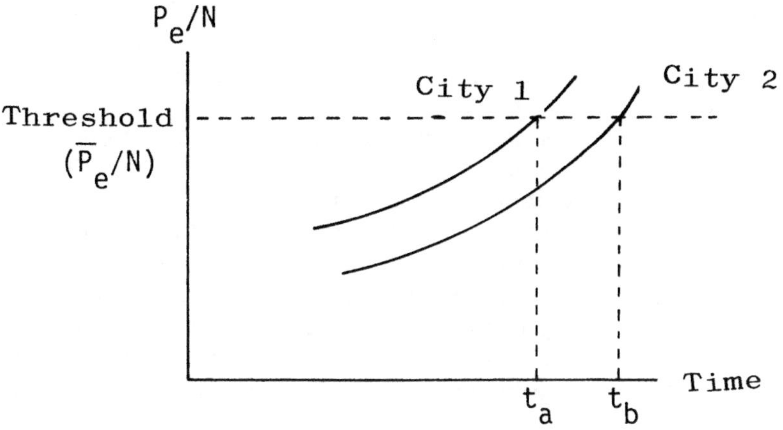

Figure 5–4. Threshold of Attractiveness

topic and found that most results lend support to the assumption. Second, in relation to our propositions, we reviewed the empirical studies that assess the impact of environmental qualities on urban wages and earnings. Third, we surveyed the empirical studies that analyze the impact of environmental quality on net urban migration rates.

We start by reviewing the literature on the relationship between city size and environmental quality. Morris (1972) developed a model for air pollution and city size using 1970 data for sulfates, particulates, and

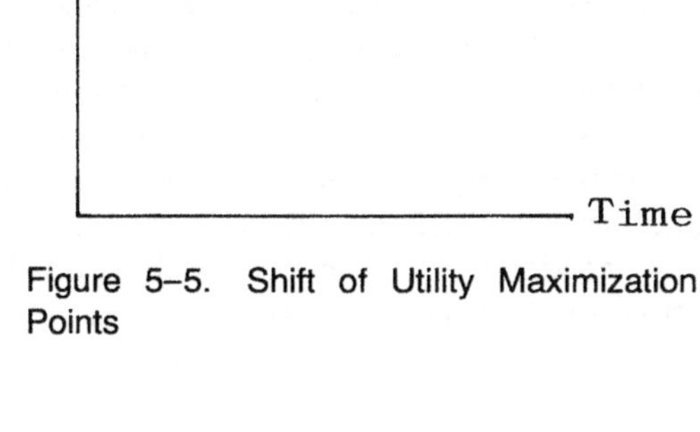

Figure 5–5. Shift of Utility Maximization Points

carbon monoxide. He found that air pollution is positively related to city size up to a point (8–10 million population), beyond which air pollution does not increase (Berry et al. 1974). However, it appears that the evidence relating city size and air pollution is weak. It is relatively difficult to establish a firm link here, relying only on cross-sectional analysis. Furthermore, the evidence is not uniform. As in Hoch's (1972) study, for instance, when additional explanatory variables for air pollution are included, the significance of city size decreases substantially with respect to nitrates and appears to drop out altogether in the case of sulfates. Morris's conclusions are somewhat suspect since, even though his model produces "adjusted" pollution levels according to city size, a strong statistical foundation relating size to the air pollution indicators (particulates, sulfates, and carbon monoxide) in the individual equations is lacking.

Water pollution constitutes a very difficult measurement problem. Nonetheless, Hoch cites some evidence that water pollution is correlated with city size — namely, that the incidence of water pollution problems increases with size. Hoch suggests that water quality declines and water quality management costs per capital increase with urban size. While engineering cost figures show economies of scale, the empirical evidence suggests that costs are U-shaped, increasing after a certain population level is reached.

The amount of solid waste produced is not itself a measure of environmental quality. We assume that the solid waste produced is collected and disposed. Hoch provides some evidence that the scale economies of disposal (landfill and incineration) are outweighed by the scale diseconomies of collection and transportation of solid waste, since collection and transportation comprise from 75 to 90 percent of the total costs of solid waste disposal. He provides some evidence that as city size increases, collection costs increase. Hoch suggests that higher wage rates, greater congestion, and greater distances to landfill sites (or, alternatively, higher land costs at any given distance from the city) explain the correlation between city size and collection costs.

Noise level by city size has not been documented sufficiently, and the evidence is fragmentary. The Environmental Protection Agency indicated that outdoor noise levels in the central districts of large cities are on the order of twice that perceived in the residential areas of those cities (i.e., approximately ten decibels higher) and twice the perceived level in suburban areas or small towns (USEPA 1971). Hoch states that the sources of loudest noise — jet airports, heavy automobile traffic, building construction and demolition — occur in large cities.

Two empirical studies have explored the impact of environmental factors on wage and earnings differentials among SMSAs. Kelley (1977) developed a labor market model designed to account for the urban area disamenities and amenities that influence the wage levels in those areas. He feels that economic welfare in urban areas may have increased more than the increases in growth of personal income since 1929 suggest. He attempts to refute another study (Nordhaus and Tobin 1972) that hypothesizes that some part of the increases in personal income merely offset unpleasant living conditions in the more densely settled areas. In essence, Kelley's model tests the impact of density, level of urbanization, and population on wages and on labor supply. Kelley finds, in contrast to the Tobin-Nordhaus hypothesis, that all three factors constitute measures of disamenities of urban living, that density is an amenity, urbanization level is a disamenity, and population is a strongly significant amenity. He concludes that urban amenities outweigh the disamenities and that despite whatever congestion, pollution, and the like result from dense populations in urban areas, people like living in these areas. Kelley finds that these urban amenities attract sufficient numbers of people to keep the market wage below what it would be without the amenities. Unfortunately, Kelley's model is not detailed enough to allow for examination of the effect of specific urban amenities or disamenities.

Kelley is criticized by Getz and Huang (1978) on the grounds that his model does not account for differences in the cost of living in different cities or differences in labor force quality. Getz and Huang developed a model that attempts to account for the factors that influence labor supply across cities. They suggest that the hedonic process for environmental attributes can be estimated by examining the compensating earnings differentials across cities. The environmental attributes set is quite large. Of particular concern to them are the four "environmental" factors that are associated with city size: air pollution, commuting time, crime rate, and "opportunity amenity." Getz and Huang find that, with the exception of the crime rate, these variables are not significant; they suggest that multicollinearity among the variables disguises their individual impact. The particular advantage of their model lies in its ability to take into account productivity through wage differentials. Nonetheless, the results leave something to be desired with respect to identifying the impact of physical environmental characteristics.

Several empirical studies have included environmental attributes and quality of life (QOL) measures in attempts to explain variations in net migration rates among SMSAs. Along these lines, Cebula and Vedder (1973) and Koshal (1976) have developed very similar migration models.

Cebula and Vedder use the following as independent variables for SMSAs over the period 1960–1968: per capita income, unemployment rate, average annual growth rate of per capita income, number of physicians per 100,000 population, crime rate, nonwhite population, temperature, and suspended particulates (air pollution). Their regression yielded an $R^2 = .647$ with only one variable — air pollution — not significant at the 12 percent level.

Koshal examines the 1960–1970 period and uses virtually the same variables as do Cebula and Vedder, except that he includes housing quality and population age structure and excludes crime rate. His results produce an $R^2 = .6275$, and all variables are significant. Koshal concludes that his analysis lends support to the hypothesis that air pollution was one of the important variables that influenced the migration pattern in the metropolitan areas of the United States during the 1960s.

AN EMPIRICAL TEST OF THE RELATION BETWEEN ENVIRONMENTAL QUALITY AND PUBLIC EXPENDITURE

We are interested first of all in providing more concrete and detailed evidence on the relationships between environmental quality and city size, since the evidence presented in other works is spotty and is, for the most part, presented in aggregate form. Our analysis of urban scale, environmental quality, and the "price" of environmental quality derives from the theoretical structure presented in this chapter and also draws on some aspects of the empirical and theoretical studies mentioned above. Our analysis is limited to five environmental quality attributes: air quality, water quality, per capita level of solid wastes, park space per 1,000 population, and noise.

The empirical analysis in the following pages has two purposes: (1) to clarify the relationship between environmental quality and public expenditure on environmental quality control, and (2) to ascertain the relationship between urban size and various measures of physical environmental quality.

We expect that time-series analysis would yield a positive relationship between environmental quality and public expenditures on the environment such that

$$\frac{dQ}{dE_Q} > 0, \qquad \frac{d^2Q}{dE_Q^2} < 0, \tag{5.4}$$

where Q and E_Q respectively denote aggregate measure of environmental quality and public expenditure for it. We were able to find time-series data on environmental quality only for air quality. This provided us with the opportunity to test the condition (5.4).

$$Q_{\text{AIR}} = e_o + e_1 E_Q, \tag{5.5}$$

where Q_{AIR} = air quality. The parameter e_1 means dQ_{AIR}/dE_Q.

In time-series analysis, we must initially face the data limitations which restrict us to using the mean (geometric) level of suspended particulates as our indicator of air quality. This kind of data is available for the years 1966 to 1977. Public expenditure data for air quality control at the county and city level are available from FY 1968–69 to FY 1975–76. It needs to be stressed at this point that expenditures at the county and city levels comprise only a little more than 10 percent of total expenditures for air quality control; the rest is concentrated at the state and federal government levels. Resource constraints do not enable us to allocate state and federal expenditures to particular SMSAs or cities. Therefore, even at this early stage, we anticipate some problems with using county and city expenditures as explanatory variables.

We expected that there would be a time lag between expenditures on environmental quality and the environmental quality level itself. We postulated that we would find a higher correlation between the expenditure of the tth year and the environmental quality of one or two years later, namely t-1 or t-2. But from the point of view of statistical significance, the result is not satisfactory, and we calculated using the unlagged data of 1968 and 1975 and obtained the results shown in Table 5–1.

The results appear to confirm our a priori conjecture that public expenditure for air quality control at the county and city levels may not be

Table 5–1. Environmental Quality and Public Expenditure

	e_o	e_l	R^2	$\bar{R}^2$	DW
Los Angeles	101.9550	22.52780	.08	−.08	2.72
	(3.75898)	(0.70674)			
New York City	119.10400	−47.82750[a]	.55	.47	2.11
	(13.46290)	(−2.69788)			
Dallas	67.87570	152.3390[a]	.57	.49	2.52
	(7.20362)	(2.79449)			

[a]Significant at the 5 percent level.

the ideal explanatory variable. Expenditures at the federal and state levels as well as regulatory policies for air pollution control may be the more important determinants of levels of air quality. However, only a closer analysis of this component of air quality control expenditures and public regulations on a city or county basis can provide us with a clearer picture of the relationship between public expenditures and air quality levels.

Even in cases in which statistically significant relationships are found, the signs of the parameters, e_1, which are supposed to measure the marginal effectiveness of expenditures, vary among cities (i.e., in some cases public expenditures affect quality levels favorably, while in others the effect is the opposite). Illustrative of such a predicament are New York City and Dallas; the effect of expenditures on air quality levels is different between these two areas.

For New York City, public expenditures for air quality control improve the level of air pollution — that is, as the amount of expenditure increases, the mean level of suspended particulates decreases. In contrast, Dallas shows the opposite trend — that is, air quality levels have not improved with increases in public expenditures.

It should be noted, however, that per capita air quality control expenditures for Dallas from 1968–1975 rose only from $.08 in 1968 to $.27 in 1975, while for the same period in New York City, expenditures ranged from $.11 in 1968 to $.93 in 1975. This may be an indication that there is a minimum quantum of public expenditures at which expenditures begin to have favorable effects on air quality levels. Closer analysis is needed in this area.

Another plausible explanation for the difference in the effect of public expenditure on air quality levels between New York City and Dallas is their difference in rates of industrial expansion and population concentrations. In New York City, industrial expansion has more or less stabilized, with firms and people moving to the suburbs or even relocating to some other cities. This may imply that the rate of increase of environmental degradation has declined. Intensified air pollution control measures, as evidenced by greatly increased public expenditures, are more capable of exerting a favorable impact on air quality levels. At the other extreme, Dallas is one of the more recent boom cities, as reflected in the continued gravitation of industries and population toward it. The rate of environmental degradation may be rapidly increasing, but, since it is of recent origin, government reaction to the problem through the allocation of more public expenditures has not really been substantial enough to offset this trend.

We assume in our theoretical formulation that city size is related to agglomeration and amenity externalities and, in particular, that in partial equilibrium, city size is a function of environmental quality.

We assume that $E = E(N)$, and $Q_e = Q(E)$. Accordingly, $Q_e = Q(N)$. The environmental quality of a city would thus be a function of its population size. On the unknown form of the function, we can suppose a similar decreasing rate of effect of the population on the environmental quality as condition (1). (See Figure 5–6.) In addition, on the basis of the regression, we could ascertain that the following form of the function has the best fit:

$$\log N = \alpha_o + \sum_i \alpha_i Q_i,$$

where i denotes the kinds of the indicator of Q.

$$\alpha_i = \frac{d \log N}{dQ_i} = \frac{1}{N}\frac{dN}{dQ_i} = \frac{1}{N}\frac{1}{\frac{dQ_i}{dN}}$$

whether

$$\frac{dQ_i}{dN} > 0 \quad \text{or} \quad \frac{dQ_i}{dN} < 0$$

is the problem. We set

$$\frac{dQ_i}{dN} = \eta_i \qquad \alpha_i = \frac{1}{N}\frac{1}{\eta_i},$$

$$\log N = \alpha_o + \alpha_1 Q_1 + \alpha_2 Q_2 + \alpha_3 Q_3 + \alpha_4 Q_4 + \alpha_5 Q_5, \qquad (5.6)$$

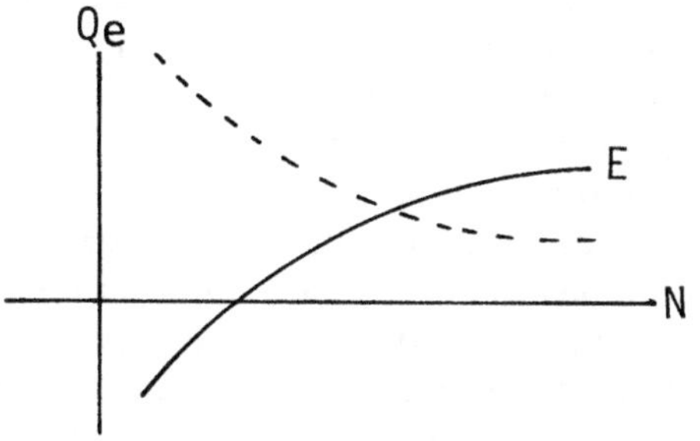

Figure 5–6. Environmental Quality and Population

where Q_1 = park area per 1,000 population, Q_2 = water pollution, Q_3 = air pollution, Q_4 = solid waste, and Q_5 = noise pollution.

Income level is added on the right-hand side to derive equation (5.7):

$$\log N = \alpha_o + \alpha_1 Q_1 + \alpha_2 Q_2 + \alpha_3 Q_3 + \alpha_4 Q_4 + \alpha_5 Q_5 + \beta_1 y. \quad (5.7)$$

In general, we expect that environmental quality is negatively related to city size. Therefore, according to these environmental variables, the coefficients for water pollution, air pollution, solid wastes, and noise are expected to have a positive sign, while park area should be negative. The income coefficient should be positive.

Our sample consists of fifty-four U.S. SMSAs in which the largest SMSAs (larger than 1.8 million population) are all represented, and some proportion of the next largest (0.5 to 1.8 million) and the medium-size SMSAs (200,000 to 500,000) are included as data on environmental quality permit. Park area indicates the amount of park and recreation area per 1,000 population for each SMSA in 1972. Water pollution is derived from a water pollution index for 1971. Air pollution consists of the mean levels of both total suspended particulates and sulfur dioxide for 1970. Solid waste represents the per capita level of solid waste produced in 1970. Noise pollution is estimated using automobile (1970) and air traffic voiumes divided by SMSA area to reflect the intensity of noise over the SMSA (1969). The regression results are shown in Table 5–2 (on the data, see Appendix 5.1).

The results indicate that the coefficient of air pollution and solid waste have the wrong sign; the solid waste coefficient is significant. These results suggest that solid waste per capita is higher in smaller SMSAs and lower in larger SMSAs. An analysis of solid wastes conducted by the state of California presents contrary evidence, although this is presented at the low end of the city spectrum (State of California 1971). It could be that in larger cities with different consumption patterns (use of individual electric garbage disposal systems and large apartment house garbage incinerators, for example), we would obtain opposite results. The lack of significance of the air pollution coefficient suggests that air pollution is not related to city size. We have not included carbon monoxide as a component of air pollution; its inclusion, since CO is produced primarily by automobiles, could possibly tip this relationship. Total suspended particulates and sulfur oxides are produced primarily by industries. This suggests that the industrial level and mix by SMSA could be important. Moreover, the local topographical and meteorological characteristics of an urban area may play a large enough part in air pollution to overcome the influence of size on pollution levels. Nevertheless, we

Table 5–2. Regression Results of the Relationship between City Size (Population) and Various Environmental Quality Variables

Equation	*Constant*	*Park Area*	*Water Pollution*	*Air Pollution*	*Solid Waste per Capita*	*Noise*	*Income*	R^2	$\bar{R}^2$
Expected sign		(−)	(+)	(+)	(+)	(+)	(+)		
(5.6)	9.30122	−0.11591	0.26221[a]	−0.11815	−0.19682[a]	0.61809[a]		.55	.50
	(106.21500)	(−1.27077)	(2.77231)	(−0.92525)	(−2.11592)	(5.58099)			
(5.7)	6.04406	−0.15314[b]	0.27036[a]	−0.04355	−0.21917[a]	0.44326[a]	6.66769×10^{-4}[a]	.67	.63
	(7.73711)	(−1.93464)	(3.31394)	(−0.39069)	(−2.76238)	(4.25303)	(4.18916)		

Note: *t*-ratios in parentheses.
[a]Significant at the 5 percent level.
[b]Significant at the 10 percent level.

find overall that the environmental variables explain about half of the differences in population size from the viewpoint of the significance level of statistics.

CONCLUSION

Despite the limited focus of this examination as well as the data constraints, we can conclude that the relationship between city size and environmental quality is not as straightforward as the research referred to in the third section indicates. It seems to be very difficult to reach general conclusions about the relationships because of the idiosyncratic nature of each city with respect to environmental quality as well as in terms of public expenditure on the environment.

However, with respect to some indicators of environmental quality, such as park area, water quality, and noise, there is an apparent basis for concluding that environmental quality declines according to city size. On the other hand, there are indicators that, at least in the case of air pollution, public expenditure should be effective, at least in matured cities such as New York. Partially because of this, city size does not appear to be related to environmental quality insofar as air quality is concerned.

Although we limit our attention to physical environmental qualities, such as open space, city size should also affect social environmental quality through other external diseconomies. Apparently, however, it is very difficult for social environmental degradation to be compensated by public expenditure.

APPENDIX 5.1: DATA

Sample Choice

In selecting the SMSAs to be included in the empirical analysis, we have used a purposive sampling method. Since our study attempts to assess the effect of environmental degradation on population decentralization (i.e., to examine the hypothesis that the negative externalities arising from population concentration eventually lead to population losses in the large cities), it is necessary that the large SMSAs (population 1.8 to 11 million) comprise part of the sample. Moreover, the cross-sectional analysis requires that we have a wide range of city sizes. Therefore, the inclusion of large SMSAs, of which there are few (only fifteen), must be ensured. In addition to the large SMSAs, smaller SMSAs were included insofar as data availability permitted. Although it is ideal to include SMSAs with populations of less than 200,000, data is unfortunately not available for some of the environmental quality indicators that we have chosen for analysis. Therefore, only thirty-nine smaller SMSAs with populations ranging from 260,000 to 1.8 million were added to our sample, making a total of fifty-four SMSAs.

Of the 243 SMSAs in the United States in 1970, 95 have populations of less than 200,000; 83 have populations of 200,000 to 500,000; 50 have populations of 0.5 to 1.8 million; and 15 have populations of 1.8 million or more. In comparison, our sample is comprised of (1) all the large SMSAs, (2) 23 SMSAs with populations of .5 to 1.8 million, and (3) 16 SMSAs with populations of 200,000 to 500,000.

In terms of geographical location, 21 percent of all SMSAs are in the Northeast, 27 percent in the North Central states, 38 percent in the South, and 15 percent in the West. In our sample, 28 percent of SMSAs are in the Northeast, 24 percent in the North Central states, 28 percent in the South, and 20 percent in the West.

Environmental Quality Data

Our data set for all environmental quality variables, with the exception of air quality, is limited to a single data time point. Air quality data were obtained from the U.S. Environmental Protection Agency on an annual basis. The geometric mean level of total suspended particulates (TSP micrograms per cubic meter) and of sulphur dioxide (also micrograms per cubic meter) constitute our measures of air quality. Water quality data were taken from a water pollution index, based on prevalence, duration, and intensity of pollution, developed by the MITRE Corporation (1971). It is converted in such a way that lower values reflect less of a water pollution problem. Solid waste data were taken from the solid waste data set (from individual multipliers) in Berry et al. (1974) and converted to a per capita basis. Park area per 1,000 population was taken directly from Liu (1975), who obtained statistics for parks and recreation areas from the U.S. Bureau of Outdoor Recreation (1972) at the county level and aggregated to the SMSA level. Noise data were obtained from Berry et al.'s (1974) noise data set, auto and traffic volumes, which we divided by SMSA area to reflect the intensity of noise over the SMSA.

All the data used correspond to 1970, with the exception of parks

(1972), water pollution (1971), and air traffic noise (1969). Net migration rate and annual average income growth data for 1970–1975 are taken from the *City and County Data Book, 1977* (U.S. Bureau of the Census 1977).

Inasmuch as our environmental quality variables have different units of measurement, it is necessary to have a common or standard measure, especially since a composite environmental quality indicator is to be derived. Therefore, we normalize each variable — that is, we compute how many standard deviations each SMSA's environmental quality level for a particular attribute is away from the sample's mean level for that attribute. After normalizing all the environmental quality variables, the composite environmental quality indicator for each SMSA can be derived by simply aggregating the various individual environmental quality variables for each SMSA.

APPENDIX 5.2: LIMIT ON THE GROWTH OF CITIES

The empirical analyses developed thus far deal with partial aspects of the theoretical formulation and are directed toward particular assumptions. In this appendix we present a differential equation to provide an overall synthetic test of the propositions developed in the chapter.

We assume as usual that the population movement is caused by the difference of the utility level of the individual, as expressed, say, by equation (5.2). In the equation, also, we suppose that,

$$dV/dP_e < 0, \qquad dV/dY > 0.$$

Furthermore, there should be some limitation in terms of population density that might express some limit of the environmental degradation determined by the idiosyncratic situation of each city.

Focusing our attention on this limit of the population density for the growth of the population in the city, we can reformulate a variant of a well-known differential equation of ecology (Hirsch and Smale 1974, p. 256). It seems to be particularly effective in revealing the empirical regularity of urbanization processes with respect to environmental degradation and to the "price" of environmental quality in the context of our theoretical propositions. We formulated a dynamic model for the change of the population with respect to time in the following differential equation:

$$N_i(t + 1) - N_i(t) = \gamma_{1i}[E - (D)_i] + \gamma_{2i}$$

$$\left(\frac{\sum_{l=1}^{k} T_{il}}{\sum_{l=1}^{k} N_{il}} - \frac{T_i}{N_i}\right) + \gamma_{3i}\left(\frac{\sum_{l=1}^{k} Y_{il}}{\sum_{l=1}^{k} N_{il}} - \frac{Y_i}{N_i}\right), \tag{5.8}$$

where N denotes population; D, density; and T, taxes.

Average income of each city is expressed by

$$\sum_{l=1}^{k} Y_{il} \Big/ \sum_{l=1}^{k} N_{il}.$$

Average tax level of each city is

$$\sum_{l=1}^{k} T_{il} \Big/ \sum_{l=1}^{k} N_{il}.$$

Sample size, l, is $k = 47$ for each city. The number of SMSAs is $i = 1, \ldots, 14$.

We estimated the parameters in order to minimize the estimation errors (Polak 1971). The estimated values of the parameters by each SMSA are shown in Table 5–3.

$$\gamma_{1i} > 0, \qquad E_i > 0.$$

In each metropolitan area, there should be a particular threshold for population density. The plus sign of γ_{1i} shows that, over this particular threshold, the population of the urban area would decrease. The special value of E means that the threshold for each city would vary by the

Table 5–3. Values of Parameters γ and E

City Number	γ_{1i}	γ_{2i}	γ_{3i}	E
1	1.000	2.000	−1.000	2.735
2	0.999	0.999	−1.000	3.524
3	1.000	1.000	−1.000	2.207
4	1.000	1.000	−1.000	1.005
5	1.000	1.000	−1.000	42.620
6	1.000	1.000	−1.000	1.883
7	1.000	1.000	−1.000	1.876
8	0.999	1.000	−1.000	17.898
9	1.000	1.000	−1.000	2.309
10	1.000	1.000	−1.000	4.221
11	1.000	1.000	−1.000	0.357
12	1.000	1.000	−1.000	0.486
13	1.000	1.000	−1.000	6.637
14	0.910	0.910	−1.000	2.645

component races of the residents, by the natural situation, such as latitude of the city, and the other idiosyncratic conditions, natural as well as societal, of each city.

$$\gamma_{2i} > 0.$$

In the process of urban development, the per capita tax rate is usually increasing. In the earlier stage of the development of the city, people are willing to pay the tax in order to enjoy the agglomeration economies and public goods produced by the government; later the tax rate becomes less effective in improving the quality of life for the residents. Thus the per capita tax rate relates positively with population increments. When the tax rate is lower than the average, the growth rate of the population increases. In contrast, when the tax rate becomes higher, the growth rate will decrease. So, when the city grows in the course of time, the difference between the average value and the then value will change from plus to minus, as illustrated in Figure 5–7. A higher tax rate is an unattractive factor in the context of city growth. Accordingly, the sign of the parameter, γ_2, is plus.

$$\gamma_{3i} < 0.$$

We assume that the per capita income of a city increases over time. If a city's per capita income is lower than the average per capita income during the period of development, people emigrate out to the higher-income areas. After the per capita income of the city becomes greater than the average in the process of development, it acts to increase the city's population. Associated with the city's growth, the sign of difference

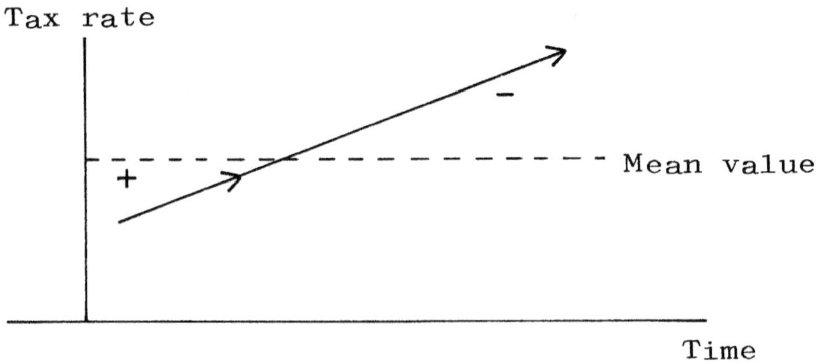

Figure 5–7. Effect of the Tax Rate on Population Change

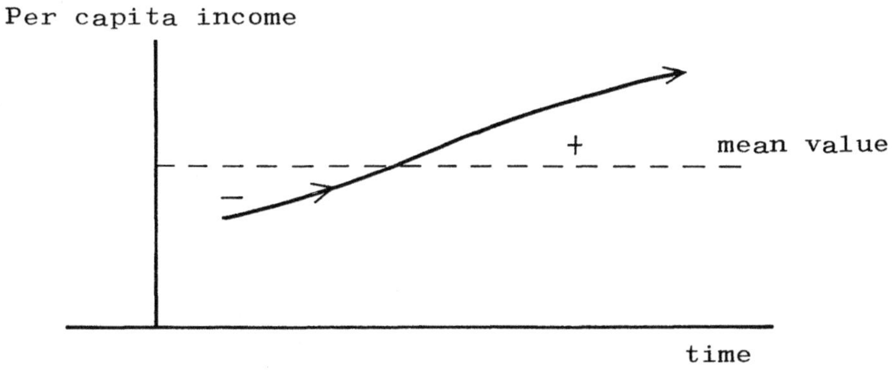

Figure 5–8. Effect of Per Capita Income on Population Change

between the average per capita income and the then values will change from minus to plus, as illustrated in Figure 5–8.

APPENDIX 5.3: STATISTICAL UNIT FOR DEFINING A CITY

The question of what kind of statistical unit most adequately defines a city for analytic research of this type is difficult to answer.

> We noted . . . that the heart of this problem lies in the appropriate designation of contiguous urban areas. This is particularly true when we examine changes in urban structure over time when political boundaries are changing. . . . In particular, city growth by annexation of adjoining (similar) territory often leaves the scale of the urban area unchanged. [Leven and Barr 1972, pp. 52–53]

Moreover, the necessary data is very hard to get. For instance, in the case of the United States, "The hard reality is that the Census simply does not have any data on the area of incorporated places before 1940, except for special studies such as the one from which the 1890 data were extracted" (Leven and Barr 1972, p. 57).

From the viewpoint of availability of information, SMSAs are more appropriate than cities. Of course, the growth rates of populations of the cities and SMSAs are different (Berry et al. 1976). In spite of these difficulties, however, it seems reasonable to think that an urban area should be considered as some kind of social entity that has particular characteristics, despite its political reorganization and the apparently arbitrary annexation of contiguous neighborhoods.

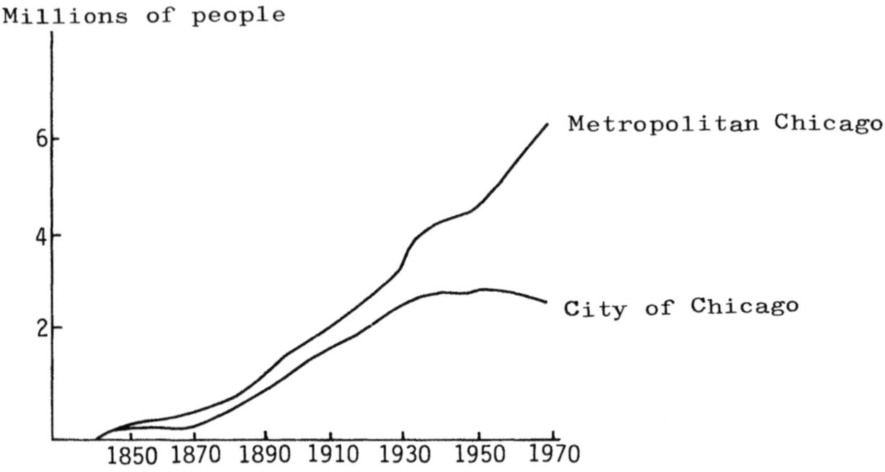

Figure 5–9. Population Change in Metropolitan Area and City Area

Figure 5–9 shows the changes in population size of metropolitan and urban Chicago from 1850 to 1970. We see that the population of the city has been tapering off or decreasing since approximately 1940, whereas the population of the metropolitan area has been growing steadily since 1850. It should be stressed that although the jurisdictional areas for the city and suburbs have differed over time, it is nonetheless possible to discern this general trend of a dwindling population in the central part of the city and a growing population in the surrounding part.

6 ENVIRONMENTAL POLICY AND IMPLEMENTATION

In the preceding chapters we have attempted to clarify, both theoretically and empirically, the substance of the urbanization process with respect to environmental degradation. In this chapter we focus on environmental policy and its implementation process; we look primarily at the elements of the social response to environmental degradation that lead to policy formulation. In trying to trace out the social responses to environmental degradation as well as the environmental policy process in general, we find that the elements of environmental policy and implementation are not easily grasped. In particular, we find that quantitative methods, such as cost-benefit analysis, do not provide an adequate means of assessing environmental quality or policy; moreover, they cannot easily encompass the intangibles of social responses to environmental degradation.

In the next section we consider the elements of social response to environmental degradation, categorize them, and observe their shifting nature in order to uncover some of the complexities of the social motivation for environmental policy formulation. Particular emphasis is given to the changing dimensions of social responses to environmental degradation. In the following section we examine the validity of cost-benefit analysis as a criterion for environmental policy. We then consider the changing characteristics of the planning and policy-implementation process in general, and specifically in the case of transportation policy. Further, in relation to the assumptions of cost-benefit analysis, we examine the shifting role of the government from a historical point of view. During the industrialization process, the government's role was confined to coordination and arbitration of conflicts arising between economic agents. However, as the production-consumption process has progressed to today's extended scale, the government's role has shifted to that of intermediary between industrial society and nature, where nature is understood as the renewable force of the environment. It is in the government's current role — mediating between industrial society and the environment — that we are skeptical of the use of cost-benefit analysis by government policymakers for environmental policy formulation and assessment, because cost-benefit analysis assumes that we can assess environmental quality. Finally, in the appendix to the chapter, in addition to presenting a general conclusion on the usefulness of cost-benefit analysis in establishing environmental policy, we focus our attention on the idiosyncratic character of the policy-implementation process of each country. We use the example of Japan to examine the suitability of cost-benefit analysis in a traditional society.

ENVIRONMENTAL DEGRADATION AND SOCIAL RESPONSES

The externalities associated with industrial, transportation, energy, and other projects and with public policy choices have emerged as a major subject of public controversy. Increased public concern for environmental quality (e.g., air, water, natural ecology resources, and noise) and the quality of life in general is evident. In this section, we are particularly interested in developing a general framework for examining these social responses to environmental degradation.

A framework for examining social responses to environmental degradation is difficult to construct because of the diverse and ambiguous nature of both social responses and environmental degradation. Several simplifications are necessary. First of all, it is appropriate, as Gakenheimer suggested (1976), to distinguish air, noise, and ecological problems from social impacts, such as damage to social cohesion and residential and job dislocation.

Second, we must recognize that any social response to environmental degradation is situational. On the one hand, social responses to pollution vary according to the level of the social unit (e.g., community, region, nation), and there is no single set of values underlying all communities. On the other hand, environmental impacts have locational contexts. Thus, most responses to an environmental problem will vary and therefore require contextual consideration.

We suggest some degree of the complexities associated with environmental quality and social responses in the matrix of elements in Table 6–1. Overall, it is necessary to identify particular physical characteristics of environmental degradation (i.e., air, water, noise pollution, etc.) as well as the origins of those elements (e.g., emissions from industrial plants, ecological disturbances caused by highway construction, etc.). We can then assess the impact on people with regard to various criteria (material damage, wealth, etc.) suggested within a spatial context of the environmental effects as well as according to sociopolitical groups. An additional dimension concerns the conflict of interests between different groups.

More concretely, we can consider the following points. First, the regional spatial distribution of each environmental quality attribute (affected by a given source or origin) has special characteristics. For instance, noise and air pollution caused by transportation facilities occur along the facilities. Water pollution of a river or an ocean might be interregional and intranational, even international.

Second, with respect to the affected area and the characteristics of the conflict of interest (columns 4 and 5 in Table 6–1), we generally find that an affected area is "local" rather than "national." For example, in the construction of an international airport, the national interest almost invariably conflicts with local interests (item 1, column 5). The emissions of a national market-oriented firm, even if it is regulated, usually conflict with the community's interest in environmental conservation (items 1 and 5 of column 5). Consider also a commuter train; the commuters can enjoy the open space of their residential area, but the residents living in the area through which the train runs suffer the negative externalities of the environmental degradation (items 3 and 4 of column 5).

Third, we recognize much variety in the permutation of the unevenly distributed elements of each category of environmental degradation since, in reality, we are often unable to isolate the various causes and effects by category and must recognize that environmental impacts in a location are mixed. Depending on our perspective, the objective environmental quality itself will be variable, or at least relative. In other words, envi-

Table 6–1. Elements Relating to Environmental Quality

Environmental Quality Attributes	*Source of Environmental Impact*	*Impact Assessment Criteria*	*Spatial Context of Effects*	*Conflict of Interest*
Physical	Industry	Material damage	National	National vs. local (1)
ecological[a]	manufacturing	Wealth	Local	Local vs. local (2)
air pollution	agriculture	Recreation	regional	Community vs. local (3)
water pollution	Transportation	Direct aesthetic pleasure	community	Community vs. community (4)
solid waste	Consumption of goods	Ideological benefits or value of the unexperienced environment		Consumer vs. producer (5)
noise				
Social				
health				
crime				

[a]The term *ecological* is used here to denote impacts that produce significant structural change in the natural environment itself (Gakenheimer 1976).

ronmental systems are said to be stochastic, nonlinear, nonseparable, often in disequilibrium; in addition, environmental quality is imperfect and uncertain (Roberts 1976).

Given the detailed network of environmental degradation suggested in Table 6–1, the characteristics of social response to environmental degradation require examination. A broad categorization of social responses includes the following:

1. Relocation (in response to environmental degradation, households and businesses can move to preferable locales);
2. Voting (e.g., electing a political representative, voting on an issue involving environmental degradation, or making a financial contribution to a lobby);
3. Direct citizen participation in the policymaking process.

Certainly in recent years public reaction to the environment has intensified and has been manifested in these three categories. There have been significant shifts in public values as citizens have become more aware of the widespread effects of certain projects, such as the construction of transportation networks, many of which increase our convenience. The differences in opinion as to which effects should be achieved are reflected in the wider variety of groups that participate in the political process. Groups have become more active and politically effective to defend what they perceive as their interests.

Heightened public awareness of environmental attributes and increased political involvement by citizen groups have induced a counterresponse by public agencies. These agencies have attempted to understand more completely project impacts on environmental quality and to provide mechanisms for reducing or completely avoiding adverse environmental effects. Furthermore, there have been efforts — for instance, with regard to transportation decisions and policy in recent years — to (1) promote early involvement of all interest groups — national, regional, and local; (2) consider a wide range of policy and project options; (3) identify the adverse impacts early so alternatives can be developed; and (4) provide just and fair compensation.

Even in the case of an environmental quality that is measured as objectively as possible, different societies or social groups may vary with respect to ways of recognition, social responses, and policy formulation. For instance, apparently the larger the per capita income level, the more sensitive is the recognition of the environment. Social response depends on the extent to which pollution or destruction of the natural ecology is recognized, as well as on the perception of individuals or groups who can affect policy changes. The relationship between environmental degradation and social responses to it is very difficult to depict by a simplified formula. Nonetheless, a simplified representation of the processes is presented in Figure 6–1; it is further explored in the following sections.

THE VALIDITY OF COST-BENEFIT ANALYSIS

The *charge strategy* is a mechanism whereby the government makes firms and other economic agents internalize an externality for which they are responsible by forcing them to pay a charge proportionate to their share of the public costs of dealing with it. This strategy has long been attractive to economists because (1) it provides a certain and graduated incentive to firms by making pollution itself a cost of production; (2) where several sources are discharging into the same medium, they will be induced to minimize the total cost of achieving any given reduction in pollution; and (3) it provides an incentive for innovation and technical change in pollution control (Portney 1978). The charge strategy is fundamentally based on the reasoning of cost-benefit analysis. We would like to make clear just where the theoretical background of cost-benefit analysis lies. The analysis presupposes the possibility of qualitative measurement of environmental degradation as well as the differentiability. As Nijkamp (1977) suggested, a cost-benefit analysis is based on the marginality principle in which a Pareto equilibrium plays a crucial role. Most of the research on environmental economics has used the following utility function:

$$U = U(X, Z),$$

where X denotes the vector of commodities, and Z denotes the vector of environmental qualities.

$$U = U(X_1, \ldots, X_m, Z_1, \ldots, Z_n).$$

Because of the diversity and unpredictability of social responses to environmental degradation, and in light of recent trends in the policy-implementation process, the validity of cost-benefit analysis for environmental policymaking has to be understood as extremely limited.

Here, we would like to examine the limitations of cost-benefit analysis on the basis of the following points: As Nijkamp (1977) suggested, in the case of non-negative land use investments, the weighted rate of interest should be equal to the aggregated marginal net benefits of the associated

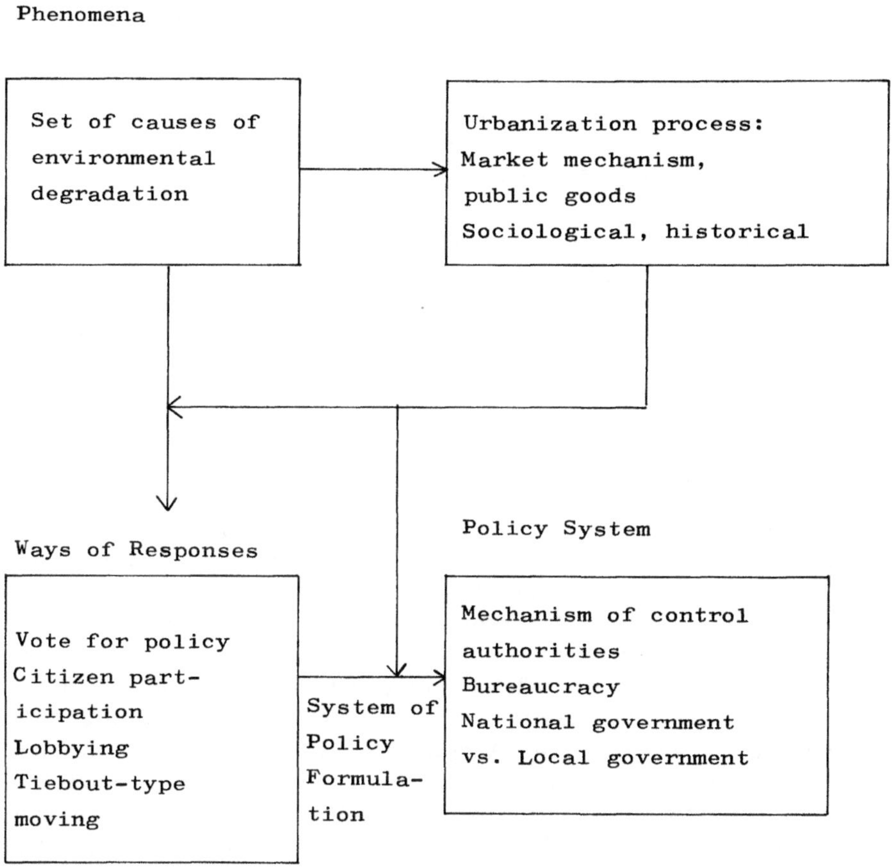

Figure 6–1. The Planning-Implementation Process

land use conversion. More precisely, the marginality principle contains the assumptions of continuity, monotonicity, and convexity. But once environmental quality becomes associated with the concept of benefit, these assumptions are not necessarily reasonable, as Roberts (1971) has noted. If environmental quality is regarded as a benefit in cost-benefit analysis, then the assumptions of marginality, continuity, monotonicity, and convexity should hold. But, as we saw in the previous section, these assumptions would be very difficult to substantiate in the case of environmental concerns.

Second, and more fundamentally, we have to consider the shifting nature of government functions and the way the government is recognized. In this regard, we would like to make clear the function of the government with respect to the environment. The government's function has been closely related with property rights, usually with the objective of helping the market to operate effectively and equitably. For the purpose of avoiding contradictions among rights or sets of rights, the government establishes a set of rules as an adjustment process for conflicts.

Generally, we can understand conflicts among rights on the basis of the concept of externality. However, the variety and extent of these conflicts are changing very rapidly, in response to, inter alia, technical innovation of the production process as well as changing consumer behavior.

In this changing context, we now recognize the environment as a self-renewing natural function that is adversely affected by urban-industrial activities. Insofar as we can recognize this function as a kind of public service, we can conceptualize the environmental problem on the basis of the concept of public goods. When we recognize that the word *environment* is a functional one that explores the relationship between human demand and the ability of living and renewing systems to respond to that demand, the function of "government" is that of an intermediary, according to the concept of externality or of public goods.

However, neither the conflicts among the rights nor the role of the self-renewing natural function of the environment is so accurately conceptualized in the usual case. Accordingly, the role of the government itself, not only as a mediator among rights in an industrial society but also as a mediator between the industrial society and the environment, is ambiguous and relative. Therefore, our point of view on the government is not necessarily simple or monotone, as we can assume various objective assessments of the environment.

CHANGING CHARACTERISTICS OF THE PLANNING AND POLICY-IMPLEMENTATION PROCESS

Generally speaking, the character of the planning and policy-implementation process in recent years has undergone considerable change. In this section, using mainly the example of transportation policy, we consider the general nature of the policy-implementation process with respect to environmental degradation.

In the case of transportation policy, the traditional conception of planning and policy implementation is very straightforward, as illustrated

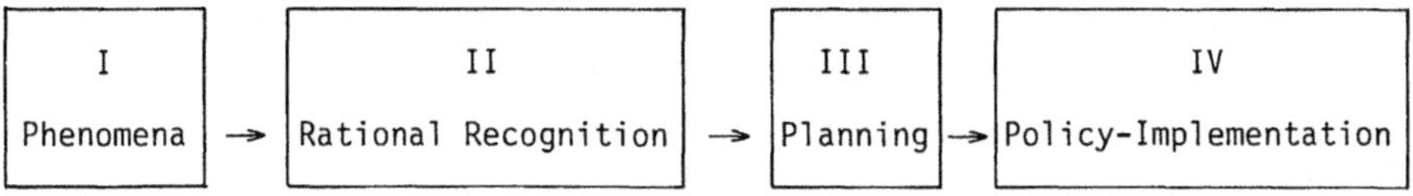

Figure 6–2. Traditional Concept of the Planning and Policy-Implementation Process

by the flow chart in Figure 6–2. (See, e.g., McEvoy 1977.) However, in view of recent trends, it is evident that this planning process is becoming increasingly complex and merits greater attention.

The characteristics of the planning and policy-implementation processes are affected by recent trends in the development of planning techniques on the one hand, and by greater social involvement in planning and implementation on the other. The two factors intermingle. As a result of the transition, changes in the planning process can be described as follows:

1. A shift from long-range planning to short-range planning;
2. A shift from central planning to coordination among many planning authorities;
3. A shift to a sequential and dynamic process motivated by sociopolitical involvement, such as community participation (Manheim and Suhribier 1978).

Transportation system management (TSM), which contains four categories of actions (actions to ensure the efficient use of existing road space, actions to reduce vehicle use in congested areas, actions to improve transit service, and actions to increase internal transit management efficiency) (Meyer and Gakenheimer 1978), provides a useful example of these kinds of changes in the planning process. This kind of planning process is a highly complicated sequential decision model. The process is not so logical, or so well defined, as that proposed recently by economists who suggest that the process can be modeled using applied optimal control theory. To use such a theory requires that the constraints be explicitly identified and confirmed. But in these sequential planning models, the contexts of the constraints as well as the elements of the objective functions are constantly changing. The emergence of a dynamic, interactive planning process necessarily affects the policy-implementation process.

One issue concerns small government versus central government. In the case of local government, a dynamic, interactive planning process appears to suit the requirements of short-term planning or community-level planning and incorporates citizen participation. In contrast, central government functions involve national equity, national perspective, long-term programming, and the iterative and sequential nature of the actual policy choices.

The political argument in favor of decentralization generally focuses on the geographic scope, although some consideration has been given to the issue of functional comprehensiveness. The basic contention has to do with the way in which citizens relate to their government. The argument is that smaller-scale governments are more open and accountable, that citizens are more involved, and that the resulting decisions are more flexible and responsive to public attitudes. Thus the problem is understood differently depending on the perspective — centralization versus decentralization.

Earlier in this chapter, we noted various kinds of conflict of interests; it is possible that the residents of one area might well utilize and enjoy facilities constructed in another region (e.g., a recreational reservoir). Less directly, the residents of one area might be made happier by vicarious enjoyment of the access of residents in another area to water-based recreation or the aesthetic pleasure of clean streams. In either case, decentralized decision making might fail to take into account the external benefits of water quality enjoyed by nonresidents. The possibility of such failure is taken as an argument for centralized, comprehensive choice, so that all benefits will be properly counted (Roberts 1970). While decentralization has virtues, there are important political goals that can best be served by centralization.

As a concluding remark to this chapter, a quote from Malthus seems appropriate: "The partial goods attained must be much more than counter-balanced by the general deterioration in the condition of the great mass of the society, and the prospect of its daily growing worse" (Malthus 1830, p. 275).

APPENDIX: A CONSIDERATION OF THE POLICY-IMPLEMENTATION PROCESS IN JAPAN

The arguments for environmental policy in Japan generally take one of two forms:

1. *Scenario One*: The response of Japanese society to environmental problems is not modern. The planning-implementation process in the United States and the other Western countries is far advanced, and the Japanese have to learn the way of the advanced countries.
2. *Scenario Two*: Japanese society is doing well on the basis of their system of administrative guidance, which is very special and superior. In contrast, the American way of solving environmental problems is ineffective.

In Japan environmental considerations in transportation problems are, year by year, increasingly acknowledged as vital. The OECD report on Japan's environmental problems aptly expresses the situation:

> The decrease in on-street traffic in Tokyo might also have contributed to these results, although lower traffic counts due to increased congestion may reflect lower speeds and thus more CO pollution. These successful results are partly due to the early implementation of CO emission standards on new cars (1966) and their subsequent strengthening. Three years have thus been necessary to have a sufficient number of clear vehicles with respect to the total stock of motor vehicles to affect the ambient concentration of CO. The development of traffic control now reinforces the emission standard approach, particularly in heavily congested and polluted areas. [OECD 1977, p. 65]

Generally, Japan's environmental policy is summarized in the OECD report as follows: (1) The Japanese approach to pollution abatement appears to be largely noneconomic; pollution abatement has been an attack against industry as much as a defense of the environment and is based more on intuitive feelings than on economics. The familiar proposition that a balance must be struck between environmental costs and economic benefits has even been officially rejected. (2) Environmental policy in Japan has focused on certain types of pollution: mercury, cadmium, polychlorinated biphenyls, sulphur dioxide, and nitrogen oxides. (3) With regard to the policy instruments utilized, Japan has preferred direct administrative controls to indirect economic incentives. The Japanese approach to pollution abatement therefore relies on "administrative guidance," in the spirit of a planned economy rather than in that of a market economy.

Generally speaking, the OECD report on environmental policy in Japan seems to be adequate. However, if we scrutinize the report in more detail, there are many ambiguous expressions, even if we limit our attention to what is the substantive character of "administrative guidance" and to what is the spirit of a market economy or of a "planned economy." Clarification of these expressions deserves to be based more fundamentally on, for example, cultural or historical studies of Japanese society. The substantive content of concepts such as "administrative guidance" and "planned economy" should derive from the fundamental structure of Japanese society.

The report also appears superficial when it says that Japanese environmental policy seems to be implemented very smoothly on the basis of the particular nature of that society. But if we look at the delay in the opening of the Narita International Airport or at other demonstrations against other transportation systems, we find that Japan is not necessarily dealing smoothly with the planning-implementation process.

The following quote broadly sketches the characteristics of Japan's institutional structure, or what we might call the exogenous sphere of implementation in Japan:

> The course to the achievement of this goal is being charted by the Japanese central government through the mechanism of national planning. The Japanese government is eminently able to mobilize the country's people and resources for the achievement of almost any national goal it may set because it stands atop a pervasive social, cultural, and political top-down hierarchy. In this position, it is, in the words of the former ambassador to Japan, Edwin Reischauer, the supreme authority in Japanese society. [Shapiro 1978]

Endogenously the Japanese bureaucracy seems to respond insufficiently to the multi-objective, multimodal age of transportation planning and implementation; the bureaucracy is mainly in charge of planning as well as implementation. In the exogenous sphere — or the particular organizational sphere of the planning-implementation process — there are, as is well known, many disputes over jurisdiction, especially when new implementation (as, e.g., of environmental acts) is required. On the other hand, an efficient bureaucratic mechanism in some sense has worked smoothly, partially backed by a highly conscientious and able cadre of career civil servants, as Shapiro (1978) points out. But this same bureaucracy was severely criticized in the name of democracy after the war, and democracy does naturally require a more egalitarian atmosphere, both institutionally and substantively. Institutionally, considering the age of the overwhelming majority of the government party in the House, political compromise should be substituted for conscientiousness in career officials.

In the general organizational sphere of the planning-implementation process, much protest has been directed toward the planning-implementation agencies. However, in the academic field, the problem of citizen participation in the planning-implementation process, except for some ideological discussion, has not yet been properly dealt with.

Accordingly, endogenously as well as exogenously, Japan's planning-implementation process seems to be in a phase of conversion, and in such a sense, the problem constitutes one of the most important subjects for research, both theoretically and practically. In conclusion, we should consider the cultural viewpoint, which is an indispensable part of this theme.

The little-understood yet fundamental elements of Japanese society are complex, and their subtle effects have hindered mutual understanding between Japanese society and Western society since Japan's industrial revolution. In Western terminology, *Rechtssoziologisch Erkennennis* ("sociological recognition of law") (Ehrlich 1911) of the basic historical elements of Japanese society is required to clarify these concepts.

As a means of understanding the basis of the Japanese choice of environmental policy instruments, let us consider the hypothesis that Japanese society has responded to its heterogeneous culture (i.e., traditional and modern/Western) by adopting a twofold psychological structure, one that adapted to and rapidly assimilated cultural innovation, and the other that stuck to traditions. The contradiction between the substance (what is at the surface) and the formal matter (what ought to be) of Japanese society has often been pointed out. We can understand that the former expresses the traditional element of the society, and the latter its modernized or Westernized element. In the terminology of *Rechtssoziology,* the former is the substantive social law, and the latter is the formal law of the society. In comparison, we point out the contradiction between the traditional German law and the Roman law that is recognized in European countries.

Of course, every developing country may have a more or less dual cultural structure. Usually the nation is split into two classes, one class representing more modernized values and the other more traditional. But the Japanese way of treating cultural duality seems to be very special. Each individual deals with Western culture by internally adopting a two-sided psychological structure. This psycho-sociological structure contains both the formal and the substantive sides, which contradict each other but are coexistent. Figure 6–3 illustrates the dual system of psycho-sociological structure of traditional society.

In the case of Japan, the multiple folds of the psychological structure of each individual are internalized, but accompanied by the usual surface struggle between social classes. When a tradition-oriented society like Japan encounters such a contradictory situation, it tends to rely on the

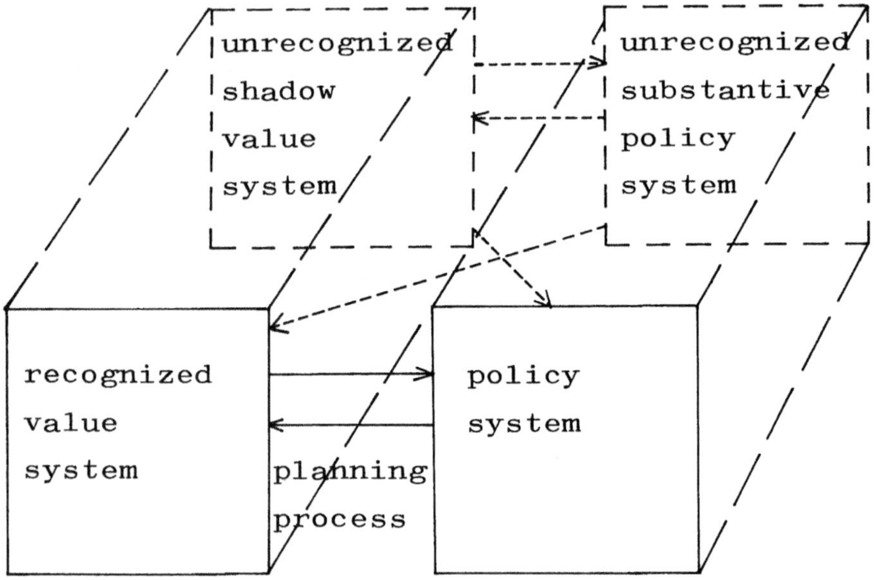

Primary Relationships of the Society

Figure 6–3. The Dual System in Traditional Society

traditional or "shadow" parts of the society, which are not necessarily adequate in terms of generating a long-run solution.

From our hypothesis that Japanese society reflects this twofold psychological structure, we observe on the one hand that the Japanese eagerly study American problem-solving methods, while on the other hand they stick to their own traditional ways. Accordingly, it is necessary to understand and introduce the theories developed in the United States and to consider in greater depth the "shadow" part of Japan's psychological structure.

Nevertheless, traditional Japanese society is more or less organizational, and these characteristics continue to dominate its political structure, although the dominance is diminishing. Hence the Japanese rely on traditional social and political organizational structure to solve their problems when they encounter difficulties.

Under the circumstances, coalition or coordination of the contradictions among the different organizations within the total society seems to be extremely difficult. Accordingly, the concepts of effective decentralization or of dependence on market mechanisms, in the case of public policy, are extremely difficult to apply in practice even if they prevail theoretically. This seems to be why the conflict of social interests can easily lead to ideological confrontation. In contrast, in societies like that of the United States, dependence on market mechanisms or cost-benefit analysis seems to be comparatively easy to achieve, even though those approaches have limitations (Roberts 1971).

For Japan, piecemeal approaches such as cost-benefit analyses are not entirely inappropriate since they serve to introduce new elements to traditional problem solving, which might otherwise lack flexibility. Japan can attempt at any time to develop a way of resolving the contradictions associated with retention of the traditional elements of society, but we should recognize that it is sometimes favorable and sometimes unfavorable. With respect to environmental policy issues, we believe that it is necessary to acknowledge and deal with these contradictions totally, not piecemeal, as far as possible. Nevertheless, in the context of Japanese environmental policy formulation, we have to devise piecemeal ways of resolving each of the contradictory factors. In contrast, the United States has to struggle to arrive at some synthetic way of resolving the issues, as Roberts correctly suggests.

STATISTICAL APPENDIX

Table A-1. Population of the Main Cities in the United States, 1900–1975

1900			1910		
Rank	City	Population	Rank	City	Population
1	New York	3437	1	New York	4767
2	Chicago	1699	2	Chicago	2185
3	Philadelphia	1294	3	Philadelphia	1549
4	St. Louis	575	4	St. Louis	687
5	Boston	561	5	Boston	671
6	Baltimore	509	6	Cleveland	561
7	Pittsburgh	452	7	Baltimore	558
8	Cleveland	382	8	Pittsburgh	534
9	Buffalo	352	9	Detroit	466
10	San Francisco	343	10	Buffalo	424
11	Cincinnati	326	11	San Francisco	417
12	New Orleans	287	12	Milwaukee	374
13	Detroit	286	13	Cincinnati	364
14	Milwaukee	285	14	Newark	347
15	Washington	279	15	New Orleans	339
16	Newark	246	16	Washington, D.C.	331
17	Jersey City	206	17	Los Angeles	319
18	Louisville	205	18	Minneapolis	301
19	Minneapolis	203	19	Jersey City	268
20	Providence	176	20	Kansas City	248
21	Indianapolis	169	21	Seattle	237
22	Kansas City	164	22	Indianapolis	234
23	St. Paul	163	23	Louisville	224
24	Rochester	163	24	Providence R.I.	224
25	Denver	134	25	Rochester	218
26	Toledo	132	26	St. Paul	215
27	Omaha	129	27	Denver	213
28	Columbus	126	28	Portland	207
29	Atlanta	118	29	Columbus, Ohio	182
30	Syracuse	108	30	Toledo	168

Table A–1. *(continued)*

1920			1930		
Rank	City	Population	Rank	City	Population
1	New York	5620	1	New York	6930
2	Chicago	2702	2	Chicago	3376
3	Philadelphia	1824	3	Philadelphia	1951
4	Detroit	994	4	Detroit	1569
5	Cleveland	797	5	Los Angeles	1238
6	St. Louis	773	6	Cleveland	900
7	Boston	748	7	St. Louis	822
8	Baltimore	734	8	Baltimore	805
9	Pittsburgh	588	9	Boston	781
10	Los Angeles	577	10	Pittsburgh	670
11	San Francisco	507	11	San Francisco	634
12	Buffalo	507	12	Milwaukee	578
13	Milwaukee	457	13	Buffalo	573
14	Washington	438	14	Washington	487
15	Newark	415	15	Minneapolis	464
16	Cincinnati	401	16	New Orleans	459
17	New Orleans	387	17	Cincinnati	451
18	Minneapolis	381	18	Newark	442
19	Kansas City	324	19	Kansas City	400
20	Seattle	315	20	Seattle	366
21	Indianapolis	314	21	Indianapolis	364
22	Jersey City	298	22	Rochester	328
23	Rochester	296	23	Jersey City	317
24	Portland	258	24	Louisville	308
25	Denver	256	25	Portland	302
26	Toledo	243	26	Houston	292
27	Providence	238	27	Columbus	291
28	Columbus	237	28	Toledo	291
29	Louisville	235	29	Denver	288
30	St. Paul	235	30	Oakland	284

1940

Rank	City	Population
1	New York	7455
2	Chicago	3397
3	Philadelphia	1931
4	Detroit	1623
5	Los Angeles	1504
6	Cleveland	878
7	Baltimore	859
8	St. Louis	816
9	Boston	771
10	Pittsburgh	672
11	Washington	663
12	San Francisco	635
13	Milwaukee	587
14	Buffalo	576
15	New Orleans	495
16	Minneapolis	492
17	Cincinnati	456
18	Newark	430
19	Kansas City	399
20	Indianapolis	387
21	Houston	385
22	Seattle	368
23	Rochester	325
24	Denver	322
25	Louisville	319
26	Columbus	306
27	Portland	305
28	Atlanta	302
29	Oakland	302
30	Jersey City	301

1950

Rank	City	Population
1	New York	7892
2	Chicago	3621
3	Philadelphia	2072
4	Los Angeles	1970
5	Detroit	1850
6	Baltimore	950
7	Cleveland	915
8	St. Louis	857
9	Washington	802
10	Boston	801
11	San Francisco	775
12	Pittsburgh	677
13	Milwaukee	637
14	Houston	596
15	Buffalo	580
16	New Orleans	570
17	Minneapolis	522
18	Cincinnati	504
19	Seattle	468
20	Kansas City	457
21	Newark	439
22	Dallas	434
23	Indianapolis	427
24	Denver	416
25	San Antonio	408
26	Memphis	396
27	Oakland	385
28	Columbus	376
29	Portland	374
30	Louisville	369

Table A–1. *(continued)*

1960

Rank	City	Population
1	New York	7782
2	Chicago	3550
3	Los Angeles	2479
4	Philadelphia	2003
5	Detroit	1670
6	Baltimore	939
7	Houston	938
8	Cleveland	876
9	Washington, D.C.	764
10	St. Louis	750
11	Milwaukee	741
12	San Francisco	740
13	Boston	697
14	Dallas	680
15	New Orleans	628
16	Pittsburgh	604
17	San Antonio	588
18	San Diego	573
19	Seattle	557
20	Buffalo	533
21	Cincinnati	503
22	Memphis	498
23	Denver	494
24	Atlanta	487
25	Minneapolis	483
26	Indianapolis	476
27	Kansas City	476
28	Columbus, Ohio	471
29	Phoenix	439
30	Newark	405

1970

Rank	City	Population
1	New York	7895
2	Chicago	3367
3	Los Angeles	2816
4	Philadelphia	1949
5	Detroit	1511
6	Houston	1233
7	Baltimore	906
8	Dallas	844
9	Washington, D.C.	757
10	Cleveland	751
11	Indianapolis	745
12	Milwaukee	717
13	San Francisco	716
14	San Diego	697
15	San Autonio	654
16	Boston	641
17	Memphis	624
18	St. Louis	622
19	New Orleans	593
20	Atlanta	582
21	Columbus	540
22	Seattle	531
23	Jacksonville	529
24	Pittsburgh	520
25	Denver	515
26	Kansas City	507
27	Atlanta	497
28	Buffalo	463
29	Cincinnati	453
30	Nashville-Davidson, Tenn.	448

1973			1975		
Rank	City	Population	Rank	City	Population
1	New York	7647	1	New York	7482
2	Chicago	3173	2	Chicago	3099
3	Los Angeles	2747	3	Los Angeles	2727
4	Philadelphia	1862	4	Philadelphia	1816
5	Detroit	1387	5	Houston	1357
6	Houston	1320	6	Detroit	1335
7	Baltimore	878	7	Baltimore	852
8	Dallas	816	8	Dallas	813
9	San Diego	757	9	San Diego	774
10	San Antonio	756	10	San Antonio	773
11	Washington, D.C.	734	11	Indianapolis	715
12	Indianapolis	728	12	Washington, D.C.	712
13	Milwaukee	691	13	Milwaukee	666
14	San Francisco	687	14	Phoenix	665
15	Cleveland	679	15	San Francisco	665
16	Memphis	659	16	Memphis	661
17	Phoenix	637	17	Cleveland	639
18	Boston	618	18	Boston	637
19	New Orleans	573	19	Jacksonville	562
20	St. Louis	558	20	New Orleans	560
21	Columbus, Ohio	541	21	San Jose	556
22	San Jose	523	22	Columbus, Ohio	536
23	Jacksonville	522	23	St. Louis	525
24	Denver	516	24	Seattle	487
25	Seattle	503	25	Denver	485
26	Kansas City	488	26	Kansas City	473
27	Pittsburgh	479	27	Pittsburgh	459
28	Atlanta	451	28	Nashville-Davidson	447
29	Nashville-Davidson	427	29	Atlanta	436
30	Cincinnati	426	30	Cincinnati	413

Source: U.S. Bureau of the Census, *Census of Population* and *Current Population Reports*.

Table A–2. Population of SMSAs, 1930–1975

(Unit: Hundred)

	1930		1940		1950		1960	
1.	NEW YORK	78,897	NEW YORK	85,165	NEW YORK	91,908	NEW YORK	95,396
2.	CHICAGO	44,496	CHICAGO	45,741	CHICAGO	51,932	CHICAGO	62,209
3.	PHILADELPHIA	31,370	PHILADELPHIA	32,000	LOS ANGELES-LB	41,873	LOS ANGELES	60,387
4.	BOSTON-L-B	25,856	BOSTON-L-B	28,840	PHILADELPHIA	36,777	PHILADELPHIA	40,343
5.	DETROIT	22,925	LOS ANGELES-LB	28,028	DETROIT	31,878	DETROIT	39,497
6.	LOS ANGELES-LB	22,084	DETROIT	25,346	BOSTON-L-B-ECT.	31,323	BOSTON	29,466
7.	PITTSBURGH	20,232	PITTSBURGH	20,817	PITTSBURGH	22,151	SAN FRANCISCO	26,487
8.	ST. LOUIS	14,303	ST. LOUIS	15,344	SAN FRANCISCO-O	21,543	PITTSBURGH	24,054
9.	NEWARK	13,142	SAN FRANCISCO-O	14,214	ST. LOUIS	17,957	ST. LOUIS	21,442
10.	SAN FRANCISCO	13,069	NEWARK	13,707	NEWARK	15,794	WASHINGTON	21,316
11.	CLEVELAND	12,882	CLEVELAND	13,238	CLEVELAND	15,390	CLEVELAND	19,094
12.	BALTIMORE	10,683	BALTIMORE	11,860	WASHINGTON	15,367	NEWARK	18,328
13.	MINNEAPOLIS-ST.P.	9,621	MINNEAPOLIS-ST.P.	10,653	BALTIMORE	14,646	BALTIMORE	18,037
14.	BUFFALO	9,117	WASHINGTON, D.C.	10,551	MINNEAPOLIS-ST.P.	12,580	DALLAS-FORT WORTH	17,379
15.	CINCINNATI	8,441	BUFFALO	9,568	DALLAS-FORT WORTH	12,267	MINNEAPOLIS	15,978
16.	MILWAUKEE	8,215	CINCINNATI	8,879	BUFFALO	10,918	HOUSTON	14,303
17.	NORTHEAST PENN.	7,837	MILWAUKEE	8,786	CINCINNATI	10,263	BUFFALO	13,069

18.	WASHINGTON	7,283	DALLAS-FORT WORTH	8,760	MILWAUKEE	10,152	MILWAUKEE	12,788
19.	KANSAS CITY	7,202	NORTHEAST PENN.	7,722	HOUSTON	9,555	CINCINNATI	12,684
20.	JERSEY CITY	6,907	KANSAS CITY	7,375	NASSAU-SUFFOLK	9,511	KANSAS CITY	11,086
21.	PROVIDENCE-W.P.	6,770	ATLANTA	6,917	ATLANTA	8,678	SEATTLE	11,072
22.	ROCHESTER	5,945	PROVIDENCE-W.P.	6,719	KANSAS CITY	8,674	SAN DIEGO	10,330
23.	ALBANY	5,801	JERSEY CITY	6,544	SEATTLE-EVERETT	8,474	INDIANAPOLIS	9,444
24.	INDIANAPOLIS	5,724	HOUSTON	6,479	INDIANAPOLIS	7,332	MIAMI	9,350
25.	DALLAS	5,519	INDIANAPOLIS	6,143	PROVIDENCE-W.P.	7,249	DENVER	9,348
26.	BIRMINGHAM	5,427	ROCHESTER	6,115	NEW ORLEANS	7,160	NEW ORLEANS	9,071
27.	SEATTLE-EVERETT	5,423	NASSAU-SUFFOLK	6,031	PORTLAND	7,095	ATLANTA	9,010
28.	NEW ORLEANS	5,262	SEATTLE-EVERETT	5,950	NORTHEAST PENN.	6,840	TAMPA-ST.PETE.	8,092
29.	ATLANTA	5,057	ALBANY-S-T	5,894	BIRMINGHAM	6,789	PROVIDENCE	8,008
30.	NASSAU-SUFFOLK	4,410	BIRMINGHAM	5,829	ROCHESTER	6,768	ROCHESTER	8,006

	1970		1973		1975	
1.	NEW YORK	99,887	NEW YORK	97,464	NEW YORK	96,352
2.	LOS ANGELES-LB	70,335	CHICAGO	69,998	CHICAGO	69,829
3.	CHICAGO	70,318	LOS ANGELES-LB	69,293	LOS ANGELES-LB	69,449
4.	PHILADELPHIA	48,313	PHILADELPHIA	48,263	PHILADELPHIA	47,972
5.	DETROIT	44,388	DETROIT	44,963	DETROIT	44,447

Table A–2. *(continued)*

6.	BOSTON-L-B	38,594	BOSTON-L-B	39,185	BOSTON-L-B-ECT.	39,146
7.	SAN FRANCISCO-O	31,139	SAN FRANCISCO-O	31,428	SAN FRANCISCO-O	31,288
8.	WASHINGTON	29,153	WASHINGTON	30,126	WASHINGTON	30,162
9.	NASSAU-SUFFOLK	25,596	NASSAU-SUFFOLK	26,212	NASSAU-SUFFOLK	26,220
10.	ST. LOUIS	24,130	DALLAS-FORT WORTH	24,652	DALLAS-FORT WORTH	25,528
11.	PITTSBURGH	24,035	ST. LOUIS	23,912	ST. LOUIS	23,694
12.	DALLAS-FORT WORTH	23,863	PITTSBURGH	23,586	PITTSBURGH	23,159
13.	BALTIMORE	20,789	HOUSTON	21,634	HOUSTON	22,973
14.	CLEVELAND	20,665	BALTIMORE	21,282	BALTIMORE	21,369
15.	NEWARK	20,621	NEWARK	20,371	MINNEAPOLIS-ST.P.	20,275
16.	HOUSTON	20,063	CLEVELAND	20,040	NEWARK	19,959
17.	MINNEAPOLIS-ST.P	19,703	MINNEAPOLIS-ST.P	20,017	CLEVELAND	19,754
18.	ATLANTA	16,039	ATLANTA	17,390	ATLANTA	18,061
19.	ANAHEIM-SA-GG	14,320	ANAHEIM-SA-GG	16,006	ANAHEIM-SA-GG	17,102
20.	SEATTLE-EVERETT	14,235	SAN DIEGO	14,579	SAN DIEGO	15,872
21.	MILWAUKEE	14,074	MILWAUKEE	14,216	MIAMI	14,386
22.	CINCINNATI	13,871	SEATTLE-EVERETT	13,927	MISWAUKEE	14,264
23.	SAN DIEGO	13,584	CINCINNATI	13,841	SEATTLE-EVERETT	14,117
24.	BUFFALO	13,512	DENVER-BOULDER	13,772	DENVER-BOULDER	14,043
25.	MIAMI	12,781	MIAMI	13,714	CINCINNATI	13,845
26.	KANSAS CITY	12,762	BUFFALO	13,452	TAMPA-ST.P.	13,654

27. DENVER-BOULDER	12,460	KANSAS CITY	13,018	BUFFALO	13,272
28. RIVERSIDE-SB-O	11,484	TAMPA-ST.P.	12,757	KANSAS CITY	12,871
29. INDIANAPOLIS	11,117	RIVERSIDE-SB-O	11,926	RIVERSIDE-SB-O	12,234
30. TAMPA-ST.P.	10,962	SAN JOSE	11,576	PHOENIX	12,175

Source: U.S. Bureau of the Census, *Census of Population* and *Current Population Reports*.

Table A–3. Value Added by Manufacture, Thirty U.S. Cities, 1947–1972

SMSA	1947	1954	1958	1963	1967	1972
1. NEW YORK	7,546.6	9,982.1	11,693.9	13,332.5	17,457.1	28,383.2
2. CHICAGO	4,964.1	6,983.9	8,296.1	10,291.1	13,755.3	17,566.8
3. LOS ANGELES–LONG BEACH	2,021.5	4,925.6	6,729.4	8,988.3	12,088.2	15,257.1
4. PHILADELPHIA	2,172.6	4,023.7	4,826.3	6,031.6	7,958.8	9,238.6
5. DETROIT	2,978.9	4,326.1	4,400.7	6,879.3	8,725.9	11,792.2
6. BOSTON	1,297.9	1,759.4	2,540.6	2,914.7	4,600.2	5,421.6
7. SAN FRANCISCO–OAKLAND	1,037.5	1,656.4	2,049.4	2,567.6	3,160.1	3,817.7
8. WASHINGTON	113.2	241.7	289.6	473.9	728.2	1,068.2
9. NASSAU–SUFFOLK	164.6	900.8	1,008.1	1,563.3	2,229.7	2,522.5
10. DALLAS–FORT WORTH	404.0	913.5	1,377.2	1,787.4	3,011.5	4,093.6
11. ST. LOUIS	1,313.9	2,123.9	2,429.3	3,133.7	4,177.0	5,190.0
12. PITTSBURGH	1,704.3	2,480.5	2,622.3	2,879.2	3,838.1	4,157.3
13. HOUSTON	394.1	1,025.9	1,358.1	1,918.5	2,813.0	4,179.5
14. BALTIMORE	926.6	1,586.5	2,003.1	2,394.1	2,858.8	3,465.7
15. MINNEAPOLIS–ST. PAUL	736.0	1,141.7	1,429.9	2,014.8	2,904.7	3,731.4

16. NEWARK	1,100.6	2,292.2	2,466.2	3,234.0	4,400.2	5,608.7
17. CLEVELAND	1,570.3	2,443.8	2,557.5	3,378.8	4,297.0	5,212.5
18. ATLANTA	263.4	597.4	785.4	1,235.6	1,306.9	2,479.2
19. ANAHEIM	31.2	115.9	315.3	1,198.1	1,963.8	2,736.6
20. SAN DIEGO	101.5	390.2	625.5	661.4	803.8	1,185.2
21. MIAMI	45.5	141.2	252.1	363.1	589.4	1,219.0
22. MILWAUKEE	1,053.4	1,558.4	1,821.4	2,313.7	2,982.5	3,696.4
23. SEATTLE-EVERETT	337.3	599.8	1,064.9	1,824.5	2,038.5	2,235.2
24. DENVER-BOULDER	190.2	320.5	562.9	929.0	1,121.1	1,853.5
25. CINCINNATI	870.2	1,354.4	1,555.3	2,057.4	2,704.1	3,565.4
26. TAMPA-ST. PETERSBURG	73.0	156.6	236.0	422.0	666.3	951.5
27. BUFFALO	1,023.2	1,677.8	1,715.6	2,068.6	2,653.5	3,145.7
28. KANSAS CITY	472.0	1,042.5	1,069.7	1,511.8	2,071.3	2,915.0
29. RIVERSIDE-SB-O	43.4	205.2	319.6	493.8	618.7	996.7
30. PHOENIX	39.7	115.3	227.7	435.6	773.3	1,379.1

Source: **Office of Management and Budget,** ***Standard Industrial Classification Manual.***

Table A–4. Total Tax Paid by SMSAs for U.S. Cities, 1929–1975

	1929	1940	1950	1959	1962	1965	1966
NEW YORK	781,238	634,395	1,585,887	2,376,000	2,876,750	3,379,986	3,637,816
CHICAGO	302,291	233,006	598,307	992,375	1,108,841	1,341,312	1,461,778
LOS ANGELES	195,048	210,225	721,742	1,452,751	1,584,412	2,136,386	2,306,481
PHILADELPHIA	151,755	128,010	322,150	550,525	615,653	723,374	789,070
DETROIT	121,163	117,039	333,417	526,030	587,335	784,076	851,969
BOSTON	175,366	148,541	360,080	634,672	739,699	874,668	977,477
SAN FRANCISCO	100,698	93,060	285,896	496,517	609,323	759,793	817,005
WASHINGTON, D.C.	58,410	81,622	255,031	503,786	612,173	817,138	903,456
NASSAU-SUFFOLK	38,608	34,488	160,410	576,935	714,890	904,230	992,240
DALLAS	23,025	21,463	86,669	164,291	188,288	237,422	264,618
ST. LOUIS	68,025	57,725	164,392	721,883	318,707	391,957	428,322
PITTSBURGH	92,029	77,979	189,531	278,465	299,375	354,404	384,784
HOUSTON	18,370	23,638	85,740	164,777	202,390	236,523	261,322
BALTIMORE	64,976	64,561	177,774	305,541	370,543	460,606	604,637
MINNEAPOLIS	52,158	47,704	154,889	282,370	371,093	458,811	509,859
NEWARK	98,441	87,642	210,365	372,551	437,834	522,079	558,827
CLEVELAND	75,045	64,086	171,343	288,607	320,488	386,461	419,966
ATLANTA	13,899	14,216	54,301	112,770	159,624	189,453	213,509
ANAHEIM	5,436	4,964	27,164	154,136	202,660	284,346	319,787
SAN DIEGO	10,810	13,530	65,693	168,015	208,664	254,411	284,852
MIAMI	7,916	13,254	53,094	129,926	153,036	191,008	207,558
MILWAUKEE	57,704	47,355	152,852	279,398	344,935	416,379	463,086
SEATTLE	22,409	21,010	69,084	130,218	154,761	178,296	207,455
DENVER	19,896	18,832	68,418	148,445	187,137	221,761	244,045
CINCINNATI	42,860	35,080	90,092	165,256	176,071	220,877	243,665
TAMPA	6,614	7,986	28,121	76,729	91,070	114,291	124,633
BUFFALO	67,954	61,479	166,842	284,793	336,806	406,279	436,855
KANSAS CITY	28,869	25,005	79,873	150,675	179,184	222,035	257,207
RIVERSIDE	12,741	14,406	63,254	165,534	179,761	257,604	281,652
PHOENIX	4,945	5,252	25,245	73,741	96,978	121,948	139,244

1967	1968	1969	1970	1971	1972	1973	1974	1975
3,996,855	4,590,143	4,966,186	5,213,363	5,362,560	5,889,465	6,234,616	6,556,427	7,040,234
1,300,813	1,665,685	1,953,756	2,410,284	2,587,546	3,148,037	3,033,796	3,341,138	3,551,680
2,369,396	2,902,601	3,090,539	3,237,796	3,396,331	4,556,582	4,135,041	4,417,212	4,956,521
844,751	915,844	985,776	1,051,986	1,203,829	1,473,847	1,603,704	1,686,690	1,819,128
889,705	1,203,948	1,306,408	1,360,227	1,531,061	1,812,852	2,026,867	2,090,160	2,135,625
1,037,858	1,207,190	1,353,559	1,484,065	1,568,088	1,860,523	1,989,484	2,164,866	2,279,918
897,097	1,056,589	1,125,667	1,192,747	1,277,299	1,509,440	1,564,442	1,656,150	1,918,870
982,422	1,123,961	1,253,857	1,376,808	1,513,218	1,687,513	1,887,331	2,075,731	2,270,889
1,090,263	1,226,263	1,431,640	1,524,523	1,603,951	1,795,158	1,961,370	2,067,968	2,214,956
296,909	336,573	380,881	409,421	427,285	747,611	534,771	601,353	666,008
462,981	494,592	551,315	639,424	685,436	751,718	815,119	866,112	933,192
408,759	440,859	465,859	497,219	581,610	759,207	834,511	887,381	947,687
267,312	325,909	362,056	405,181	437,492	504,839	560,016	659,290	764,939
561,992	673,287	730,553	790,159	834,633	912,977	990,889	1,103,603	1,205,754
535,742	616,997	704,577	758,071	829,991	981,400	1,012,276	1,187,723	1,307,332
598,645	647,955	703,302	753,591	805,097	855,932	907,276	987,538	1,061,096
438,676	477,058	513,452	529,972	549,141	649,630	738,656	802,760	850,651
266,464	266,813	308,108	348,359	374,811	334,160	510,531	570,133	610,987
368,956	448,321	494,781	534,690	574,157	704,462	757,794	829,701	980,966
319,384	394,079	435,777	465,894	510,055	608,009	646,956	691,844	811,350
231,980	267,513	312,716	351,526	385,235	444,576	519,808	561,196	592,300
509,740	549,589	587,409	614,107	644,340	718,529	830,741	904,257	971,650
231,488	257,215	276,971	279,848	283,817	301,584	334,950	375,029	426,672
263,089	298,157	349,216	379,487	433,792	504,701	576,682	639,921	708,836
258,078	278,954	305,055	325,997	344,310	384,612	431,014	475,131	509,901
136,139	155,213	176,230	199,506	220,911	260,237	313,374	348,523	378,052
465,976	510,354	580,612	601,106	631,378	688,325	762,685	804,451	861,850
274,012	292,051	318,666	337,875	377,032	427,006	473,528	497,926	542,255
319,207	369,482	405,611	445,113	475,946	594,573	592,500	645,547	742,406
164,453	178,703	212,283	249,451	268,315	322,076	373,056	432,880	455,199

Source: U.S. Bureau of the Census, Census of Governments, *Compendium of Government Finances*; *Historical Statistics on Government Finances and Employment*; and *Government Finances*.

Table A–5. Highway Expenditures for SMSAs, 1932–1972

	1932	1942	1957	1962	1967	1972
NEW YORK	34,843	NA	109,832	207,359	137,835	218,727
CHICAGO	913	5,213	38,006	47,844	48,904	73,376
LOS ANGELES	14,144	5,836	78,558	38,770	61,143	78,843
PHILADELPHIA	1,633	1,444	3,796	5,963	7,217	16,619
DETROIT	5,743	10,581	26,172	29,962	47,459	67,806
BOSTON	181	407	1,364	3,006	2,327	3,253
SAN FRANCISCO	4,139	1,783	6,667	7,566	13,976	16,993
WASHINGTON, D.C.	NA	NA	25,091	73,614	72,403	101,055
NASSAU-SUFFOLK	932	2,219	15,164	21,537	22,163	45,079
DALLAS	1,770	NA	7,709	12,241	11,269	35,702
ST. LOUIS	1,004	1,424	11,300	12,774	18,317	24,160
PITTSBURGH	4,486	1,839	7,968	8,010	11,863	14,017
HOUSTON	598	NA	11,578	17,157	16,122	19,957
BALTIMORE	5,099	1,937	13,327	17,304	22,977	39,505
MINNEAPOLIS	1,430	1,890	8,747	16,424	20,899	35,649
NEWARK	2,005	1,392	5,309	6,381	10,308	17,231

CLEVELAND	1,575	2,277	13,363	11,162	11,564	15,247
ATLANTA	1,525	1,437	7,282	13,017	18,683	17,268
ANAHEIM	1,024	474	2,730	4,350	8,354	8,926
SAN DIEGO	1,450	898	3,993	6,257	12,198	12,077
MIAMI	177	499	2,328	4,720	6,615	7,528
MILWAUKEE	936	1,151	11,180	21,272	34,036	32,425
SEATTLE	1,248	1,371	7,217	7,810	10,240	26,116
DENVER	498	436	3,936	4,756	5,634	9,263
CINCINNATI	1,385	1,554	6,018	7,108	9,980	14,748
TAMPA	420	472	3,086	4,601	5,135	8,433
BUFFALO	2,424	1,662	6,655	7,808	10,918	21,589
KANSAS CITY	1,173	760	4,321	4,950	5,485	15,230
RIVERSIDE	1,106	1,130	9,786	8,515	13,312	17,081
PHOENIX	237	434	4,746	3,710	5,691	8,541

Sources: U.S. Bureau of the Census, Census of Governments, *Compendium of Government Finances* and *Government Finances*. U.S. Bureau of Economic Analysis, *Survey of Current Business*.

Table A–6. Population Density, New York City Tracts, 1920–1970

	Distance from MANHATTAN(MILES)	1920 DENSITY	1930 DENSITY	1940 DENSITY	1950 DENSITY	1960 DENSITY
1.	0	39,869.0	26,691.0	16,737.0	12,218.2	3,306.7
2.	0	50,943.5	20,723.0	30,491.2	37,166.3	28,146.4
3.	2.7	29,205.0	20,965.0	41,299.4	48,819.4	17,066.7
4.	3.1	97,984.8	114,227.9	112,721.0	109,747.9	90,483.0
5.	3.2	110,286.8	185,619.5	80,768.8	72,910.0	60,417.5
6.	3.3	109,020.0	67,560.0	50,460.0	42,740.0	38,060.0
7.	3.5	111,137.4	71,067.8	47,805.2	55,847.0	44,327.0
8.	4.0	161,474.4	161,474.4	87,842.0	85,873.4	89,794.4
9.	4.1	125,365.6	68,539.5	72,022.3	79,479.1	84,093.0
10.	4.3	110,162.1	79,195.9	76,997.0	67,692.3	52,594.9
11.	4.5	178,614.9	132,571.4	138,240.0	121,856.0	113,792.0
12.	4.7	120,335.6	113,139.5	105,959.0	92,409.8	85,962.9
13.	4.9	67,367.6	67,337.1	71,024.8	66,209.5	58,636.2
14.	5.2	96,218.5	97,264.4	96,811.7	87,055.6	77,252.7
15.	5.3	109,129.7	95,631.5	97,648.5	88,281.2	82,831.5
16.	5.3	67,546.7	53,294.5	45,246.1	45,246.1	39,796.4
17.	5.5	42,016.0	38,224.0	33,936.0	33,776.0	29,120.0
18.	5.8	60,666.0	63,494.0	56,796.3	58,641.9	51,453.0
19.	6.0	24,424.5	40,751.0	38,530.6	33,423.7	32,496.3
20.	6.3	11,298.0	28,303.7	25,952.7	25,260.4	23,327.3
21.	6.6	17,432.6	796.1	190.7	178.0	152.6
22.	7.7	28,398.4	38,919.2	38,122.3	40,899.6	39,921.5
23.	8.1	38,927.1	42,139.6	41,951.4	43,419.6	38,964.7
24.	8.4	35,963.9	39,143.2	32,578.1	29,729.0	30,286.5
25.	8.5	22,128.0	24,592.0	19,664.0	21,648.0	19,456.0
26.	8.6	32,563.8	36,007.6	37,516.2	41,523.8	39,131.4
27.	8.9	30,408.6	38,988.1	36,601.1	38,711.4	36,168.6

28.	9.0	39,149.7	37,961.1	40,320.0	40,320.0	35,145.1
29.	9.3	26,505.4	28,425.4	28,082.0	28,082.0	27,707.3
30.	9.6		27,553.7	29,221.1	29,211.1	27,806.3
31.	9.8	14,927.6	28,315.7	27,952.4	27,952.4	30,080.0
32.	9.8	14,131.9	28,436.8	28,713.5	28,713.5	26,983.8
33.	9.9	10,740.4	25,309.1	27,159.3	27,159.3	26,891.6
34.	10.2	10,553.2	25,164.3	25,164.3	25,695.3	24,796.6
35.	10.5		24,273.2	24,757.1	24,117.1	24,257.6
36.	10.9	47,320.8	38,217.1	40,058.8	38,021.2	34,102.9
37.	11.1		27,752.7	29,242.2	28,904.7	26,205.1
38.	11.4		18,425.3	22,214.7	19,098.9	17,835.8
39.	11.6		13,789.1	16,363.6	15,985.5	14,516.4
40.	11.8	8,298.7	31,110.8	37,034.7	39,957.3	36,501.3
41.	12.0		15,081.0	19,593.8	21,431.8	25,682.1
42.	12.3	2,428.7	16,827.8	13,047.6	23,451.1	22,596.2
43.	13.2		28,966.9	29,699.0	34,346.7	41,584.8
44.	13.4		48,896.0	70,362.4	70,476.2	85,470.5
45.	13.8		22.5	16.8	3,525.6	4,474.4

Sources: W. Laidlaw, ed., *Population of the City of New York, 1880–1930*. New York State Secretary, *Manual for the Use of the Legislature*. (For more detail, see Appendix 3.3.)

Table A–7. Population of the Thirty Largest Japanese Cities, 1888–1975

	1888		1893		1903	
1.	TOKYO	1,376	TOKYO	1,276	TOKYO	1,804
2.	OSAKA	472	OSAKA	484	OSAKA	989
3.	KYOTO	280	KYOTO	317	YOKOHAMA	325
4.	NAGOYA	157	NAGOYA	191	NAGOYA	285
5.	KOBE	135	KOBE	153	KOBE	284
6.	YOKOHAMA	122	YOKOHAMA	152	KYOTO	278
7.	KANAZAWA	97	KANAZAWA	92	NAGASAKI	153
8.	HIROSHIMA	85	HIROSHIMA	91	HIROSHIMA	121
9.	SENDAI	78	SENDAI	74	SENDAI	100
10.	TOKUSHIMA	60	NAGASAKI	65	KANAZAWA	100
11.	TOYAMA	55	HAKODATE	64	HAKODATE	85
12.	HAKODATE	53	KUMAMOTO	62	OKAYAMA	81
13.	KUMAMOTO	52	TOKUSHIMA	61	OTARU	79
14.	FUKUOKA	49	TOYAMA	58	FUKUOKA	71
15.	KAGOSHIMA	48	FUKUOKA	58	SASEBO	68
16.	SAKAI	45	KAGOSHIMA	56	KURE	66
17.	NIIGATA	45	OKAYAMA	52	TOKUSHIMA	64
18.	NAGASAKI	44	NIIGATA	50	NIIGATA	60
19.	OKAYAMA	44	SAKAI	46	KUMAMOTO	60
20.	SHIZUOKA	41	FUKUI	43	KAGOSHIMA	59
21.	FUKUI	40	SHIZUOKA	37	TOYAMA	56
22.	TAKAMATSU	38	KOCHI	35	SAPPORO	55
23.	MATSUYAMA	34	MATSUYAMA	35	MORIOKA	50
24.	MORIOKA	33	UTSUNOMIYA	35	SAKAI	50
25.	MATSUE	33	TAKAMATSU	35	SHIZUOKA	49
26.	SHIMONOSEKI	32	MATSUE	35	HAMAMATSU	46
27.	KOCHI	31	KOFU	34	KOFU	44
28.	HIROSAKI	30	OTARU	34	MAEBASHI	42
29.	YAMAGATA	29	SHIMONOSEKI	34	GIFU	40
30.	AKITA	29	MAEBASHI	33	YAMAGATA	40

Table A-7. *(continued)*

	1908		1913		1918	
1.	TOKYO	1,626	TOKYO	2,036	TOKYO	2,332
2.	OSAKA	1,218	OSAKA	1,389	OSAKA	1,633
3.	KYOTO	441	KYOTO	508	KYOTO	669
4.	YOKOHAMA	393	NAGOYA	448	KOBE	591
5.	KOBE	377	KOBE	441	YOKOHAMA	446
6.	NAGOYA	374	YOKOHAMA	396	NAGOYA	434
7.	NAGASAKI	176	HIROSHIMA	167	NAGASAKI	190
8.	HIROSHIMA	143	NAGASAKI	161	HIROSHIMA	162
9.	KANAZAWA	111	KANAZAWA	130	KANAZAWA	159
10.	KURE	101	KURE	128	KURE	155
11.	SENDAI	98	SENDAI	104	HAKODATE	134
12.	SASEBO	93	HAKODATE	100	SASEBO	124
13.	OKAYAMA	93	FUKUOKA	97	SENDAI	123
14.	OTARU	91	SAPPORO	97	OTARU	102
15.	HAKODATE	89	SASEBO	95	FUKUOKA	99
16.	FUKUOKA	82	OTARU	93	NIIGATA	97
17.	YOKOSUKA	71	OKAYAMA	87	OKAYAMA	96
18.	SAPPORO	70	YOKOSUKA	85	SAPPORO	95
19.	TOKUSHIMA	66	KAGOSHIMA	76	KAGOSHIMA	92
20.	KAGOSHIMA	64	SHIMONOSEKI	72	YAHATA	89
21.	NIIGATA	62	MOJI	72	YOKOSUKA	89
22.	SAKAI	61	TOKUSHIMA	70	SAKAI	75
23.	KUMAMOTO	61	SAKAI	68	KUMAMOTO	74
24.	SHIMONOSEKI	58	KUMAMOTO	68	SHIZUOKA	74
25.	TOYAMA	57	NIIGATA	67	MOJI	73
26.	MOJI	56	TOYAMA	65	TOKUSHIMA	73
27.	SHIZUOKA	54	SHIZUOKA	64	TOYAMA	73
28.	FUKUI	50	ASAHIKAWA	63	OMUTA	72
29.	OTARU	49	FUKUI	56	ASAHIKAWA	69
30.	UTSUNOMIYA	47	TOYOHASHI	55	SHIMONOSEKI	68

Table A–7. *(continued)*

	1920		1925		1930	
1.	TOKYO	3,359	TOKYO	4,110	TOKYO	4,987
2.	OSAKA	1,768	OSAKA	2,115	OSAKA	2,454
3.	KYOTO	702	KYOTO	826	KYOTO	952
4.	KOBE	644	NAGOYA	784	NAGOYA	926
5.	NAGOYA	620	KOBE	704	KOBE	788
6.	YOKOHAMA	579	YOKOHAMA	595	YOKOHAMA	704
7.	HIROSHIMA	194	HIROSHIMA	239	HIROSHIMA	270
8.	NAGASAKI	190	FUKUOKA	209	FUKUOKA	250
9.	FUKUOKA	181	NAGASAKI	202	NAGASAKI	218
10.	KURE	160	HAKODATE	170	HAKODATE	204
11.	HAKODATE	150	SENDAI	169	SENDAI	196
12.	KANAZAWA	147	KURE	169	KURE	190
13.	SENDAI	140	KUMAMOTO	158	KUMAMOTO	176
14.	KUMAMOTO	139	KANAZAWA	158	SHIZUOKA	175
15.	SHIZUOKA	130	SHIZUOKA	156	SAPPORO	174
16.	KAGOSHIMA	129	KAGOSHIMA	153	YAHATA	171
17.	SHIMONOSEKI	128	SAPPORO	149	KANAZAWA	168
18.	OKAYAMA	119	SHIMONOSEKI	148	KAGOSHIMA	166
19.	YOKOSUKA	118	OKAYAMA	134	SHIMONOSEKI	157
20.	YAHATA	114	OTARU	134	OKAYAMA	149
21.	SASEBO	111	YAHATA	131	KAWASAKI	148
22.	OTARU	108	YOKOSUKA	126	SASEBO	147
23.	SAPPORO	105	SASEBO	123	YOKOSUKA	147
24.	SAKAI	104	SAKAI	123	OTARU	145
25.	TOYOHASHI	102	TOYOHASHI	119	TOYOHASHI	139
26.	TOKUSHIMA	97	KAWASAKI	113	SAKAI	135
27.	NIIGATA	92	NIIGATA	109	HAMAMATSU	128
28.	MOJI	89	HAMAMATSU	108	NIIGATA	125
29.	ICHINOMIYA	87	TOKUSHIMA	106	GIFU	117
30.	KAWASAKI	85	GIFU	106	TOKUSHIMA	114

Table A–7. *(continued)*

	1935		1940		1945	
1.	TOKYO	5,896	TOKYO	6,779	TOKYO	4,556
2.	OSAKA	2,990	OSAKA	3,252	OSAKA	1,690
3.	NAGOYA	1,110	KYOTO	1,328	KYOTO	1,053
4.	KYOTO	1,081	NAGOYA	1,090	NAGOYA	916
5.	KOBE	912	KOBE	990	YOKOHAMA	859
6.	YOKOHAMA	797	YOKOHAMA	968	KOBE	685
7.	HIROSHIMA	310	HIROSHIMA	344	FUKUOKA	348
8.	FUKUOKA	291	FUKUOKA	323	SENDAI	307
9.	KURE	231	KAWASAKI	301	KAWASAKI	278
10.	NAGASAKI	225	KURE	276	SAPPORO	269
11.	SENDAI	220	YAHATA	261	YOKOSUKA	269
12.	HAKODATE	217	SENDAI	255	KUMAMOTO	253
13.	YAHATA	212	NAGASAKI	253	AMAGASAKI	249
14.	SHIZUOKA	201	SAPPORO	223	HIROSHIMA	246
15.	SAPPORO	197	SHIZUOKA	212	KANAZAWA	246
16.	KUMAMOTO	192	KUMAMOTO	210	SHIZUOKA	220
17.	KAWASAKI	192	SASEBO	206	HAKODATE	213
18.	SASEBO	188	HAKODATE	204	NIIGATA	211
19.	YOKOSUKA	187	SHIMONOSEKI	196	NAGASAKI	209
20.	KAGOSHIMA	182	YOKOSUKA	193	HIMEJI	201
21.	KANAZAWA	176	KAGOSHIMA	190	SAKAI	199
22.	SHIMONOSEKI	171	KANAZAWA	186	KURE	189
23.	SAKAI	160	SAKAI	182	KOKURA	182
24.	HAMAMATSU	155	AMAGASAKI	181	YAHATA	181
25.	OTARU	154	KOKURA	179	SHIMONOSEKI	181
26.	TOYOHASHI	141	OMUTA	177	OMUTA	180
27.	NIIGATA	135	GIFU	172	SASEBO	179
28.	GIFU	129	HAMAMATSU	166	GIFU	178
29.	KOKURA	129	OKAYAMA	164	KAGOSHIMA	176
30.	AMAGASAKI	126	OTARU	164	OTARU	170

Table A–7. *(continued)*

	1950		1955		1960	
1.	TOKYO	5,385	TOKYO	6,969	TOKYO	8,303
2.	OSAKA	1,956	OSAKA	2,547	OSAKA	3,012
3.	KYOTO	1,106	NAGOYA	1,337	NAGOYA	1,592
4.	NAGOYA	1,031	KYOTO	1,210	YOKOHAMA	1,375
5.	YOKOHAMA	951	YOKOHAMA	1,144	KYOTO	1,285
6.	KOBE	805	KOBE	986	KOBE	1,114
7.	FUKUOKA	393	FUKUOKA	544	FUKUOKA	647
8.	SENDAI	342	KAWASAKI	446	KAWASAKI	633
9.	KAWASAKI	319	SAPPORO	427	SAPPORO	524
10.	SAPPORO	314	SENDAI	380	HIROSHIMA	431
11.	HIROSHIMA	286	HIROSHIMA	361	SENDAI	425
12.	AMAGASAKI	276	KUMAMOTO	348	AMAGASAKI	406
13.	KUMAMOTO	268	AMAGASAKI	336	KUMAMOTO	394
14.	KANAZAWA	252	NAGASAKI	304	NAGASAKI	344
15.	YOKOSUKA	251	SHIZUOKA	296	SAKAI	340
16.	NAGASAKI	242	HIMEJI	294	HAMAMATSU	333
17.	SHIZUOKA	239	HAMAMATSU	290	YAHATA	332
18.	HAKODATE	229	YAHATA	286	SHIZUOKA	329
19.	KAGOSHIMA	229	KANAZAWA	286	HIMEJI	329
20.	NIIGATA	221	NIIGATA	279	NIIGATA	315
21.	SAKAI	214	YOKOSUKA	279	GIFU	304
22.	GIFU	214	KAGOSHIMA	274	KANAZAWA	299
23.	HIMEJI	212	SASEBO	264	KAGOSHIMA	296
24.	YAHATA	210	SAKAI	259	YOKOSUKA	287
25.	KOKURA	199	HAKODATE	243	KOKURA	286
26.	SASEBO	194	KOKURA	242	NISHINOMIYA	263
27.	SHIMONOSEKI	194	OKAYAMA	236	SASEBO	262
28.	OMUTA	192	SHIMONOSEKI	233	OKAYAMA	261
29.	KURE	188	UTSUNOMIYA	227	SHIMONOSEKI	247
30.	OTARU	178	GIFU	226	HAKODATE	243

Table A–7. *(continued)*

	1965		1970		1975	
1.	TOKYO	8,638	TOKYO	8,656	TOKYO	8,493
2.	OSAKA	3,156	OSAKA	2,944	OSAKA	2,740
3.	NAGOYA	1,965	YOKOHAMA	2,230	YOKOHAMA	2,558
4.	YOKOHAMA	1,726	NAGOYA	2,038	NAGOYA	2,081
5.	KYOTO	1,381	KYOTO	1,433	KYOTO	1,456
6.	KOBE	1,182	KOBE	1,269	KOBE	1,323
7.	KAWASAKI	835	SAPPORO	990	SAPPORO	1,178
8.	SAPPORO	779	KAWASAKI	956	KAWASAKI	984
9.	FUKUOKA	762	FUKUOKA	843	FUKUOKA	930
10.	AMAGASAKI	516	SAKAI	594	HIROSHIMA	832
11.	HIROSHIMA	515	HIROSHIMA	551	SAKAI	716
12.	SENDAI	496	AMAGASAKI	545	CHIBA	614
13.	SAKAI	474	SENDAI	532	SENDAI	576
14.	KUMAMOTO	418	CHIBA	487	AMAGASAKI	538
15.	NAGASAKI	414	HAMAMATSU	438	OKAYAMA	501
16.	HAMAMATSU	398	KUMAMOTO	436	KUMAMOTO	467
17.	GIFU	377	NAGASAKI	424	HAMAMATSU	467
18.	SHIZUOKA	371	SHIZUOKA	422	NAGASAKI	446
19.	HIMEJI	371	KAGOSHIMA	413	KAGOSHIMA	444
20.	NIIGATA	356	HIMEJI	409	SHIZUOKA	444
21.	KAGOSHIMA	340	GIFU	398	HIMEJI	432
22.	KANAZAWA	337	NIIGATA	387	NIIGATA	413
23.	NISHINOMIYA	334	OKAYAMA	381	GIFU	407
24.	CHIBA	332	NISHINOMIYA	371	KURASHIKI	391
25.	YOKOSUKA	320	KANAZAWA	361	NISHINOMIYA	384
26.	OKAYAMA	316	KURASHIKI	356	KANAZAWA	383
27.	MATSUYAMA	293	YOKOSUKA	348	YOKOSUKA	382
28.	SASEBO	277	MATSUYAMA	331	MATSUYAMA	365
29.	SHIMONOSEKI	266	ASAHIKAWA	301	UTSUNOMIYA	335
30.	UTSUNOMIYA	264	UTSUNOMIYA	300	ASAHIKAWA	316

Sources: Statistics Bureau, Japanese Prime Minister's Office, *Census*; *Survey of Permanent Residents*; and *Population Registered as Residents*. Japan Association of City Mayors, *Municipal Yearbook of Japan*.

REFERENCES

Alonso, W. 1964. *Location and Land Use — Toward a General Theory of Land Rent*. Cambridge, Mass.: Harvard University Press.

Anderson, R. J., Jr., and T. D. Crocker. 1972. "Air Pollution and Property Values: A Reply." *Review of Economics and Statistics* 1972: 470–73.

Andrews, R. B. 1953. "Mechanics of Urban Economic Base: Historical Development of the Base Concept." *Land Economics* 29: 161–67.

Arrow, K. J., and G. Debreu. 1954. "Existence of an Equilibrium for a Competitive Economy." *Econometrica* 22: 265–90.

Balasko, Y. 1975. "Some Results on Uniqueness and Stability of Equilibrium in General Equilibrium Theory." *Journal of Mathematical Economics* 2: 95–118.

Baumol, W. J., and W. E. Oates. 1975. *The Theory of Environmental Policy — Externalities, Public Outlays, and the Quality of Life*. Englewood Cliffs, N.J.: Prentice-Hall.

Beckmann, M. 1958. "City Hierarchies and the Distribution of City Size." *Economic Development and Cultural Change* 6: 243–48.

———. 1970. "City Size Distribution in a Central Place Hierarchy: An Alternative Approach." *Journal of Regional Science* 10(1): 25–34.

———. 1972. "A Regional Growth Model." Mimeographed.

Bergstrom, T. C. 1976. "Collective Choice and the Lindahl Allocation Method."

In S. A. Y. Lin, ed. *Theory and Management of Economic Externalities.* New York: Academic Press.

Berry, B. J. L., et al. 1974. *Land Use, Urban Form and Environmental Quality.* University of Chicago, Department of Geography, Research Paper No. 155.

———, Irving Cutler, Edwin H. Draine, et al. 1976. *Chicago: Transformation of an Urban System.* Cambridge, Mass.: Ballinger.

———, and Q. Gillard. 1977. *The Changing Shape of Metropolitan America — Commuting Patterns, Urban Fields, and Decentralization Processes, 1960–1970.* Cambridge, Mass.: Ballinger.

Bos, H. C. 1965. *Spatial Dispersion of Economic Activity.* Rotterdam: Rotterdam University Press.

Brady, E. E. 1967. "A Sectoral Econometric Study of the Postwar Residential Housing Market." *Journal of Political Economy* 75: 147–58.

Brigham, E. E. 1965. "The Determinants of Residential Land Values." *Land Economics* 41: 325–34.

Buchanan, J. M. 1965. "An Economic Theory of Clubs." *Economica* 32: 1–14.

Cebula, R. J., and R. K. Vedder. 1973. "A Note on Migration, Economic Opportunity and the Quality of Life." *Journal of Regional Science* 13(2): 205–11.

Chapin, F. S., Jr. 1965. *Urban Land Use Planning.* Champaign: University of Illinois Press.

Christaller, W. 1933. *Die zentralen Orte in Süddeutschland.* Stuttgart: Gustav Fischer.

Clark, C. 1951. "Urban Population Densities." *Journal of the Royal Statistical Society,* Series A, Vol. 114, Part IV.

———. 1968. *Population Growth and Land Use.* New York: Macmillan.

Courant, R., and D. Hilbert. 1953. *Methods of Mathematical Physics,* Vol. 1. New York: Wiley-Interscience.

Debreu, G. 1970. "Economics with a Finite Set of Equilibria." *Econometrica* 38: 387–92.

———. 1972. "Smooth Preferences." *Econometrica* 40: 603–16.

———, and I. N. Herstein. 1953. "Nonnegative Square Matrices." *Econometrica* 21: 597–607.

Dendrinos, D. S., and H. Mullally. 1981. "Fast and Slow Equations: The Development Patterns of Urban Settings." *Environment and Planning* 13.

Dennison, E., and W. Chung. 1976. "Economic Growth and Its Sources." In H. Patrick and H. Rosovsky, eds. *Asia's New Giant.* Washington, D.C.: Brookings.

Domencich, T. A., and D. McFadden. 1975. *Urban Travel Demand.* Amsterdam: North-Holland.

Ehrlich, E. 1911. "Die Erforschung des lebenden Rechts." *Schmoller's Jahrbuch für Gesetzgeburg* 35 S. 129.

Ellickson, B. 1973. "A Generalization of the Pure Theory of Public Goods." *American Economic Review* 63: 417–32.

Fales, R. L., and L. N. Moses. 1972. "Thünen, Weber and the Spatial Structure of the Nineteenth Century City." In M. Perlman, D. L. Leven, and B. Chintitz, eds. *Spatial Regional and Population Economics*. New York: Gordon and Breach.

Foley, D. K. 1976. "Resource Allocation and the Public Sector." *Yale Economic Essays* 7: 45–98.

Gakenheimer, R. 1976. *Transportation Planning as Response to Controversy: The Boston Case*. Cambridge, Mass.: MIT Press.

Gale, D. 1960. *The Theory of Linear Economic Models*. New York: McGraw-Hill.

Getz, M., and Y.-C. Huang. 1978. "Consumer Revealed Preferences for Environmental Goods." *Review of Economics and Statistics* 60(3): 449–58.

Glickman, N. J. 1979. *The Growth and Management of the Japanese Urban System — The Spatial Structure of Japanese Cities*. New York: Academic Press.

Harrison, D., and J. F. Kain. 1974. "Cumulative Urban Growth and Urban Density Functions." *Journal of Urban Economics* 1: 61–98.

Hirsch, M. W., and S. Smale. 1974. *Differential Equations, Dynamical Systems, and Linear Algebra*. New York: Academic Press.

Hoch, I. 1972. "Urban Scale and Environmental Quality." In R. G. Ridker, ed., Commission on Population Growth and the American Future. *Research Reports of the Commission on Population Growth and the American Future*, Vol. 3.

Holley, J. L. 1952. "Dynamic Model: I, Principles of Model Structure." *Econometrica* 20(4): 616–42.

Hoover, E. M. 1937. *Location Theory and the Shoe and Leather Industries*. Cambridge, Mass.: Harvard University Press.

Houthakker, H. S. 1952. "Compensated Changes in Quantities and Qualities Consumed." *Review of Economic Studies* 19(50): 155–64.

Isard, W. 1959. *Location and Space-Economy — A General Theory Relating to Industrial Location, Market Areas, Land Use, Trade, and Urban Structure*. Cambridge, Mass.: MIT Press.

———. 1969. *General Theory, Social, Political, Economics, and Regional*. Cambridge, Mass.: MIT Press.

———, R. A. Kavesh, and R. E. Kuenne. 1953. "The Economic Base and Structure of the Urban-Metropolitan Region." *American Sociological Review* 18: 317–21.

Japan Association of City Mayors. 1966. *Municipal Year Book of Japan*. Tokyo: Inoue.

Kelley, K. 1977. "Urban Disamenities and the Measure of Economic Welfare." *Journal of Urban Economics* 4: 378–88.

Koopman, T. C., P. A. Diamond, and R. E. Williamson. 1964. "Stationary Utility and Time Perspective." *Econometrica* 32: 82–100.

Koshal, R. 1976. "Urban Growth and Environment." *Growth and Change* 6 (January): 34–38.

Laidlaw, W., ed. 1932. *Population of the City of New York, 1880–1930*. New

York: New York City Census, Inc.

Lancaster, K. J. 1966. "A New Approach to Consumer Theory." *Journal of Political Economy* 74: 132–57.

Leven, C. L., and L. M. Barr. 1972. "Spatial Dimension of the Economy: As a Social Outcome — Some Theoretical and Empirical Issues." In M. Perlman, ed., *Spatial, Regional and Population Economics*. New York: Gordon and Breach.

Liu, B.-C. 1975. *Quality of Life Indicators in U.S. Metropolitan Areas, 1970: A Comprehensive Assessment*. New York: Praeger.

Lösch, A. 1954. *The Economics of Location*. New Haven, Conn.: Yale University Press.

Maisel, S. J. 1964. "Price Movements of Building Sites in the United States; A Comparison Among Metropolitan Areas." *Papers of the Royal Statistical Society* 12.

Malthus, T. R. 1830. *An Essay on the Principle of Population and a Summary View of the Principle of Population*. Harmondsworth: Penguin Books, 1970.

Manheim, M. L., and J. H. Suhribier. 1978. "The Automobile and the Environment: Implications for the Planning Process." In R. Gakenheimer, ed. *The Automobile and the Environment: An International Perspective*. Cambridge, Mass.: MIT Press.

McDonald, J. F., and H. W. Bowman. 1976. "Some Tests of Alternative Urban Population Density Functions." *Journal of Urban Economics* 3: 242–52.

McEvoy, L. J., III, ed. 1977. *Handbook for Environment Planning — The Social Consequences of Environmental Change*. New York: Wiley.

McGillivray, R. G. 1970. "Demand and Choice Models of Modal Split." *Journal of Transport Economics and Policy* 4: 192–207.

Meyer, M., and R. Gakenheimer. 1978. *Participating Agencies in TSM; An Update of the Boston TSM Experience*. MIT Working Paper No. 78–4. MIT.

Mills, E. S. 1972. *Studies in the Structure of the Urban Economy*. Baltimore: Johns Hopkins University Press.

———. 1978. *The Economics of Environmental Quality*. New York: Norton.

Ministry of Construction. 1978. *Statistical Year Book of Roads*. Tokyo: Kensetsubukkachosakai.

MITRE Corporation. 1971. *The PDI Index*. Working Paper 7963.

Morris, D. E. 1972. "The Cost of Controlling Air Pollution: A Study in Economics of City Size." Unpublished paper.

Muellbauer, J. 1974. "Household Production Theory, Quality and the 'Hedonic Technique.'" *American Economic Review* 64: 977–94.

Muth, R. F. 1960. "The Demand for Non-Farm Housing." In A. C. Harberger, ed. *The Demand for Durable Goods*. Chicago: University of Chicago Press.

———. 1961. "The Spatial Structure of the Housing Market." *Papers and Proceeding of Regional Science Association* 7.

———. 1969. *Cities and Housing — The Spatial Pattern of Urban Residential Land Use*. Chicago: University of Chicago Press.

Newling, B. E. 1969. "The Spatial Variation of Urban Population Densities." *Geographical Review* 59: 242–52.

Nijkamp, P. 1977. *Theory and Application of Environmental Economics.* Amsterdam: North-Holland.

Nikaido, F. 1959. *Mathematical Methods of Modern Economics.* Tokyo: Iwanami.

Nordhaus, W., and J. Tobin. 1972. "Economic Growth." National Bureau of Economic Research, Fiftieth Anniversary Colloquium, Vol. 5. New York: Columbia University Press.

OECD. 1977. *Environmental Policies in Japan.* Paris: OECD.

Orishimo, I. 1971. "Factors Affecting the Fluctuations of Land Prices in Japanese Cities." *Papers and Proceedings of the First Pacific Regional Science Conference.* Tokyo: University of Tokyo Press.

———. 1973. "Land Use and Land Price." *Appraisal Journal of Property* 5: 40–57.

Polak, E. 1971. *Computational Methods in Optimization.* New York: Academic Press.

Portney, P. R., ed. 1978. *Current Issues in U.S. Environmental Policy.* Baltimore: Johns Hopkins University Press.

Quandt, R., and J. Baumol. 1966. "The Demand for Abstract Transport Modes: Theory and Measurement." *Journal of Regional Science* 6: 13–26.

Reichman, S., and P. Stopher. 1971. "Disaggregated Stochastic Models of Travel Mode Choice." *Highway Research Record* 369: 91–103.

Richter, D. K. 1978. "Existence and Computation of a Tiebout General Equilibrium." *Econometrica* 46: 45–98.

Roberts, M. J. 1970. "River Basin Authorities: A National Solution to Water Pollution." *Harvard Law Review* 83(7): 1527–56.

———. 1971. "Environmental Quality — Discussion." *American Economic Review* 61(2): 174–77.

———, and M. Spence. 1976. "Effluent Charges and Licenses under Uncertainty." *Journal of Public Economics* 5: 193–208.

Schweizer, U., P. Variya, and J. Hartwick. 1976. "General Equilibrium and Location Theory." *Journal of Urban Economics* 3: 285–303.

Seyfried, W. R. 1963. "The Centrality of Urban Land Values." *Land Economics* 39: 275–84.

Shapiro, H. 1978. "Japan: Torn between Its Economy and Its Environment." *Planning* (November): 15–18.

Smale, S. 1974. "Global Analysis and Economics II A, Extension of a Theorem of Debreu." *Journal of Mathematical Economics* 1: 5.

Smith, B. A. 1978. "Measuring the Value of Urban Amenities." *Journal of Urban Economics* 5: 370–87.

State of California. 1971. *California Solid Waste Management Study 1968 and Plan 1970.* USEPA Report SW-2T SG, Solid Waste Management Office. Washington, D.C.: U.S. Government Printing Office.

Stewart, P. 1950. "Development of Social Physics." *American Journal of Physics* 18: 239–53.

Thom, R. 1975. *Structural Stability and Morphogenesis — An Outline of a General Theory of Models*. Translated by D. H. Fouler. New York: Benjamin.

Tiebout, C. M. 1956. "A Pure Theory of Local Expenditures." *Journal of Political Economy* 64: 416–24.

U.S. Bureau of the Census. 1976. *Historical Statistics of the U.S., Colonial Times to 1970*. Washington, D.C.: Government Printing Office.

———. 1977. *City and County Data Book*. Washington, D.C.: Government Printing Office.

U.S. Bureau of Outdoor Recreation. 1972. *Public Outdoor Recreation Areas and Facilities Inventory*. Washington, D.C.: Government Printing Office.

U.S. Environmental Protection Agency. 1971. *Report to the President and Congress on Noise* (as required under PL91-604). December 31. Washington, D.C.: Government Printing Office.

———. 1973. *The Quality of Life Concept — A Potential New Tool for Decision-Makers*. Washington, D.C.: Government Printing Office.

Vining, D. R. 1977. "Rank-Size Rule in the Absence of Growth." *Journal of Urban Economics* 4(1): 15–19.

Ward, D. 1971. *Cities and Immigrants*. New York: Oxford University Press.

Wilkenson, T. O. 1968. *The Urbanization of Japanese Labor, 1968–1955*. Amherst: University of Massachusetts Press.

Wingo, A. R. 1962. "Housing Space Demand, A Cross-Section Analysis." *Land Economics* 38: 33–41.

Zeeman, E. C. 1977. *Catastrophe Theory*. Reading, Mass.: Addison-Wesley.

———, and C. A. Isnard. 1974. "Some Models from Catastrophe Theory in the Sciences." In L. Collins, ed. *Use of Models in the Social Sciences*. London: Tavistock.

Zipf, G. K. 1941. *National Unity and Disunity*. Bloomington, Ind.: Principia Press.

INDEXES

NAME INDEX

SUBJECT INDEX

GPSR Compliance

The European Union's (EU) General Product Safety Regulation (GPSR) is a set of rules that requires consumer products to be safe and our obligations to ensure this.

If you have any concerns about our products, you can contact us on ProductSafety@springernature.com

In case Publisher is established outside the EU, the EU authorized representative is:

Springer Nature Customer Service Center GmbH
Europaplatz 3
69115 Heidelberg, Germany

Batch number: 10830939

Printed by Printforce, the Netherlands